GIANNI SIMONE

# OTAKU JAPAN

## The Fascinating World of Japanese Manga, Anime, Gaming, Cosplay, Toys, Idols and More!

TUTTLE Publishing

Tokyo | Rutland, Vermont | Singapore

# CONTENTS

## INTRODUCTION

### JAPAN'S OTAKU CULTURE HAS CONQUERED THE WORLD 006



## CHAPTER 1

### TOKYO AND THE SURROUNDING REGION 016

## CHAPTER 2
## THE KANSAI REGION: OSAKA, KYOTO AND KOBE 056



## CHAPTER 3
## OTHER REGIONS OF JAPAN 090

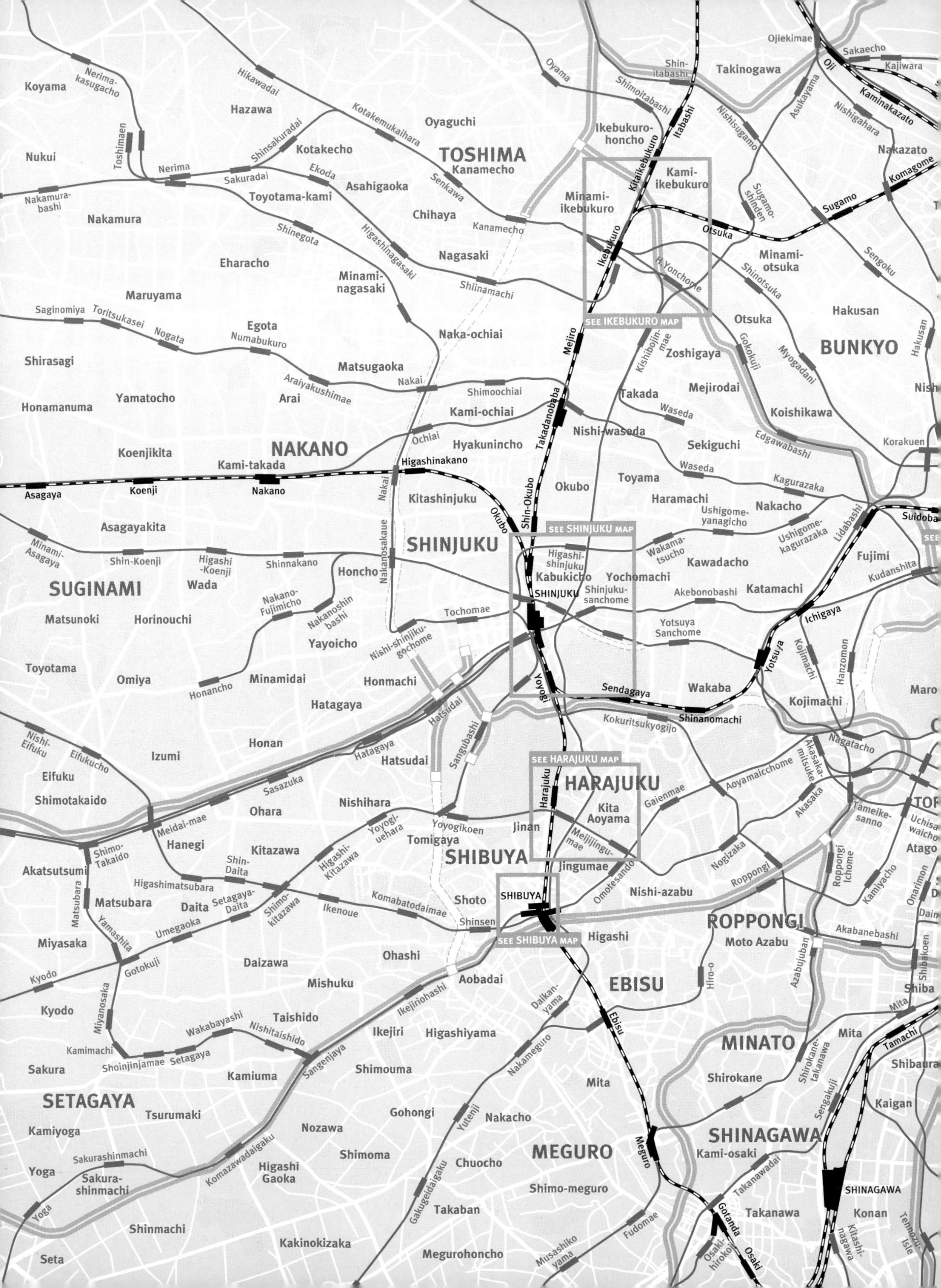

TOSHIMA
NAKANO
SHINJUKU
SUGINAMI
SHIBUYA
HARAJUKU
ROPPONGI
EBISU
MINATO
SETAGAYA
MEGURO
SHINAGAWA
BUNKYO
SEE IKEBUKURO MAP
SEE SHINJUKU MAP
SEE HARAJUKU MAP
SEE SHIBUYA MAP
SHINJUKU
SHIBUYA
SHINAGAWA
Ikebukuro
Mejiro
Takadanobaba
Shin-Okubo
Okubo
Yoyogi
Harajuku
Ebisu
Meguro
Gotanda
Osaki
Higashinakano
Nakano
Koenji
Asagaya
Otsuka
Sugamo
Komagome
Yotsuya
Ichigaya
Iidabashi
Suidobashi
Sendagaya
Shinanomachi
Tamachi
Koyama
Nukui
Nakamura
Hazawa
Oyaguchi
Kotakecho
Asahigaoka
Chihaya
Nagasaki
Eharacho
Maruyama
Egota
Shirasagi
Yamatocho
Arai
Honamanuma
Koenjikita
Kami-takada
Asagayakita
Wada
Honcho
Matsunoki
Horinouchi
Yayoicho
Toyotama
Omiya
Minamidai
Honmachi
Hatagaya
Honan
Izumi
Eifuku
Shimotakaido
Ohara
Nishihara
Hatsudai
Hanegi
Akatsutsumi
Matsubara
Daita
Kitazawa
Tomigaya
Jinan
Shoto
Miyasaka
Daizawa
Ohashi
Aobadai
Mishuku
Kyodo
Taishido
Ikejiri
Higashiyama
Sakura
Kamiuma
Shimouma
Tsurumaki
Kamiyoga
Gohongi
Nozawa
Nakacho
Shimoma
Chuocho
Yoga
Sakura-shinmachi
Higashi Gaoka
Takaban
Shinmachi
Kakinokizaka
Meguro-honcho
Seta
Mita
Shimo-meguro
Kami-osaki
Takanawa
Konan
Shirokane
Kaigan
Shibaura
Moto Azabu
Nishi-azabu
Higashi
Jingumae
Kita Aoyama
Wakaba
Kojimachi
Fujimi
Katamachi
Kawadacho
Yochomachi
Kabukicho
Okubo
Toyama
Haramachi
Nakacho
Sekiguchi
Nishi-waseda
Koishikawa
Mejirodai
Takada
Zoshigaya
Otsuka
Hakusan
Minami-otsuka
Ikebukuro-honcho
Kami-ikebukuro
Minami-ikebukuro
Takinogawa
Nakazato
Kami-ochiai
Hyakunincho
Matsugaoka
Naka-ochiai
Minami-nagasaki
Kitashinjuku

Tokyo

# JAPAN'S OTAKU CULTURE HAS CONQUERED THE WORLD

Not only can the words "manga" and "anime" be found in most dictionaries, but otaku culture is celebrated in countless conventions around the world, and Japanese comics and animation are widely available in many languages—from the giant robot sagas that first became popular in the West to *shojo* manga for girls and "boys' love" homoerotic stories. Online communities have popped up everywhere, and many countries now have *dojinshi* fairs and cosplay events. Some people even go so far as to learn the Japanese language so they can enjoy manga and anime in their original versions.

But it wasn't always like this. Back in 1983, when the word "otaku" first appeared in print, people's attitudes toward hardcore manga and anime fans were not so forgiving. Indeed, when essayist Nakamori Akio used the term in *Manga Burikko* magazine, his aim was to criticize all those "socially inept young males" who were guilty of seeking refuge in a fantasy world made of video games, toys and cute girls.

From that less than stellar beginning, things got even worse, and more than 20 years passed before the slow acceptance of the otaku community began, mainly thanks to the *Densha Otoko* (Train Man, 2004) phenomenon. This allegedly true story of a 20-something geek who falls in love with a girl was born on the 2channel Internet forum. From there it spread like wildfire, eventually becoming a novel, a movie and a TV series, all of them extremely successful—showing in the process that otaku were not so dangerous after all, and some were actually quite appealing.

Now those dark days seem all but forgotten. Some people in Japan still have mixed feelings about the subject; highbrow culture, on the other hand, has fully embraced the otaku world. Internationally renowned artist Murakami Takashi has cleverly exploited manga's popular appeal in his Superflat works; the well-respected Venice Biennale has featured an otaku-themed exhibition (the 2004 Japanese pavilion was titled "Otaku: Persona = Space = City"); and even the otaku concept of *moe* (a feeling of strong affection for female characters) is now discussed by cultural critics and sociologists with the same gravity once only granted to *wabi-sabi* and other philosophical ideas from Japan.

Most importantly, the rest of the world has embraced otaku culture beyond everybody's expectations. Foreign fans have never had any problems with the concept to begin with, and have wholeheartedly used the term to describe themselves. In Europe, Japanese animation first appeared on French and Italian television in the second half of the

Manga and anime characters can be found everywhere, from kids' socks (below) to posh department store windows (left).

Japanese otaku are not afraid to show off their predilections anymore.

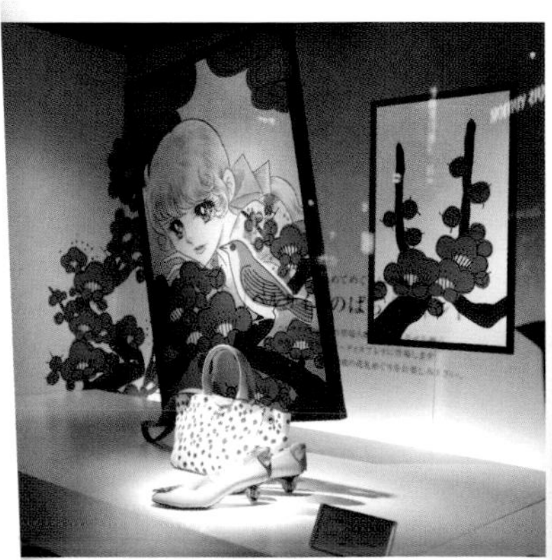

1970s, and much of the under-40 generation in those countries has been raised on a steady anime diet. In the United States, even 10 years before *Densha Otoko*, many American fans who attended early anime conventions like Otakon used to proudly display the "O" word on their T-shirts. And even in China—where *Astro Boy* first aired on TV in the '80s—the so-called One-Child Generation born at the end of the last century has found ways to circumvent government bans and restrictions on Japanese pop culture by pirating copies of popular anime and organizing their own *dojin* fairs.

In other words, today it's much easier to get your daily fix of your favorite otaku genre. However, you can't really say you have fully experienced otaku culture until you have made a pilgrimage to the holy land of manga and anime. A trip to Japan really makes apparent how much otaku "sights and sounds" are part of Japanese life, from giant billboards and graffiti to the jingles in some train stations. Manga, anime and other pop-culture icons are now so embedded in the Japanese psyche that they are used to advertize train lines, warn people against crime and even help the armed forces' recruiting campaigns. A few years ago, even Disney went so far as to produce an anime-styled TV commercial to attract more people to its Tokyo Disney Resort.

The international appeal of Akihabara's maids has helped put otaku culture on the world map.

**ABOVE** *UFO Robot Grendizer* led the anime invasion of Europe in the summer of 1978. In France the series was known as *Goldorak*, while in Italy it became famous as *Goldrake*. **RIGHT AND BOTTOM RIGHT** From vending machines to bus decorations, manga and anime imagery in Japan is inescapable.

Otaku often draw manga and anime characters on the *ema* (votive wooden plaques) they hang at Shinto shrines with their prayers or wishes.

ABOVE An otaku's room is like a small museum where they can display their huge collections of anime, manga, games and figures, decorating every available space.

Otaku is everywhere in Japan. These two young women are celebrating Halloween in Nagoya, a city which has come to be considered Japan's cosplay capital.

Obviously Tokyo remains the capital of Otakudom, and is the number-one destination for foreign fans. The range and depth of otaku delights on offer is just unbeatable, and one trip is simply not enough to experience them all. Otaku culture is everywhere in Japan. Osaka is as good as Tokyo in terms of quality and range; Kyoto is the unofficial headquarters of the foreign indie game community; and Nagoya can be justly considered the world's cosplay capital. Fukuoka is a very convenient destination if you arrive from mainland Asia, and has enough to satisfy any taste; and Sapporo in winter is the go-to place for Hatsune Miku devotees. The list of otaku places could go on forever, because really, from the northern tip of Hokkaido to Japan's southernmost reaches, you can find manga and game shops of all kinds, wonderful museums and libraries devoted to particular authors and characters, and fun otaku and cosplay events nearly everywhere and all year round.

This guide has been made with the specific purpose of showing you the wide variety of otaku-related things to do, see and enjoy throughout Japan, and it will no doubt whet your appetite for all things otaku. If you have any suggestions, criticisms or ideas, or you know a place that you feel should be covered in future editions of this book, please get in touch with me at **bero_berto@ yahoo.co.jp**

## How to Use This Book

This book is about Japan. There are several shops that specialize in, for instance, American toys, but I chose to focus on made-in-Japan goods and the world of Japanese comics and animation. That's why you will find precious little information on foreign-made otaku products. Big chain stores with many branches around Japan (e.g., Animate), are covered in chapter 1; opening times and addresses of many of the other branches are provided.

The listings in each chapter are arranged alphabetically or, in a few cases, by genre (manga, video games, etc.). The details were accurate at the time of writing. Sometimes the sign in front of the shop is written in Japanese, in which case I have provided the Japanese version (that's the one you have to look out for) and its alphabet version Websites listed here are mostly in Japanese. Few shops have English pages.

Japanese names are written according to the Japanese order, with the surname coming before the name.

Some small shops don't keep regular hours or stick to their posted opening schedule. If you plan to visit an indie shop that's off the beaten track, try calling in advance.

WARNING: Like living organisms, Tokyo and other big cities change constantly and more rapidly, with new places always opening and others disappearing for good. This means that by the time this guide is out, a few of the stores listed here will have probably closed down.

There are so many otaku shops and eateries in Japan, we couldn't possibly cover them all. The first chapter, in particular, is a sort of "best of" compilation—the proverbial tip of the iceberg. For more exhaustive coverage of otaku Tokyo, please check out my companion volume *Tokyo Geek's Guide*.

GUIDE TO SYMBOLS USED

* This place was included in the Anime Tourism 88 list.

(1) and other bracketed numbers indicate the contents of a museum. Number references are listed on the facing page.

Numbers in red boxes refer to map locations.

# Otaku Museums and Libraries

Manga and anime in Japanese culture are so pervasive that people often take these forms of expression for granted and only see them as part of something else, be it art, education or tourism (promoting a certain region). Because of their high level of recognition and acceptance, they are often used by politicians to explain their agendas, or by companies to convince consumers to buy their products.

But what are they, really? And what separates them from other creative endeavors? For those who want to know more about their history and better understand of their peculiarities and inner workings, museums and libraries offer a unique experience that, at its best, is able to engage both your senses and your intellect.

Considering how manga and anime are important features of Japanese popular culture, it is somewhat surprising that most related museums have opened only in the last 20 years. For a long time, even in Japan, comic art was considered a rather lowbrow form of entertainment that didn't deserve a serious academic approach. Luckily, there are now places where these publications (rare and historically important titles, in particular) are collected, preserved, studied and shown to the public together with original art, manuscripts and, in the case of animation, cels and production-related props. Some places even go so far as to collect character- and story-related materials such as figures, badges and other manga merchandise.

While manga museums are a recent phenomenon, they are widespread. There are now about 70 manga museums in Japan, many devoted to a local author, with the aim of celebrating their art and attracting tourists. Kochi prefecture, for instance, is definitely off the beaten track, but in the last 15 or 20 years many manga fans have traveled all the way to its location on the island of Shikoku to visit a couple of museums devoted respectively to the creator of Anpanman (Yanase Takashi) and Fukuchan (Yokoyama Ryuichi).

While the main purpose of libraries is to make reading and study material available to researchers and the general public, the collections and organization of museums are directed toward one or more of the following objectives:

(1) Displaying art (much like fine art museums, they mainly display the original pictures on which manga are based and generally focus on the artistic part of the medium)

(2) Introducing a particular author's life and work

(3) Showing the unique features of manga and how they are made

(4) Providing a full-immersion experience in the world of a particular manga or its author's philosophy

(5) Selling goods

Each of the museums listed in this guide has been number-coded so you can get a quick idea of what you can expect there.

An asterisk * next to the name of a place indicates that it was included in the Anime Tourism 88 list.

Otaku-themed exhibitions are by no means limited to the institutions covered here. Every year several mainstream museums and galleries (e.g., the Mori Arts Center Gallery, the Museum of Contemporary Art, the Kawasaki City Museum, etc.) attract thousands of people, especially—but not only—during the spring and summer school holidays. All these exhibitions are regularly listed online. Two of the more useful websites for identifying such events are **metropolisjapan.com** and **tokyoartbeat.com.**

Manga libraries are invaluable sources of reading and study material for both researchers and the general public.

# THE WONDERFUL WORLD OF OTAKU CAFÉS

Tokyo is famous for its many theme bars and restaurants, and maid, butler and *danso* cafés are a popular form of otaku entertainment dining. They're a typical example of how the Japanese manage to think out of the box and come up with seemingly outlandish but ultimately successful enterprises They also cater to the Japanese love of uniforms and cosplay. The manga café is a lot different—think of it as a uniquely Japanese take on the Internet café. The Japanese are famous for tinkering with other people's ideas and coming up with even better versions, and the local joints—called manga cafés (漫画喫茶 *manga kissa*)—offer a lot more than simple Internet connection. That's why, even in the age of smartphones, these places are still going strong and can be found everywhere.

**ABOVE** In gender-confused Otakuland, *danso* (girls dressed as boys) are only one of many possible permutations. **BELOW LEFT AND RIGHT** Manga cafés offer private booths. Many places offer an all-night stay, but only a thin five-foot-high wall separates you from the other cubicles.

## Manga Cafés

A typical manga café is, more than anything else, a place for relaxation and entertainment. Besides a PC, unlimited Internet access and free WiFi, some things you will find at nearly all of them (for no extra fee) are thousands of manga, books and magazines; DVDs; and unlimited soft drinks and coffee. Many cafés offer all-you-can-eat soft-serve ice cream, sell instant meals and junk food, and even let you charge your phone and print things out from your PC.

When you arrive at a manga café, you'll be offered a range of time and seating options. Most people choose the private booth, which comes with either a reclining chair or a flat mat. In the 2000s, with the local economy going down the drain and a sharp increase in the number of working poor, many people in their 20s and 30s began to use these cafés as alternative lodgings, becoming so-called net café refugees. Since then, the authorities have countered this phenomenon with new laws (for instance, you can't be admitted unless you prove you have a legal address) but now many places offer "night packs" (a six- or nine-hour all-night stay), free luggage storage and even showers (for an extra fee), so that people who have missed the last train home can crash there for the night. Most cafés are very clean, and this is definitely an only-in-Japan kind of experience you may want to try. Just remember that only a thin five-foot-high plastic wall separates you from the other cubicles, so in some cafés you may not be able to sleep a lot, what with ambient lighting you can't turn off, muffled but constant background noise and the occasional snoring.

A few good chains are:

**Bagus bagus-99.com/internet_cafe/shops**
**Media Café POPEYE media-cafe.ne.jp**
**Manga Kissa GeraGera geragera.co.jp/store**

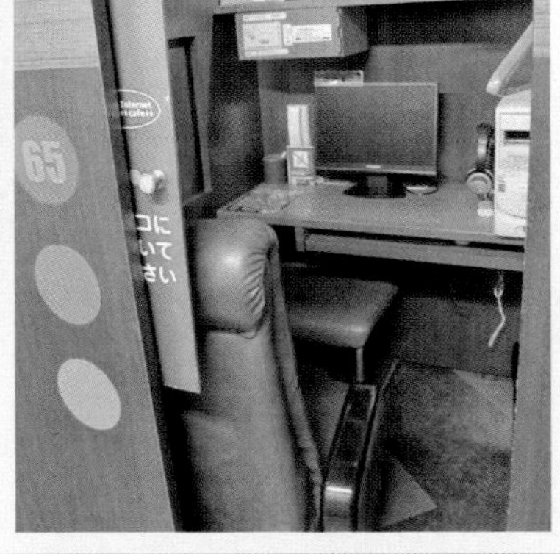


## Maid, Butler and Danso Cafés

Tokyo is famous for its many theme bars and restaurants, and maid, butler and *danso* cafés are a popular form of otaku entertainment dining. They're a typical example of how the Japanese manage to think out of the box and come up with seemingly outlandish but ultimately successful enterprises. They also cater to the Japanese love of uniforms and cosplay.

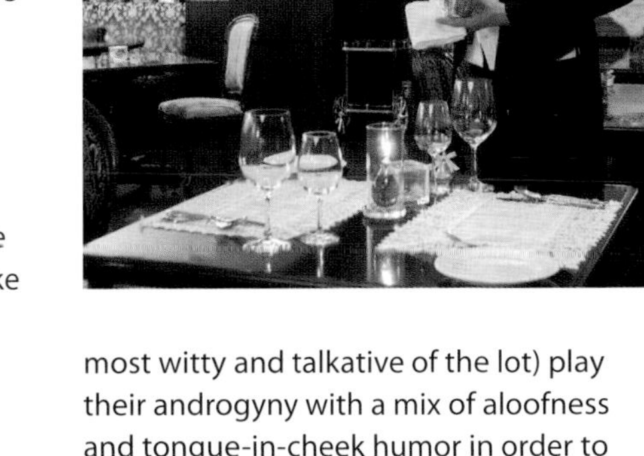
At butler cafés, female customers are treated like royalty.

Maid characters became popular in the 1990s with the PC dating-simulation game *Welcome to Pia Carrot!!* The first permanent maid café, Cure Maid Café, appeared in 2001. This novel idea became so successful that, according to business-news website SankeiBiz, in the following decade 282 similar establishments opened in Akihabara alone. Many of them didn't survive the intense competition, but maid cafés are still one of Akiba's more recognizable features. In the process they have somewhat broken out of the *moe* stereotype; now many places are frequented by women, students, couples and tourists.

A typical maid café is a small room with simple chairs, small tables and decor that, though minimal, often manages to be garish and over the top. Some even have a tiny stage for singing and dancing performances. The maids will welcome you with a high-pitched "*Okaerinasaimase, goshujin-sama / ojo-sama*" (welcome home, master / mistress). You can order a la carte—typical dishes are *omu-raisu* (omelette over rice), curry and cakes—but they usually recommend a set menu, which may include one dish, one drink and a photo with a maid of your choice. On average the food is unremarkable and quite expensive compared to regular eateries—but most people don't come here for the food. Also, don't be disappointed if the maids look overly childish and unskilled. In Japan, being hapless and sloppy is a sure sign of cuteness. A sophisticated, articulate hostess can be intimidating, but a young and inexperienced girl is the epitome of *moe*-ness. They will lead you in singing a "spell" that will make your food taste better (something like *Moe-moe kyuuuun!* or *Pyoko-pyoko pyonpokorin!*) while shaping your hands into a heart, or play (for a fee) some innocent game like Rock, Scissors, Paper or Pop-Up Pirate.

While maid cafés enjoy the lion's share of the costumed café industry, they have been joined by places where impeccably dressed and mannered butlers wait on a mainly female clientele, and by *danso* cafés staffed by girls dressing and behaving like boys. Both venues have a rather different character. While some maid cafés frankly look a little tacky, butler and *danso* cafés feature a more restrained and elegant décor. Also, the maids' (feigned) inexperience is replaced by the expertise of highly trained butlers who wouldn't look out of place in an English country house. Meanwhile, *danso* (who are, according to many, the most witty and talkative of the lot) play their androgyny with a mix of aloofness and tongue-in-cheek humor in order to attract clients of both sexes.

A lot has been said about these places' appeal—especially the kind of ritualized, mediated intimacy that prevails in maid cafés—while media reports often hint at their potential erotic nature. The important thing to remember, though, is that the maids are just waitresses and their main job is to sell food and beverages—albeit in a weird fantasy setting. While a hostess bar, for instance, is a place where you are supposed to playfully flirt with a sophisticated-looking woman, you can't flirt with a maid or ask for her personal contact information, let alone touch her. You can't even take pictures inside the café, except of the food you have ordered. If you break those rules, they are going to kick you out. That said, these are all spaces of fantasy and play that reward open-minded people, so just relax and have fun.

All these bars and cafés welcome foreigners. Some places now even hire foreign girls who can speak Japanese (probably for that added exotic touch), but almost all maids are Japanese who, though they generally don't speak English, will go out of their way to overcome any communication problems. Anyway, don't worry, because you won't need to speak Japanese to have fun.

**ABOVE & LEFT** At maid cafés, a set menu may include one dish such as *omu-raisu* (omelette over rice), one drink, and a photo with a maid.

# VISITING A GAME CENTER

Video game arcades—or game centers, as they are called in Japan—used to dot cities and shopping malls around the world. Most of that scene has now disappeared, replaced by home consoles, PC software and portable devices. Only in Japan does time seem to have stopped, as many people still enjoy their weekly (sometimes daily) commute to those loud, crowded and mesmerizing temples to electronic fun. The secret of their longevity is the clever way in which game producers and arcade owners have managed to create a kind of experience that goes beyond the games themselves and can only been enjoyed in the arcade environment.

**ABOVE** Game centers are loud, crowded, and mesmerizing temples to electronic fun.

Japanese game centers can be either one-floor mazes or multi-story fun palaces, but their basic layout is about the same anywhere you go. Let's take as an example a medium-sized three-story Taito arcade in suburban Tokyo. The first floor is crammed with a couple of Taiko no Tatsujin (Drum Master) machines (a very popular game a few years ago, as it attracted players regardless of age or sex), a few kids' attractions such as card-based games, and a whole lot of UFO catchers (crane-and-claw games). These cabinets are strategically placed near the entrance because they're more likely to attract casual passersby, young couples and families. UFO catchers come in different varieties, but whatever the type, they should be avoided like the plague because they are nothing but coin suckers. Though it looks easy, your chances of nabbing one of those cute stuffed toys are close to nil. It's not a coincidence that revenues from UFO catchers can represent as much as 40 percent of all game revenues at arcades in Japan.

Going upstairs, the second floor (and in bigger arcades, the third and possibly even the fourth) features what many consider the heart of a game center. It is here, in fact, that you'll find the typical games that most people identify with arcade fun: shooting games, fighting games and dedicated cabinets. These genres have evolved dramatically since the first hit games appeared in the late 1970s (remember Space Invaders?). Shooting games (known in Japan as STGs), for instance, have always been the dominant arcade games, but the newer ones can be so complicated that they only attract hardcore players (some would call them maniacs), as it takes a lot of time and money to memorize their amazingly intricate patterns. Fighting games, of course, include perennial classics such as Street Fighter, Tekken and Virtua Fighter, in ever-new versions.

When it comes to virtual brawls, one of the more interesting features in

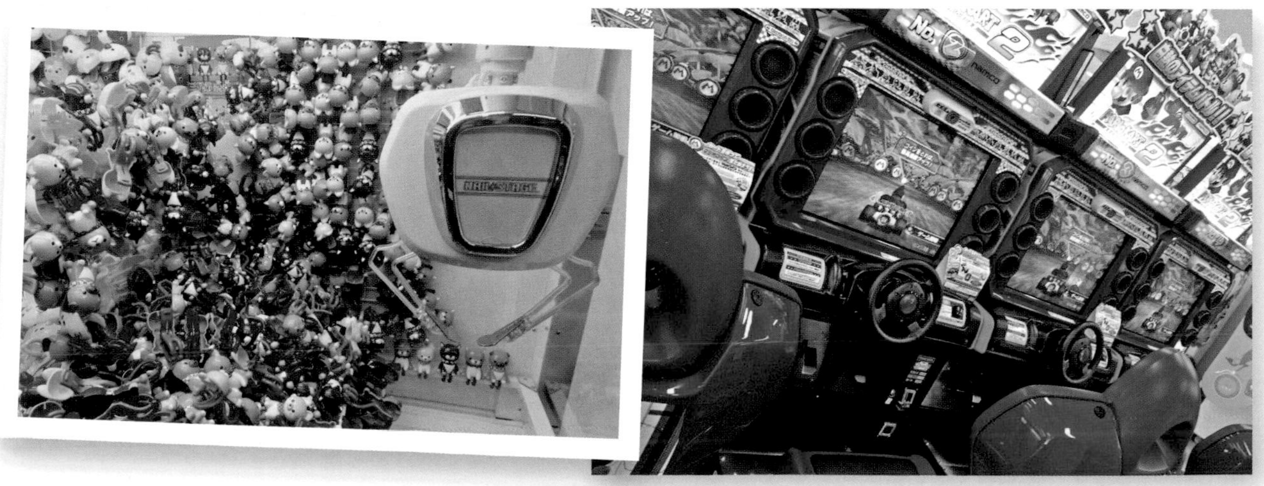

Japanese arcades is that many—if not most—cabinets are connected to common motherboards. This allows you to challenge one of the players on the opposite row, adding a thrilling note to the already exciting situation. The downside is that if you're unlucky enough to be challenged by a master player, you will likely walk out of the game center with empty pockets and a bruised ego.

If you want to avoid this embarrassment, you can always take refuge in one of the many dedicated cabinets; i.e., games housed in a specific casing that offer a quintessential arcade experience. These driving, flying and gun-shooting games offer a degree of sensory immersion and emotional involvement that cannot be duplicated at home.

While the kinds of games mentioned above have been around forever, you have to go upstairs to see the hottest fun in town. It's on the semi-dark third floor that you'll find the huge variety of music-based games. This genre is relatively new, but it has proved extremely successful in luring new customers to Japanese arcades. The games are roughly divided into three groups: dance games, music simulators and rhythm games. Dance games used to rule in the late 1990s, but have recently been replaced by Groove Coaster, Jubeat and the Sound Voltex series—games in which you manipulate knobs and hit buttons in order to match a certain rhythmic or musical pattern.

You'll notice that some people pull out a smart card every time they play a game. These so-called e-Amusement cards, which cost 300 yen, are part of an online service that players use to save their progress between games, keep track of their statistics and ranking, and access exclusive features like special songs. Certain arcades even let card holders try new games for free. Just swipe your card on the reader and get a one-time free game!

These are the main arcade features. A typical game center has even more to offer, but it's either games of chance (things like electronic mahjong and pachinko . . . not terribly exciting stuff) or card-based games, which obviously require the cards on top of understanding what the hell is going on in order to enjoy them.

Much better to finish your arcade full immersion with a visit to the *purikura* or photo-sticker booths (you can find them either on the first or top floor) that let you choose a background, scribble digital notes, add decorations to the pictures and even retouch your face and body so that you can look like a model. Just be warned that some *purikura* do not allow men unless they are accompanied by a female.

## VR Game Centers

Since 2016, virtual reality has become the new frontier in the ever-evolving world of video games. While those futuristic-looking head-mounted displays (HMDs) are still quite expensive to buy, you can enjoy VR games for a lot less in VR game centers. All the places mentioned here are located in Tokyo and have detailed English websites. Just remember that most of them require visitors to have at least some Japanese language ability.

### VR Zone Shinjuku

**Fee:** *6-ticket set: 6,200 yen; 4-ticket set: 4,400* **Hours:** *10:00–22:00* **Access:** *1-29-1 Kabukicho*
**vrzone-pic.com**

### Sky Circus Sunshine 60 (Ikebukuro)

**Fee:** *Admission: 1,200 yen (900 yen for high school and university students, 600 yen for elementary and junior high students); attractions: 400–600 yen*
**Hours:** *10:00–22:00* **Access:** *60F Sunshine City, 3-1 Higashi-Ikebukuro*
**sunshinecity.jp/en/observatory**

### VR Park Tokyo (Shibuya)

**Fee:** *Weekdays: 2,900 yen; Saturdays, Sundays, national and school holidays: 3,300 yen for a 110-minute all-you-can-play set* **Hours:** *10:00–23:20* **Access:** *4F Adores, 13-11 Udagawacho*
**adores.jp/vrpark/en/shibuya.html**

### Zero Latency VR (Odaiba)

**Fee:** *Admission: 800 yen (500 for 7- to 17-year-olds); attractions: 600 yen; Passport Ticket (all included): 4,300 yen (3,300 for 7- to 17-year-olds); show your passport and get a 300-yen discount* **Hours:** *10:00–22:00* **Access:** *Joypolis 3-5F Decks, 1-6-1 Daiba*
**tokyo-joypolis.com/language/english/attraction/1st/zerolatency/index.html**

LEFT Game centers include a variety of games and experiences, from UFO catchers (crane-and-claw games) to driving and flying games and *purikura* or photo-sticker booths. The second and third floors of a game center is where you'll find the typical games that most people identify with arcade fun: shooting games, fighting games and dedicated cabinets.

# *The Prince of Tennis* and 2.5-D Musicals

For centuries, the Japanese have been enthusiastic theatergoers, equally enjoying kabuki and noh, modern theater, and the only-in-Japan all-female Takarazuka troupe. Musical is another extremely popular genre, with major productions regularly selling out and enjoying long runs. This doesn't really come as a surprise, because many of the above-mentioned genres mix drama and music to great effect. What is rather surprising, though, is the clever way in which manga, anime and video game story lines are being adapted to the musical form, creating a new kind of entertainment that is uniquely Japanese. Called 2.5-D musicals, these productions have successfully mixed 3-D stage acting and 2-D illustration-like gimmicks.

The originator and by far the most popular of these works is the *Prince of Tennis Musical*, a stage adaptation of Konomi Takeshi's hit manga of the same title. After a slow start in 2003, *Tenimyu* (short for Tennis Musical), as it is affectionately called by local fans, has proved increasingly popular, particularly among girls who make up most of the audience at every sold-out performance. Although the manga ended its run in 2008, the stage version (which was composed of 22 different musicals) lasted until 2010, requiring in the process double casting of characters and live streaming in multiple theaters in order to satisfy the growing demand. It was followed by a second series in 2011–2014, while a third one premiered in 2015.

The story of a teenage boy who first fights his way into his junior high school's prestigious tennis club and then goes on to lead his team to capture the national title would seem an odd choice as the basis for a musical, but it has proved the right mix of drama, quirky humor, songs and dance numbers.

At the heart of each performance are the choreographed tennis scenes where the actors—a parade of cool *ikemen* (handsome boys; hence the franchise's popularity with girls)—jump around the almost empty stage while hitting an imaginary ball. Then they suddenly stop to create surreal and highly dramatic freeze-frame effects, turning the frantic on-stage action into a manga-like tableau. It is this mixture of 3-D performance and 2-D sensibility that makes these 2.5-D musicals so engaging. Of course, this being a musical, each scene is accompanied by over-the-top tunes and exciting songs that are compiled into sought-after CDs (likely to be found in many Otome Road shops in Ikebukuro).

This novel formula has proven so successful (*Tenimyu* has sold more than two million tickets so far) that the ad-hoc Japan 2.5-Dimensional Musical Association has since come up with a seemingly endless stream of new productions, adapting to the stage such otaku heavyweights as *Sailor Moon*, *Naruto*, *Haikyu!!*, *Sengoku Basara* and *Death Note*. Many of them are staged at the AiiA 2.5 Theater in Kobe, and at a number of venues around Japan including THE GALAXY THEATER and the Shinagawa Prince Hotel Stellar Ball in Tokyo. Check the 2.5-D Musical website for details.

**AiiA 2.5 Theater Kobe**
*2F Kotonohako Kobe, 1 Kitanocho, Chuo-ku*
*aia-theater.com*

***Prince of Tennis* Musical**
*tennimu.com*

**2.5-D musical lineup**
*j25musical.jp*

# Dojinshi Self-Publishing

Independent publishing is alive and well in Japan, and this being the Land of the Otaku, the great majority of small-press titles are devoted to manga, anime and video-game stories and characters. Thousands of so-called *dojinshi*—self-published manga, magazines or novels—are produced everywhere and openly sold online, in dedicated stores and at *dojin* fairs. The *dojinshi* market, in fact, is nearly as large as the official manga industry.

To be sure, the *dojin* community encompasses all kinds of independent productions, from video games, DVDs and illustrations to music CDs, clothes and accessories, but the overwhelming majority of *dojin* works are comic books and magazines. This category, in particular, is further divided in two groups: original stories and *niji sosaku*, which are parodies of mainstream anime, manga and video games. This latter subgenre is by far the biggest and most popular among fans. At the biannual Comiket in Tokyo, for instance, six halls are devoted to parodies, versus just two for original titles.

The problem with *niji sosaku* is that most of them are technically illegal, as they rework copyrighted stories, creating alternate plots and using their characters in unorthodox ways.

Then there's the problem with pornography, as many *dojinshi* feature very explicit art. Surprisingly, though, all the buying and selling goes on undisturbed while publishers and the authorities usually look the other way. The artists themselves, with a few exceptions, seem to be mostly flattered by the obvious popularity their works enjoy among fans.

There are so many *dojin* fairs in Japan that nearly every week one or more takes place around the country. If you can read Japanese, the best way to keep yourself updated is to sign up with the *dojin* portal Circle.ms (circle.ms) so you will automatically get news on any upcoming events.

If you don't have the time or are too intimidated to brave the masses of hardcore *dojin* fans in Odaiba, you can still get your fair share of zines in the many specialized *dojinshi* stores. These shops have so many titles that making sense of the way in which they are organized is not easy. They may be arranged by genre and/or circle. Popular series are further divided by Character Pairing (CP). Of course, everything is written in Japanese, so unless you know the katakana syllabic system, you will hardly find anything on your own. Better ask the staff, so don't forget the artist's or circle's name and the zine's original Japanese title.

Most new *dojinshi* are priced between 500 and 900 yen depending on size (A5 or, more commonly, B5), page count (30 to 40 pages), the author's popularity and the artistic level. Compilations are more expensive (1,000 to 2,000 yen). Also, the same publication can be priced differently depending on the shop. Ideally you will want to check a few places before making your purchase. In this respect, Ikebukuro's Otome Road is the perfect place to shop, as all the *dojinshi* stores are bunched up in the same area.

I mentioned pornography earlier. If you are interested in this genre, be sure to take a valid ID with you, because you may be asked to show proof of your age. Apparently Toranoana is particularly strict in this sense.

One last word of warning: All *dojinshi* are sealed, so if you find an interesting-looking zine by an unknown circle there's no way you can check its contents out. Whatever you do, you'd better not try to tear open the clear bags, because (as every shop makes clear) if you get caught you'll be kicked out for good.

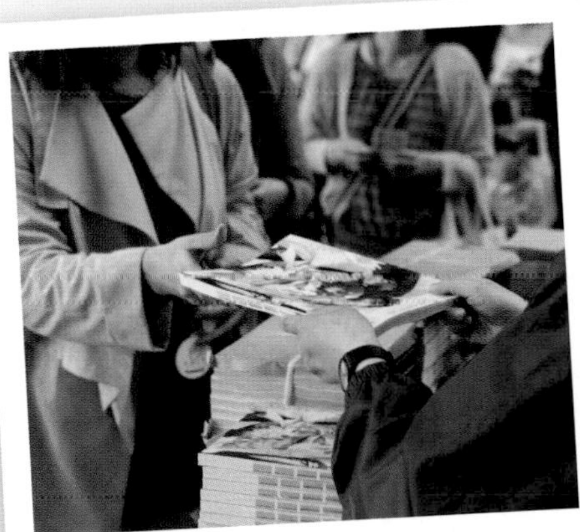

At Super Comic City you'll find independently produced comics and other goods for otaku.

# CHAPTER 1

# TOKYO and the

# Surrounding Region

# AKIHABARA: THE CENTER OF THE OTAKU UNIVERSE

In the 1980s, journalist Vittorio Zucconi spent a few years in Tokyo as a reporter for a major Italian newspaper. As he later recalled in the book he wrote about his experiences, the first time he gazed at the Tokyo cityscape from a plane he thought it looked like a giant toy box turned upside down. While his words were meant as an unflattering comment on the city's chaotic urban sprawl, they aptly describe Akihabara. Indeed, the district today is nothing but a treasure trove of "toys," its streets filled with people who are constantly looking for old and new manga, anime, figures and whatever else the otaku industry has come up with. However, Akihabara hasn't always been like this. Today's futuristic otaku capital of the world is just the latest in a series of the neighborhood's iterations, which have one thing in common: introducing the latest technology in order to fulfill people's desires.

**A Little History**

Akihabara's history as "Electric Town" began after World War Two, when many radio technicians who had returned from the front began to sell radio components in the black market that had quickly developed under the elevated railway. They were later joined by students from the electronic schools who began to build and sell radio sets.

The "electronic heart" of the district has survived the many transformations the area has witnessed since then. Even today, people who try to find their way at Akihabara Station are directed to the Electric Town Exit (電気街口), and the Radio Center and Denpa Kaikan (the Radio Wave building) can still be found under the tracks and alongside the Sobu-Chuo line respectively. If you want to devote all your precious time to manga- and game-hunting, you can easily skip this part of Akihabara, but even if plugs, LEDs and connectors bore you to tears, I suggest you stop by and pay homage to the core of the area, where everything got started.

While the hunger for cheap entertainment was behind the radio craze of the postwar years, the 1960s saw a growing demand for TVs and so-called "white goods" (large household electrical appliances), driven by the economic boom. Whole families would trek to Akihabara in order to acquire fridges and washing machines, and the original hobby shops made way for stores selling these new status symbols. This trend peaked during the 1970s, when as many as 10 percent of all household appliances sold in Japan were bought in Akihabara.

First a black market for radio components, then a center for household appliances, Akihabara is now famed for computer-related shops and its thriving otaku culture.

The "electronic heart" of Akihabara still exists and has survived the area's many transformations.

The next big turning point in Akihabara's history came along in the early 1980s. When all the major household-appliance chain stores began to move to the suburbs, closer to where people lived, the void left by these companies was quickly filled by a new kind of shop, thanks to the birth of the FamiCon game console and an increased popular interest in home computers. Then, in the early 1990s, the big guns began to move in, with computer giant Laox opening its main store not far from the station in 1990; Sofmap established its first branch on Chuo-dori three years later. This process culminated in 1994, when computer-related sales surpassed other consumer electronics for the first time.

Even though 21st-century Akihabara is better known for its thriving otaku culture than computers, this relatively small district still boasts what is arguably the greatest concentration of computer-related shops in the world, with brand new PCs being sold on Chuo-dori and secondhand stuff being peddled in the small shops in the backstreets, while spare parts of all kinds can be found in the narrow, low-ceilinged corridors near the station.

Though computer hobbyists resembled the people who used to tinker with radios back in the 1950s, many of them were also into manga, anime and video games. As a consequence, the new DIY PC era saw a gradual transformation of Akihabara: with the release of a new generation of game consoles (Sega Saturn, PlayStation and Nintendo 64) more and more retailers started to sell game software, including manga- and anime-based products.

Everybody seems to agree that the single most important event behind this transition was the huge success of the TV anime series *Neon Genesis Evangelion*, first aired in 1995. Subsequent reruns and the 1997 feature movie helped elevate the show's cult status. Meanwhile, the huge amount of money the title generated (an estimated 20 to 30 billion yen from books, plastic models and other goods) was a bonanza for otaku-oriented shops, and more and more of them were drawn to Akihabara.

Since then, the thriving Japanese and international otaku communities have turned the place into their capital. After the turn of the century, computer and hi-fi shops have been increasingly replaced by stores—big and small—selling manga, anime, video games and other otaku-related music and video products, including more controversial adult stuff.

Though Akihabara's association with otaku culture has brought the district huge financial gains and unprecedented global fame, mainstream Japanese society initially had a hard time accepting a community that since 1989 (the year serial killer Miyazaki Tsutomu—the "Otaku Killer"—was arrested) had been seen as a bunch of creepy antisocial nerds. That changed, however, in 2005 with the unexpected success of the *Densha Otoko* (Train Man) book/TV drama/film saga, which signaled the popular acceptance of otaku.

The nation-wide *moe* boom that followed has continued to shape the look and character of the district as an otaku mecca. It was also in 2005 that major electronics chain retailer Yodobashi Camera opened its mammoth Yodobashi Akiba store on the former site of an old freight depot; at the end of that year idol girl-group AKB48 debuted at their AKB48 Theater on the eighth floor of the local Don Quijote store. Since then Akihabara has become a sort of wonderland where otaku of every persuasion not only have a chance to get their most outlandish desires fulfilled, but can discover things they never dared to dream up.

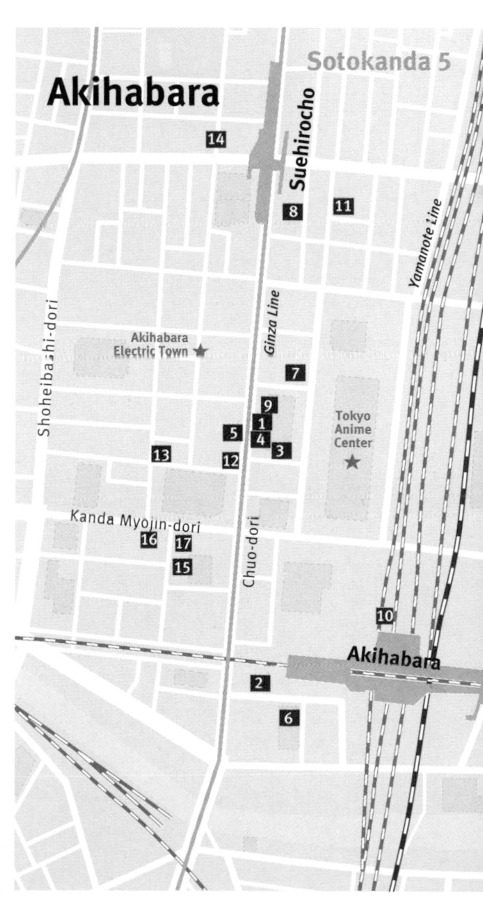

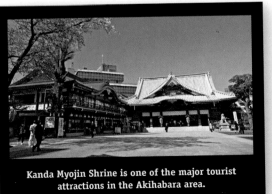


Kanda Myojin Shrine is one of the major tourist attractions in the Akihabara area.

# EXPLORING AKIHABARA

One good thing about Akihabara is that most of the shops are concentrated in a relatively small area west of the station, and even the most distant can be reached on foot in five to ten minutes. Chuo-dori (the main avenue) is home to many of the bigger stores. You can use it as your main reference point and branch off to the back streets on either side in order to explore the smaller niche shops. Be prepared for tremendous visual and aural overload, with garishly colored giant billboards, neon lights and loud music assaulting you from every direction.

Even though Akihabara's core area is just half a square mile (150,000 square meters), the sheer number of shops means it's impossible to see everything in a few hours. So unless you can make more than one trip, you'd better plan your visit carefully. Be ready to climb stairs and ride elevators. This is nothing less than a treasure hunt, after all.

Even though the place is crowded on Sundays, that may be a good time to explore the neighborhood and take in the whole scene, as Chuo-dori is closed to traffic. All the singing and dancing has been outlawed, but you still have a chance to catch sight of some wandering party of cosplayers.

## East of Chuo-dori

### General

**1 Animate**

Since opening its first store in Ikebukuro in 1983, Animate has become Japan's largest retailer of anime, manga and video games, with branches everywhere. The Akiba shop is a little smaller than the main store in Ikebukuro, but it still features seven floors of everything, including some goods found only at this location. The event space on the seventh floor hosts authors and voice actors for autographs and hand-shaking. This is by no means the cheapest place in Akihabara, but the range of goods on offer is hard to beat.

**Hours:** *10:00–21:00* **Access:** *4-3-2 Soto-Kanda* **animate.co.jp**

**2 Gamers**

Gamers, born as a joint venture between Animate and media company Broccoli (hence its original name AniBro), focuses on manga, anime and games. On the upper floors they often collaborate with different creators (e.g., visual novel maker Nitroplus) on so-called Museum special events (original picture displays, card game tournaments, etc.).

**Hours:** *9:00–22:00 (1F), 10:00–21:00 (2-7F)* **Access:** *1-14-7 Soto-Kanda* **anibro.jp**

### Manga

**3 4 5 Comic Toranoana**

A visit to this place (founded back in 1994, when "otaku" still was a bad word) is a must if you are into the fan-generated comics known as *dojinshi*. Stores A and B are next to each other. Store A stocks mainstream manga as well, but has become universally—and deservedly—famous for its huge ***dojinshi*** catalogue (11,000 titles for a total of 1.2 million copies). If

ABOVE Toranoana is a paradise for fans of indie comics and dojinshi. RIGHT When visiting Akihabara be prepared for tremendous visual and aural overload.

you are hunting for vintage issues or signed editions, this is the place for you. Store B specializes in CDs, DVDs and Blu-rays, including ***dojin*** audio and video works. And if you don't have the time to visit Akiba (just kidding!) they have more shops scattered around and near Tokyo (see list at toranoana.jp/shop).

**Hours:** *10:00–22:00* **Access:** *4-3-1 Soto-Kanda*
**toranoana.jp**

### 6 K-Books

While better described as a general store selling character goods, *mecha* models, CDs, video games and the like, K-Books' Akiba branch is better known for stocking a staggering 200,000 to 300,000 publications of all kinds: collected manga and *dojinshi*, illustrated books, and more than 100 new light novels (short young-adult novels mainly targeting middle- and high-school girls) every month.

**Hours:** *11:00–20:00* **Access:** *3–4F Radio Kaikan, 1-15-16 Soto-Kanda*
**k-books.co.jp**

## Anime and DVDs

### 7 Heroine Tokusatsu Kenkyujo

ヒロイン特撮研究所

The Heroine Special Effects Research Center is the door to a different, slightly darker side of Akihabara. Ever heard of such masterpieces as Zen Pictures' *Enormous Breasts Squadron Fiber Star* or *Hyper Sexy Heroine Cyber Soldier Etoile*? If you're interested in Power Rangers parody, Sailor Moon–like characters and masked-girl fighters, Studio 2.5's wacky Akiba-kei action porno flicks and other low budget V-Cinema (straight-to-video) stuff, this store could change your life. They even sell the original costumes used during the shoots.

**Hours:** *11:00–22:00* **Access:** *B1 Matsui Bldg., 4-4-9 Soto-Kanda* **heroinetokusatsu.jp**

## Toys

### 6 Kaiyodo Hobby Lobby Tokyo

Japan's only retail shop for this popular figure and model maker can be found on the fifth floor of the famed Radio Kaikan building. Kaiyodo is synonymous with beautifully crafted figures. Their works are so realistic that their dinosaur models, for instance, were reportedly used as the basis for the CG design of the monsters in *Jurassic Park*. The Revoltech series of figures featuring the company's unique "Revolver Joint" articulation system are also famous. Last but not least, the garage kits displayed every year at the Wonder Showcase (see the **Wonder Festival** entry) can also be bought here.

**Hours:** *11:00–20:00 (closed irregularly for events, etc.)* **Access:** *5F Radio Kaikan, 1-15-16 Soto-Kanda*
**kaiyodo.co.jp/kaiyodo_HB/TK_topics**

**ABOVE** Event and new product information is plastered on every available surface in Akihabara. Unfortunately, very little of this information is in English.

### 8 Toys Golden Age

This the place if you are into retro toys. The tiny, cramped shop is bursting at the seams with all the classic products Japan is famous for: *Godzilla*, *Ultraman*, *kaiju*, *Kamen Rider*, *Mazinger Z* and other *sofubi* and *chogokin*; minicars; Candy Candy and other girls' toys; tin toys; magazines for kids; bromides (old photo portraits of idols) . . . It literally has things you won't find anywhere else in Akiba. Enough said.

**Hours:** *11:30–21:00; closed on Tuesdays*
**Access:** *4-7-2 Soto-Kanda*
*(No website—they are old school, after all)*

Toys Golden Age is the first place you should check out if you are into retro toys.

## Idols

### 9 AKB48 Theater

Since 2005, this small venue on top of the Don Quijote discount store has been the home base of AKB48, the most popular Japanese idol group of the decade; it also hosts the other member groups of the AKB galaxy whenever they are on tour in Tokyo. The theater seats only 145 people and has a total capacity of 250, making each concert a rather intimate experience (even though two big pillars near the stage partially block your view if you happen to get the wrong seat). The bad news—especially if you are in Tokyo on a trip—is that tickets are assigned by random lottery after you have applied through their website. Considering the group's popularity, you have between a 1:50 and a 1:200 chance at getting one. Good luck! (To learn how to apply for tickets, see the **HKT48 Theater** sidebar in the Fukuoka chapter.)

**Hours:** *17:00–20:00 (weekdays), 12:00–19:00 (weekends and national holidays)* **Access:** *8F Don Quixote Bldg., 4-3-3 Soto-Kanda*
**akb48.co.jp/theater**

Mandarake is Akiba's largest seller of used manga- and aniime-related goods.

LEFT AKB48 costumes; BELOW AKB48coasters. RIGHT Manga characters adorn advertising posters for otaku superstore Sofmap.

## Eateries

### 10 Gundam Café

Next door to the AKB48 Café, this popular joint can be a pretty underwhelming experience for the casual visitor, but if you are a Gundam fan you'll love it no matter what. Besides the obligatory big screen playing videos nonstop, you can admire several model kits on display. The food and drink are far from memorable, but fans will surely be impressed by the staff (who are clad in Gundam-like uniforms) and the funky toilet featuring special sound effects. And the attached shop sells limited-edition goods, along with more food, including *gunpla-yaki*, the Gundam twist on traditional *taiyaki* cakes filled with sweet bean paste and whipped cream.

**Hours:** *10:00–22:30*
**Access:** *1-1 Kanda-Hanaokacho* **g-cafe.jp**

## Other Venues

### 11 Akiba Joshi-ryo あきば女子寮

Here's your chance to infiltrate a girls' dormitory (*joshi-ryo*) where the pajama-wearing "resident" girls, instead of screaming and calling the cops, are more than happy to engage you in conversation and play games. The "dorm" has several rooms furnished in different ways—one for each girl. The basic course, which costs 1,880 yen for 30 minutes, consists of chatting and playing analog and/or video games with the girl of your choice. There are plenty of additional options (1,000 to 3,000 yen each), including light massages, photo-taking and even being slapped across the face (!).

**Hours:** *13:00–21:30* **Access:** *3F, 4-8-3 Soto-Kanda* **planetplan.net**

## West of Chuo-dori

## General

### 12 Akiba Sofmap #1

アキバ☆ソフマップ1号店

If you are really in a hurry and can only hit one shop, this one may be your best choice. Taking center stage on Chuo-dori, it's a sort of otaku supermarket with a little bit of everything: manga, character goods, J-Pop and idol CDs and DVDs (including an AKB48 special corner), *pla-mo*, cards and even light novels. The seventh and eighth floors are event spaces.

**Hours:** *11:00–20:00* **Access:** *3-13-12 Soto-Kanda* **sofmap.com**

### 13 Mandarake Complex

Housed in a menacing-looking black monolith nicknamed "Treasure Mountain," Mandarake is Akiba's largest seller of used manga- and anime-related goods. Each of its eight floors is devoted to a different genre. While their selection does not compare to that of more specialized retailers, their prices are often cheaper. And if you can't make it all the way to Japan, they also ship abroad. Just check their excellent English website. WARNING: If erotic stuff makes you uncomfortable,

BELOW A long queue outside Sofmap, a sort of otaku supermarket with something for all tastes.

you may want to avoid the "men's entertainment" on the fourth floor.
**Hours:** *12:00–20:00* **Access:** *3-11-12 Soto-Kanda* **mandarake.co.jp** *(English)*

## Video Games

### 14 Friends フレンズ

You might think this small, unassuming place run by an old lady and her husband isn't worth your time. Think again, because this is a Holy Land for retro-game hunters, and its ever-changing selection includes games for less popular consoles. Most importantly, their prices are unbeatable (they even have bins filled with loose cartridges you can get for as cheap as 100 yen), so if you find what you want here, don't bother looking for a better deal.
**Hours:** *11:00–20:00; closed on Tuesdays.* **Access:** *2-3F, 2 Shin-Etsu Kanda Bldg., 6-14-13 Soto-Kanda* **gameshop.ocnk.net**

### 15 Super Potato スーパーポテト

This is perhaps the most famous of the retro game shops in Akiba. When the area is featured on TV, chances are this place will be shown. They have practically EVERYTHING, including Neo Geo and PC Engine games and very rare (i.e., very expensive) goods. They even sell game-related items (strategy guides, T-shirts, Super Mario glasses, etc.). The downside is that their prices are 25 to 30 percent higher than the competition. That said, they do have two- or three-day bargain sales, which usually take place during holidays (Golden Week in early May; Obon in mid August; and New Year). There's even a small game center on the top floor, complete with glass-topped cabinets for that old '70s feeling.
**Hours:** *11:00–20:00 (weekdays), 10:00–20:00 (weekends)* **Access:** *3-5F 1-11-2 Soto-Kanda* **superpotatoakiba.jp**

## Game Centers

### Club Sega

**Hours:** *10:00–1:00* **Access:** *1-10-9 Soto-Kanda* **bpnavi.jp/toru/ssc/shop/1186**

### Taito HEY

**Hours:** *10:00–24:00* **Access:** *1-10-5 Soto-Kanda* **taito.co.jp/gc/store/00001703**

### Tokyo Leisure Land

**Hours:** *10:00–1:00* **Access:** *1-9-5 Soto-Kanda* **llakihabara.sakura.ne.jp**

## Idols

### 16 Akiba Cultures Theaters

The Akiba Cultures Zone building is home to many otaku shops, but the most interesting place is in the basement. If you are among the many people who couldn't get hold of an AKB48 concert ticket, your best chance to catch a live performance in Akihabara is to check out the Akiba Cultures Theater, a 220-seat venue that holds concerts almost every day. You can buy tickets from their website, from the Ticket Pia ticket agency and even at the door, and with a rotating lineup of up-and-coming idol groups, you may be lucky enough to see the superstars of tomorrow.
**Access:** *B1F Akiba Cultures Zone, 1-7-6 Soto-Kanda* **akibalive.jp**

ABOVE A maid touts for customers. BELOW Super Potato may be the most famous of Akiba's retro game shops.

## Eateries

### 17 @home café

This maid café has a dedicated army of 170 maids ready to entertain the honorable *goshujin-sama* (master)—but only for one hour at a time, and there's a 600-yen cover charge. The main location (there is another inside Don Quijote) is divided into three areas: Classical (mainly eating and drinking in a quiet environment); Entertainment (for chatting and playing games with the maids); and Bar. Depending on the course menu one chooses, it is also possible to have your picture taken and/or play games with a maid.
**Hours:** *11:00–22:00; closed irregularly* **Access:** *4–7F Mitsuwa Building, 1-11-4 Soto-Kanda* **cafe-athome.com**

# EXPLORING JIMBOCHO

Tokyo is a city of specialized neighborhoods, each one devoted to a particular trade (musical instruments in Ochanomizu, kitchen utensils in Kappabashi, textiles in Nippori, etc.), and if you are a lover of secondhand or rare books you must pay a visit to Jimbocho. Once the home of many samurai (its name derives from one of them, Jimbo Nagaharu), in the late nineteenth century it began to attract many intellectuals, as three of Tokyo's most prestigious universities (Meiji, Nihon and Chuo) were founded here. After a fire destroyed most of the district in 1913, a university professor named Iwanami Shigeo opened a bookstore which eventually became Iwanami Shoten, one of the country's more prestigious publishing houses.

If you are a lover of secondhand or rare books, you must come to Jimbocho, a neighborhood that has one of the highest concentrations of booksellers and publishers in the world.

Others followed his example, and today Jimbocho has one of the world's highest concentrations of sellers and publishers of books, including major manga companies Shueisha (famous for its *Jump* magazine series) and Shogakukan, whose offices are only a short walk south of Jimbocho's main intersection and subway station, on the right side of Hakusan-dori. Fans of Urasawa Naoki's *20th Century Boys*, a comic that was originally published by Shogakukan, will remember that the company's building was actually featured (and destroyed) in those pages—an example of the sort of in-jokes that manga and anime creators often like to slip into their stories.

Even today the area is very popular with college students and book lovers in search of a good read, and is further renowned for its eateries and cafés. Book shops run the gamut from big multi-story establishments selling new titles (Sanseido) to elegant antiquarian stores (Kitazawa Shoten) and tiny hole-in-the-wall sellers. Admittedly, for people who don't read Japanese it can be rather frustrating, as the places that sell foreign-language books are very few and specialize in rare, high-quality (therefore expensive) books. Still, otaku fans will surely have fun checking out the shops listed below. All the stores are close to Jimbocho Station on the Tokyo Metro Hanzomon Line.

**Note:** You can visit the Shueisha Gallery on the first floor of the Shueisha building at 3-13 Kanda-Jimbocho, on weekdays from 9:30 to 17:30.

### 1 ARATAMA

One of the best shops in the area for goods related to idols and gravure models, the first floor has DVDs, pictures, photo books (often of the naughty variety) and magazines, while the Poster Collection on the second floor has a huge stock of posters (a rare Morning Musume signed poster sells for 50,000 yen), calendars, trading cards, telephone cards and ephemera.
**Hours:** *11:00–20:00 (Monday through Saturday), 11:00–19:00 (Sun)* **Access:** *1-3-5 Kanda-Jimbocho* **aratama.com**

### 2 Bunken Rock Side
ブンケン・ロック・サイド

Easily recognizable by its bright red front, this shop specializes in music magazines, but if you dig around you will find many idol and anime mags as well.
**Hours:** *10:30–19:30 (Monday through Saturday), 11:00–19:00 (Sundays and national holidays)* **Access:** *2-3 Kanda-Jimbocho* **bunken-shoin.co.jp**

### 3 Comic Takaoka コミック高岡

This store specializes in brand-new comic books, magazines and light novels. The first floor sells manga for men, while the basement floor has works for women (including BL comics) and reprinted classics by famous authors like Tezuka Osamu and Nagai Go.
**Hours:** *11:00–21:00 (weekdays), 11:00–19:30 (Saturdays), 12:00–18:30 (Sundays and national holidays)* **Access:** *1-9 Kanda-Jimbocho* **comic-takaoka.jp**

### 4 Kanke Shobo かんけ書房

Located inside a nondescript red-brick building (don't miss the tiny sign at the entrance reading 古本・かんけ書房・2F), this shop carries a small but interesting selection of boys' and girls' manga, old issues of *Garo* and *COM* (these were the two best alternative comic anthologies in the late '60s-early '70s, and are definitely worth your yen), and other vintage delights.

Atom Boy and other vintage comics on display in a Jimbocho shop window.

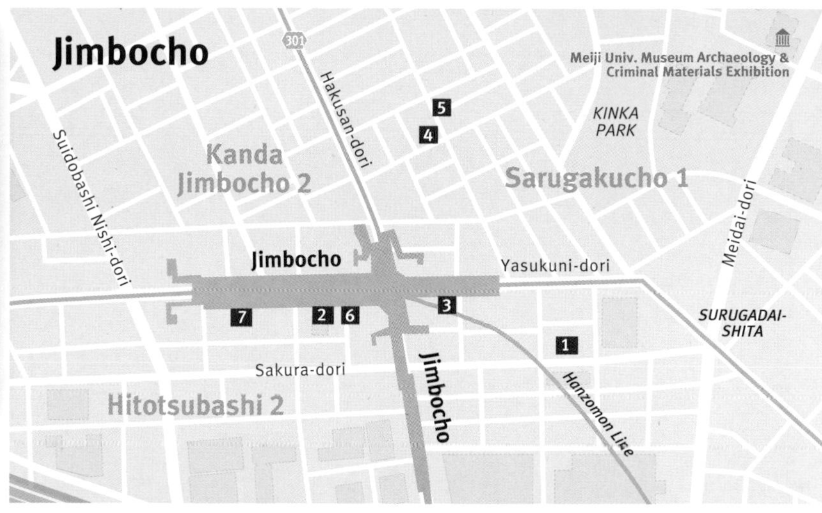


**Hours:** *11:00–16:30 (Monday through Saturday), 11:00–14:30 (Sundays and national holidays); closed on the third Sunday of every month* **Access:** *2F, 1-32 Kanda-Jimbocho*
**kanke.news.coocan.jp**

### 5 Kasumi Shoboカスミ書房

Next door to Kudan Shobo (see below), this shop stocks an interesting mix of books and magazines on anime, *tokusatsu*, SF and music.
**Hours:** *13:00–18:00; closed Sundays* **Access:** *3F, 1-34 Kanda-Jimbocho*
**ne.jp/asahi/kasumi/syobo**

### 5 Kudan Shoboくだん書房

Hidden on the third floor of a small derelict building on the right side of the street (look for a small くだん書房 sign near the entrance), Kudan Shobo is a place for connoisseurs. From comic books and magazines to dojinshi and *kashihon* (rental books), this tiny, messy shop is all about girls' manga, and it's very well worth a visit.
**Hours:** *11:00–19:00 (Monday through Saturday); closed on Sundays and national holidays* **Access:** *3F, 1-34 Kanda-Jimbocho*
**kudan.jp**

### 6 Nakano Shoten Manga Store 中野書店漫画部

If you only have time for one place, this is it. The most famous old-style vintage manga store in the neighborhood is a paradise for serious collectors with lots of money to spend. For instance, this is the store where you have the best chance of finding Tezuka Osamu's first editions. *Lost World* and *Treasure Island* will likely be priced around 100,000 yen. On the cheaper side, they have old issues of *Garo* and *COM* going for 1,000 to 2,000 yen depending on their rarity and condition. This shop sells anime cels and a lot more as well.
**Hours:** *10:00–18:30 (Monday through Saturday), 11:00–17:30 (Sundays and national holidays); closed on the third Sunday of every month* **Access:** *2F Kanda Kosho Center, 2-3 Kanda-Jimbocho*
**nakano.jimbou.net/catalog/index.php**

### 7 Vintage

Covers about the same genres as Bunken Rock Side (listed above).
**Hours:** *11:00–19:00 (Monday through Saturday), 12:00–19:00 (Sundays and national holidays)* **Access:** *2-5 Kanda-Jimbocho*
**jimboucho-vintage.jp**

**LEFT** Signboards for Kudan Shobo (left) and Kasumi Shobo. **RIGHT** Jimbocho is a treasure trove of vintage and retro publications.

# EXPLORING HARAJUKU

Walking through Youth Fashion Central these days, it's hard to believe that during the feudal period, ninja were quartered here and even had their own shrine (Onden Jinja, 5-26-6 Jingumae), while the local farmers cleaned their rice and milled their flour at the watermill on the Shibuya River. Today JR trains, not water, run under the Harajuku bridge, but the real action happens on the bridge itself, with tribes of Lolitas (both cute and gothic), French maids and other assorted cosplayers vying for attention. If quirky, loud, cute fashion is your thing, then forget the rest of Tokyo and head directly here. The back streets east of Meiji-dori in particular (Jingumae 3- and 4-chome—the very same area the ninja turned into a maze of narrow winding streets in order to make life difficult for possible invaders), now known internationally as Ura-Harajuku, are full of small, independent fashion shops.

**ABOVE** Takeshita-dori is an unavoidable stop for Harajuku pilgrims. **LEFT** Doll lovers should make a beeline for Volks Tenshi no Mado.

More orthodox otaku treasure hunters may be a little disappointed by what they find here, as several shops and cafés have moved to Akihabara (including Blister and Hello! Project) or Ikebukuro (Evangelion) while others have closed for good (Edelstein). But if you're after toys and figures, Harajuku is still very much worth a visit, as the district has established itself as the best place in Tokyo for serious toy collectors.

### 1 Spinns

Spinns is one of the favorite fashion brands of the hip Harajuku crowd. In Japan you can see several different trends and styles at the same time, and people are not afraid to experiment and mix them all together. The fashion sold here is a mix of street culture, anime characters and other otaku themes. Harajuku has two Spinns stores: Chucla by Spinns and another one in Takeshita-dori, both a five-minute walk from JR Harajuku Station.

**Chucla by Spinns** **Hours:** *12:00–20:00* **Access:** *2F, 1-15-2 Jingumae* **chucla.stores.jp**

**Spinns Harajuku Takeshita-dori** **Hours:** *12:00–20:00* **Access:** *2F, 1-7-1 Jingumae* **twitter.com/spinns_tkst**

### 2 6%DOKIDOKI

More than 20 years have passed since artist and designer Sebastian Masuda dropped his version of "*kawaii* anarchy" in the middle of the unsuspecting Harajuku crowd. Many things have changed since then (most notably Masuda's collaboration with Kyary Pamyu Pamyu) but his pink-and-yellow (!!!) boutique is still the go-to place for outrageously cute clothes and accessories.

**Hours:** *12:00–20:00* **Access:** *2F, 4-28-16 Jingumae (two minutes' walk from Tokyo Metro Meiji-Jingumae Station, Chiyoda and Fukutoshin lines)* **dokidoki6.com**

### 3 Johnny's Shop Harajuku

While female idol heavyweights AKB48 and Hello! Project fight for prominence in Akihabara, boy idol kingpin Johnny Kitagawa has opened his official store in this quiet backstreet location. Here you will find countless photos and all the SMAP, Arashi and Tokio merchandise you've ever dreamed of.

**Hours:** *10:00–19:00* **Access:** *1-14-21 Jingumae (four minutes' walk from JR Harajuku Station)* **johnnys-net.jp/page?id=shop**

### 4 Kawaii Monster Café

Art director Sebastian Masuda, of 6%DOKIDOKI fame (see entry 2), has come up with yet another outrageous idea to further expand his own peculiar *kawaii* agenda. This somewhat twisted version of Alice in Wonderland is divided into four different zones and is patrolled by five Monster Girls. Primary colors abound everywhere, including the rather expensive food. There's a 500-yen charge per person if you don't fill all the seats at your booth or table, and a 90-minute time limit.

**Hours:** *11:30–22:30* **Access:** *4F, 4-31-10 Jingumae (three minutes' walk from Tokyo Metro Meiji-Jingumae Station, Chiyoda and Fukutoshin lines)* **kawaiimonster.jp**

ABOVE Tokyo's oldest toy shop, Kiddy Land, is a landmark on scenic Omotesando avenue.

ABOVE LEFT Harajuku Bridge (properly called "Gorin Bridge") became famous when cosplayers used to gather there on weekends.
ABOVE Primary colors abound at the Kawaii Monster Café.

**5** **Kiddy Land**
When Kiddy Land opened more than 60 years ago, it was the first big toy shop in Tokyo. While not particularly large by today's standards, its five floors are packed with toys, stationery, clothes and any kind of character goods. The first floor showcases what's currently trendy in Japan, while the second floor is a riot of *kawaii* character goods. Things get even more interesting on the third floor, with toys, figures and dolls for boys, girls and even adults, while on the top floor you'll find the Hello Kitty shop. A complete floor guide can be found on the website.
**Hours:** ***11:00–21:00; closed irregularly***
**Access:** ***6-1-9 Jingumae (three minutes' walk from Tokyo Metro Meiji-Jingumae Station, Chiyoda and Fukutoshin lines)***
**kiddyland.co.jp**

**6** **Sailor Moon Store**
The world's first permanent Sailor Moon store opened in 2017 to celebrate the 25th year since the first broadcast of the original TV series. Always packed with fans, the store may be small, but it sells an astonishing variety of goods ranging from key chains and smartphone cases to books, clothes and accessories, including a number of exclusive items that can only be found at this store.
**Hours:** ***11:00–21:00*** **Access:** ***B0.5F Laforet Harajuku, 1-11 Jingumae (three minutes' walk from Tokyo Metro Meiji-Jingumae Station, Chiyoda and Fukutoshin lines)***
**sailormoon-official.com/store**

**7** **Unbreakable 5**
This paradise for indie *sofubi* lovers even sells posters, original T-shirts and other gadgets. If this store doesn't meet all your needs, try Secret Base in Ginza (7F Hankyu Men's Tokyo 2-5-1 Yurakucho, Chiyoda-ku). **Hours:** ***10:00–19:00*** **Access:** ***B1F, 3-22-8 Jingumae (six minutes' walk from Tokyo Metro Meiji-Jingumae Station, Chiyoda and Fukutoshin lines)***
**secret-b.com**

**8** **Spiral Toy Store おもちゃや Spiral**
Some people claim that this little shop might be the mother of all Tokyo's toy stores for girls. Whatever the case, don't be fooled by its diminutive size—it's a treasure trove of *kawaii* goods, and all the available space is taken by toys and anime-inspired figures. They have a lot of vintage dolls and American collectibles like Doughboy, Popples, Smurf, Troll, etc.
**Hours:** ***12:00–20:00*** **Access:** ***3-27-17 Jingumae (eight minutes' walk from Tokyo Metro Meiji-Jingumae Station, Chiyoda and Fukutoshin lines*** **spiral-toy.com**

**9** **Volks Tenshi no Mado 天使の窓**
Located just down from Johnny's Shop is one of those Tokyo oddities, a strange building in neoclassical Western style. Welcome to Volks Tenshi no Mado, Tokyo's biggest Super Dollfie (SD) store. This is a sort of temple devoted to Volks's famous dolls and their owners. On the first floor is an SD display corner; a dress and wig shop is on the second. The basement floor is a rental space where doll fans can organize parties, ceremonies and photo shoots.
**Hours:** ***11:00–20:00; closed Wednesdays and the third Tuesday of every month***
**Access:** ***1-12-1 Jingumae (four minutes' walk from JR Harajuku Station)***
**volks.co.jp/jp/tenshinomado**

# EXPLORING SHIBUYA

Though Shibuya ward is not particularly famous as an otaku spot, it actually has a lot to offer to treasure hunters and urban explorers alike. Many things have happened since the 17th century, when the district was a strategically important castle town tasked with the defense of Edo. Its complete destruction by US air raids during the Second World War was the starting point for rapid development by the Tokyu Corporation, which turned Shibuya station into one of Tokyo's main transportation nodes.

Even today, in order to access Otaku Shibuya you only need to step out of the JR station's Hachiko exit. The area in front of the station, including its world famous scramble crossing, has been featured in countless stories, probably starting with 1985 OVA *Megazone*. More recently the district has been featured in the *Ghost in the Shell: Stand Alone Complex* series, episodes of *Tokyo ESP* and *Sengoku Collection*, and most importantly in the visual novel *Chaos;Head* and Hosoda Mamoru's 2015 feature film *The Boy and the Beast*. On the other side of the scramble, another anime icon is the Q-Front building. A visit to the big **Tsutaya** store inside will give you a good idea of which manga are currently hot in Japan, since they prominently display the newest popular titles, while from the ever-busy Starbucks you can enjoy the same view of the crossing that was used in the Sophia Coppola movie *Lost in Translation*.

Shibuya has been a late addition on the *kaiju* front, but Godzilla and company have wasted no time in giving the neighborhood the royal treatment, beginning with *Gamera 3: The Revenge of Iris* (1999), in which our favorite giant flying turtle disposes of a couple of Gyaos—but only after destroying Shibuya Station, the Hachiko statue and Shibuya 109, and killing 20,000 people in the process. Then, one year later, in *Godzilla vs. Megaguirus*, the district is literally flooded during the fierce battle between the Big G and its foe.

### 1 BEAM building

This is another hotbed of otaku activity. Here, for instance, you will find the most atmospheric of Tokyo's three **Mandarake** stores (12:00–20:00), at the bottom of two dark flights of stairs. The slightly sinister atmosphere is lightened by some loud anime music coming out of the PA system. With its meandering corridors and dim lights, the store can be rather confusing, but you'll have a lot of fun checking out all the goods. This place is particularly famous for its huge stock of used manga and *dojinshi* of any kind. When you are finished there, don't forget to explore the rest of the building, which also houses an **Animate** store on the third floor (11:00–22:00), a **RECOfan** branch on the fourth (11:30–21:00) selling thousands of new and used CDs (including lots of anime soundtracks), and a stylish manga café on the fifth.

***Access:** 31-2 Udagawacho (five minutes' walk from Shibuya Station)* **shibuya-beam.com**

ABOVE The Mugiwara Store is Tokyo's only authorized One Piece store. TOP An artist's impression of Shibuya's famous scramble crossing. RIGHT Galaxxxy, where "otaku" and "cool" are not mutually exclusive.

### 2 galaxxxy

The galaxxxy store is proof that "otaku" and "cool" are not mutually exclusive concepts. Besides its popular DINO character, the Shibuya-based fashion brand excels in design collaborations with an ever-expanding lineup of popular titles like Hello Kitty, Dirty Pair, Creamy Mami, Inferno Cop, Papillon Rose and manga artist Azuma Hideo. Anyone who has ever dreamed of owning a backpack shaped like a Dreamcast controller will definitely have to pay a visit to this stylish boutique.

**Hours:** ***11:00–19:00; closed Saturdays and Sundays*** **Access:** ***10-18 Maruyamacho (ten minutes' walk from Shibuya Station)*** **joe-inter.co.jp/galaxxxy**

### 3 Marui department store

Easily recognizable by its OIOI logo, this department store is mainly devoted to men's and ladies' fashion, but the seventh floor has a few otaku shops very well worth your attention. Most people, of course, come here for the **One Piece Mugiwara Store** (mugiwara-store.com). Guinness World Records recognized Oda Eiichiro's mega-hit manga as the comic book series with the most copies published by a single author (440 million as of May 2018), and a bout of binge shopping at Tokyo's only authorized store is a great way to celebrate. You can choose from an endless array of toys, figures, plushies, clothes, stickers, stationery and even character-shaped snacks and chocolates. Next to One Piece, you'll find a **Namco CharaPop Store** (Namco キャラポップストア) (bandainamco-am.co.jp) and the **I.G Store** (ig-store.jp/about/english). **CharaPop** mixes anime- and game-themed original goods (T-shirts, stickers, postcards etc.) with lotteries and other game attractions. **I.G Store**, Production I.G's official shop, sells merchandise from the anime studio's famous works (*Kuroko's Basketball, Haikyu!!, Psycho-Pass, the Ghost in the Shell* franchise, the *Joker* 

Project 1/6 is the original flagship store for Medicom, famous for its Kubrick and Be@rbrick collector series.

*Game* series, etc.) including some special exclusives. They also have an exhibition space where they show a few impressive items such as a model of the Logicoma from *Ghost in the Shell: Arise*. The eighth floor features a few event spaces which are often devoted to anime and manga characters.

**Hours:** ***11:00–21:00 (to 20:30 on national holidays)*** **Access:** ***1-22-6 Jinnan (five minutes' walk from Shibuya Station)*** **0101.co.jp/013**

### 4 Project 1/6

This is the original flagship store for Medicom, which is deservedly famous among toy and figure lovers for its ever-expanding Kubrick and Be@rbrick collector series, and most people come here to drool over their weirdly cute original designs. But there's a lot more, including other character-based toys (Doraemon, Peanuts, Pixar, Disney, Evangelion, Hello Kitty) each one showcased in a beautiful museum-like display.

**Hours:** ***11:00–20:00*** **Access:** ***37-10 Udagawacho (ten minutes' walk from Shibuya Station)*** **medicomtoy.co.jp/official_shop/more.php**

### 5 Tokyu Hands

DIY-inclined otaku (cosplayers, manga artists, etc.) better check out this amazing "creative life department store" because they have practically everything—including many items you didn't even suspect existed. Anything connected with paper, leather, wood, textiles, etc., can be found here. They sell toys, too. There are six more branches in central Tokyo alone, but this nine-story building is their home base.

**Hours:** ***10:00-20:30*** **Access:** ***12-18 Udagawacho (seven minutes' walk from Shibuya Station)*** **shibuya.tokyu-hands.co.jp/en/index.html** ***(English)***

### 6 Village Vanguard

Apparently the Shibuya store is the biggest branch of this funky chain. Village Vanguard calls itself an "exciting book store," but it actually sells much more, from otaku goods (toys, character T-shirts, anime etc.) to wigs, clocks and junk food. Their stock is so random that you can find Gothic paraphernalia sharing space with lava lamps. There are about 30 branches in Tokyo alone (each one with a slightly different stock and atmosphere) but this one is particularly recommended, with a larger than average collection of new and vintage manga that runs the gamut from a boxed set of Miyazaki Hayao's *Nausicaa of the Valley of the Wind* to several books by maverick comic author Maruo Suehiro.

**Hours:** ***10:00–23:00*** **Access:** ***B1–2F Udagawacho (four minutes' walk from Shibuya Station)*** **village-v.co.jp**

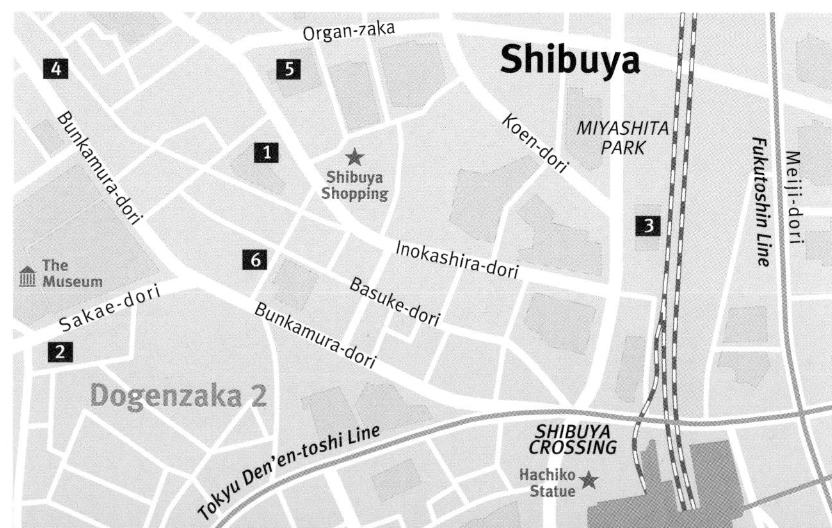

# EXPLORING SHINJUKU

ABOVE Famous as a business and entertainment center, Shinjuku is also the seat of the Tokyo government offices. BOTTOM RIGHT Takadanobaba is worth a visit to admire the beautiful mural outside the station.

Shinjuku doesn't have a great otaku pedigree, and few people would dare to put it on the same level with Tokyo's main otaku centers. To be sure, this bustling district is more famous as a business and entertainment center than for any manga- or anime-related connections. However, in the last few years several shops have opened in the area east of the station, and though their number is still far smaller than Akihabara or Ikebukuro, there are enough interesting places to keep you busy for a whole day. What really sets the place apart from the competition is the sheer number of otaku bars and cafés. For many years now the Kabukicho district on the other side of Yasukuni-dori has been synonymous with nightlife, and it is here that you will find a surprisingly high number of game- and anime-themed bars that stay open all night. Here we introduce just a short selection; for more information check out the *Tokyo Geek's Guide*.

### 1 Artnia

From the outside, the official Square Enix shop looks like a slightly squashed egg; inside resembles a jewelry store-cum-museum. They even found enough space for a café. The gift shop (selling the company's popular character goods) is rather small, but this place is so stylish it certainly deserves a visit.

**Hours:** *11:00–22:00* **Access:** *6-27-30 Shinjuku (five minutes' walk from Higashi-Shinjuku Station, Tokyo Metro Fukutoshin and Toei Oedo lines)* **jp.square-enix.com/artnia**



### 2 Kinokuniya Annex

Respected bookseller Kinokuniya has two big stores in Shinjuku, but this annex is the go-to place if you are hunting for otaku goods. The M2 floor mainly sells CDs and DVDs, while the manga, art books, magazines, video game guides, etc., are upstairs. The store is even decorated with signing boards from visiting artists.

**Hours:** *10:00–21:00* **Access:** *M2F–2F Adhoc Bldg., 3-15-11 Shinjuku (seven minutes' walk from JR Shinjuku Station)*

### 2 Sanrio Gift Gate adhoc Shinjuku

There are many similar shops in Japan (about 10 in central Tokyo alone; see the website for details) but this particular branch is perfect for taking commemorative photos since its entrance is guarded by the biggest Hello Kitty statue in the world.

**Hours:** *10:00–21:00 (weekdays), 10:00–20:00 (weekends and holidays)* **Access:** *Adhoc Bldg, 3-15-11 Shinjuku (seven minutes' walk from JR Shinjuku Station)*
**sanrio.co.jp/english/store** *(English)*

### 3 Shinjuku Marui Annex

If Shinjuku streets seem to be devoid of otaku shops, it's because most of them have been crammed into this one building. At the entrance you'll find the world's first **Godzilla Store** (godzilla.store/Tokyo). Here you'll find not only the usual T-shirts, smartphone cases, mugs and calendars, but even quirkier items such as Godzilla-embroidered jackets and weird collaboration goods like the Sanrio-Godzilla series featuring the Big G hanging out with Hello Kitty. The first floor also boasts an ultra-cute **Cinnamoroll Café**, while on the third you'll find **FewMany** (fewmany.com), an eclectic shop-cum-gallery selling stationary, original art, cute figures and Medicon toys. The fifth floor is taken up entirely by otaku mini-mar-

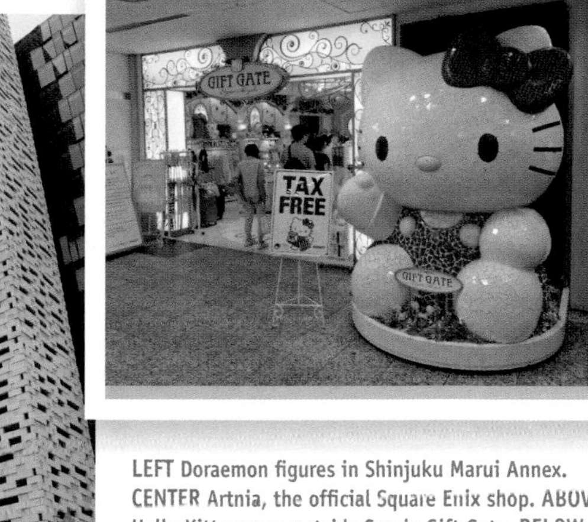

LEFT Doraemon figures in Shinjuku Marui Annex. CENTER Artnia, the official Square Enix shop. ABOVE Hello Kitty waves outside Sanrio Gift Gate. BELOW The Golden Gai bar area is home to many tiny drinking establishments, including Bar Uramen (see page 32).

ket **Surugaya**, while the sixth houses an **Animate** collaboration café (cafe.animate.co.jp/shop) and female-oriented video-game maker **Otomate**'s one and only official store (otomate.jp/otomate_store). Lastly, on the seventh floor, check out craft and model shop **Mokei Factory** (mokei-factory.com), Blythe doll store **Junie Moon** (shinjuku.juniemoon-shop.com), cosplay shop **Swallowtail**, and a couple of uber-*kawaii* Lolita-style boutiques, **Angelic Pretty** (angelicpretty.com) and **Baby the Stars Shine Bright** (babyssb.co.jp).

**Hours:** *11:00–21:00* **Access:** *3-1-26 Shinjuku (two minutes' walk from Shinjuku-Sanchome Station, Tokyo Metro Marunouchi Line)*

## Takadanobaba

Just a couple of Yamanote Line stations north of Shinjuku, Takadanobaba was, until 15 years ago, a minor otaku destination, with several small shops selling used video games and CDs for a few hundred yen. Nearly all the shops are gone now, but you may want to pay a quick visit anyway to admire the beautiful mural in front of the station's main (north) exit, underneath the tracks, portraying many Tezuka Osamu characters. Tezuka's studio was located in Takadanobaba between 1976 and 1988, and even now its head office is here. On the west side of the station, the posts on either side of the main street (Waseda-dori) are decorated with banners featuring Astro Boy, Black Jack, Kimba, Princess Knight and the Three-Eyed One. Keep walking for a few more minutes; the nondescript building on the right past Tomod's is the Seven Building, where Tezuka Productions used to be located. When you return to the JR station, pay attention to the melody used to signal train departures: it's the theme song to *Astro Boy*, composed by Takai Tatsuo for the first animated TV series. Actually, the music is arranged slightly differently for the inbound and outbound trains.

# Otaku Bars and Cafés

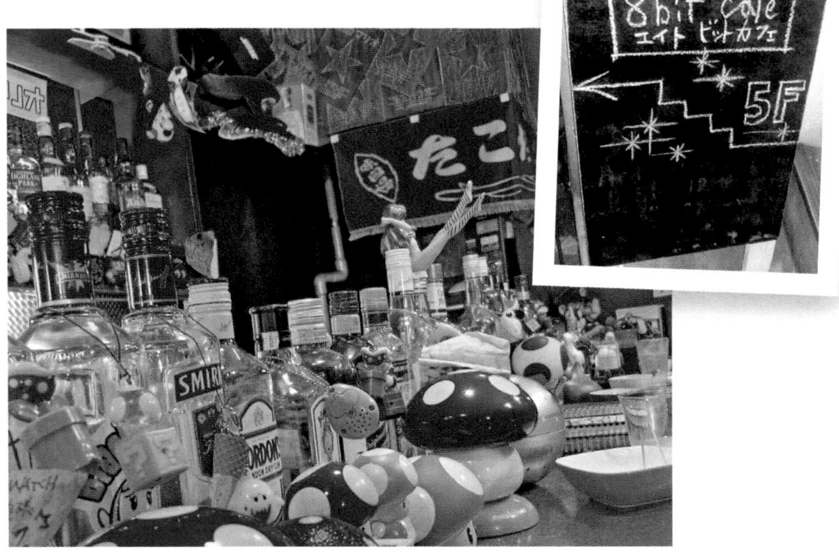


**ABOVE LEFT** Star Club Shinjuku is small and dark with a rather chic atmosphere. **ABOVE RIGHT** 8-Bit Café is one of the oldest and most popular game bars in Tokyo.

### 4 8-bit Café

One of the oldest game bars in Tokyo is also one of the most popular, even among the local expat community. This place is like its website: geeky, elegant and retro in equal measures. Mainly dedicated to 1980s subculture (the so-called Famicon/NES generation), it has tons of new and rare games and consoles and even a tabletop arcade game, along with a 5-foot (1.5-meter) tall giant Nintendo Game Boy on which you can actually play original games you'll find nowhere else. They often hold music DJ events, too (techno, electronica, etc.). Most drinks and food are between 500 and 900 yen, and there's a 500-yen seat charge.

**Hours:** *18:00–24:00, 18:00–5:00 on Fridays; closed on Tuesdays.* **Access:** *5F, 3-8-9 Shinjuku (a minute's walk from Shinjuku-Sanchome Station, Tokyo Metro Marunouchi Line)*
**8bitcafe.net**

### 5 Bar Uramen

Once upon a time there was a tiny bar called Qunai Bros. It was hidden under street level in the famous Golden Gai bar area and boasted a collection of hundreds of Famicon games. Well, that bar is still there; only its name has changed. And according to its very minimal website, the collection is now nearly up to 600 games. Drinks from 400 yen, plus an 800-yen seat charge.

**Hours:** *19:00–the morning after; sometimes closed on Sundays and holidays*
**Access:** *Golden Gai B1-A, 1-1-7 Kabukicho (seven minutes' walk from Shinjuku Station)*
**971.jp**

### 6 Hunters Bar Monhan Sakaba モンハン酒場

Fan-favorite Capcom Bar was recently replaced by this *Monster Hunter*–themed eatery. Different subject but same concept, with an atmospheric interior, game-inspired food and drinks, a few consoles to play, staff dressed as guild receptionists, and—the biggest draw for many—lots of MonHan goods on sale.

**Hours:** *17:00–23:00 (Mon–Thu), 17:00–4:00 (Fridays), 11:00–4:00 (Saturdays), 11:00–23:00 (Sundays)* **Access:** *1-3-16 Kabukicho (ten minutes' walk from Shinjuku Station)*
**paselaresorts.com/collaboration/mhsb**

### 7 Neo Black Sigma ネオ・ブラックシグマ

Join the Black Sigma crew in their karaoke all-nighters and be part of their secret plan to conquer the world through anime and *tokusatsu* songs. For 1,200 yen (600 for gals) you can sing your heart out for either 90 or 60 minutes, depending on whether you enter their underground secret base before or after midnight. Soft drinks cost 600 yen, while booze starts from 700 yen.

**Hours:** *19:00–early morning* **Access:** *B2F Miyata (ミヤタ) Bldg., 1-4-12 Kabukicho (seven minutes' walk from Shinjuku Station)*
**blacksigma.jp**

### 8 New Type Shinjuku サブカルカフェ & BAR New Type 新宿

This subculture bar is similar to others in the area, but it's larger, and even has a second floor that can be rented for private events. You can borrow one of their costumes if you are in a cosplay mood.

**Hours:** *18:00–2:00 (Mon–Thurs), 18:00–5:00 (Fri–Sat), 18:00–23:30 (Sundays)*
**Access:** *Dash Bldg., 5-12-16 Shinjuku (five minutes' walk from Shinjuku-Sanchome, Tokyo Metro Marunouchi Line)*
**ces-n.com/nt**

### 9 Star Club Shinjuku スタア倶楽部

If you are wondering what happened to the Muteki Mario ("Invincible Mario") shot bar, well, it's still in the same place, still run by the same video-game developer from Osaka, still devoted to Nintendo's most popular character. Only its name has changed (perhaps because of copyright issues?) and "Muteki Mario" is now just one of their original cocktails. Inside it's small and dark, with a rather chic atmosphere. Booze is 700–800 yen; food is around 500 yen; and there's a 500-yen cover charge.

**Hours:** *20:00–4:00 (Mon–Sat), 20:00–1:00 (Sundays and holidays)* **Access:** *2F, 3-11-1 Shinjuku (one-minute walk from Shinjuku-Sanchome, Tokyo Metro Marunouchi Line)*
**bar-starclub.com**

# Trading Card Games

Trading card games (TCG) (also called collectible card games) are big in Japan and their popularity goes well beyond the usual world-famous titles (*Pokemon, Yu-Gi-Oh!, Magic: The Gathering*, etc.) to include many anime-based games. The main TCG-selling chains (**Yellow Submarine, Amenity Dream** and **Big Magic**) have many branches around Tokyo and are pretty similar. They sell both sets and singles, with sets collected in binders and rare and/or popular cards displayed in showcases. They even have quite a few English cards, as apparently some Japanese players prefer to use them. If you are looking for something in particular, you can make a list and give it to a member of staff who will try and find it for you. Just be warned that on average, singles in Japan tend to cost more than in other countries. One more tip on TCG is good manners: You will rarely see Japanese players trade cards inside shops, and actually some stores explicitly forbid trading on the premises.

Many TCG shops have tables to play games, and their websites offer information on upcoming tournaments. Most of these are small events. Signing up is quite cheap, and if you do well you can get some cool prizes like deck boxes, card sleeves and binders. Obviously almost all participants are Japanese, but don't worry—they are very welcoming and curious about foreign players, and even if you don't speak Japanese, card language is rarely a problem. For more information on playing in Japan (especially *Pokemon*) check out Finnish champion Esa Juntunen's blog (thedeckout.blogspot.jp)

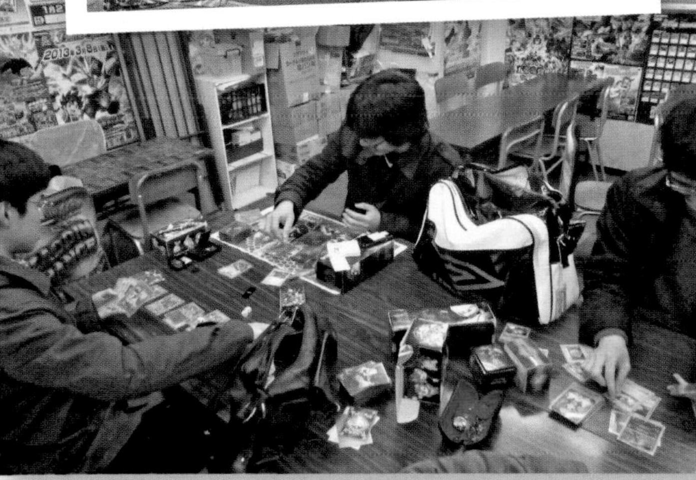

TCG stores in Tokyo are typically located close to each other, so if you don't like the prices or selection at one store you can always try your luck at another one nearby. One of the more convenient places is Radio Kaikan in Akihabara. The 10-story building houses six *toreka* (トレカ, as they are called in Japanese) shops including **Yellow Submarine** (sixth floor) and **Big Magic** (ninth). And if that's not enough, in the building in front of Radio Kaikan there's another shop, **Cardkingdom.**

# EXPLORING NAKANO

If Akihabara is the official, attention-hungry side of Otaku Tokyo, Nakano is its opposite, both geographically and temperamentally, going about its business without fanfare, yet attracting thousands of dedicated manga and anime fans with its offerings. Even though Nakano is a five-minute train ride from Shinjuku, it couldn't be more different from its glitzy, naughty neighbor.

The shopping mall Nakano Broadway, at the north exit of Nakano Station is one of Japan's major centers of otaku activity.

From an otaku perspective, its centerpiece is **Nakano Broadway**, a former luxury apartment complex that was built in 1966. It was here that in 1980 former *Garo* magazine contributor Furukawa Masuzo opened a second-hand manga store called **Mandarake**. This tiny shop (only 70 feet [6.6 meters] square) proved so successful that more and more otaku outlets followed Furukawa's example, turning Nakano Broadway into one of Japan's major centers of otaku activity, probably second only to Akihabara.

## A Visit to Nakano Broadway

The JR Chuo Line divides Nakano into two: the sleepy residential south side and the fun-loving north side; the latter is where you should head. Nakano Broadway is beyond the glass-covered Sun Mall shopping arcade. Most of the otaku shops are on the second to fourth floors. The mall's layout is rather haphazard and the hallways have been arranged with the apparent purpose of making you lose your way. Try to avoid weekends and holidays when its aisles and stores become seriously crowded. Also, remember that most otaku shops are closed on Wednesdays (unless noted otherwise). For more information: **nakano-broadway.com**

**Aloha Toy アロハトイ (2F)**
This female-oriented shop is packed with manga-, anime- and game-related toys and goods (dolls, figures, badges, posters, key chains, cards, etc.). If you're into things like *otome* games, BL (boys' love) manga and light novels, this is a real Aladdin's cave.
**Hours:** ***12:00–20:00***

**Alphaville アルファヴィル (3F)**
The keyword here is *bishojo* (beautiful young girls). This is a veritable *bishojo* gamer paradise, with tons of PC games, from mainstream titles to more maniac stuff (both new and secondhand) but also DVDs, adult and PC magazines, game instruction books, etc., all piled up in a relatively spacious but messy store. The store prides itself on carrying products that can be found hardly anywhere else.
**Hours:** ***13:00–19:00; irregular holidays***

**Anime Shop Apple Symphony (4F)**
If you have been mourning the demise of anime cel shop Commit, don't worry: it's still there—only the owner and name have changed. Hundreds (thousands?) of those beautiful hand-drawn and painted cels are either collected in binders or displayed in bins. Here you will find both prohibi-

**BELOW** The stunning-looking Hen-ya is one of the 25 Mandarake shops inside Nakano Broadway.

This Fujiko Fujio magazine from 1957, and other rare collector's items available at Mandarake, will cost you a small fortune!

tively expensive rare items (Studio Ghibli, Dragon Ball, Sailor Moon, Gundam, etc.) and equally beautiful but much cheaper cels from less famous anime.
**Hours:** ***10:00–19:00***

### Decotrand (4F)
For all the gals out there who fancy looking like Sailor Moon or some other ultra-cute anime character, this tiny shop sells original accessories and gadgets as well as plush toys. Hotcake-shaped pendants and brooches, anyone? How about triangular hairpins with *naruto* decorations, or teddy bear-ice cream bracelets?
**Hours:** ***13:00–20:00***
**decotrand.ocnk.net**

### Gaocchi (3F)
Showa-era (1950s–'70s) retro bonanza is the name of the game here. The list is endless: dolls, *menko* playing cards, character masks, *shokugan* (food toys), monster *sofubi* soft vinyl toys, Sanrio and Sailor Moon toys. Add in Gundam-, Kinnikuman- and Super Car–shaped erasers, Bikkuri Man stickers, and the like and you'll have just a few of the nostalgia-inducing items you can buy. They make for nice souvenirs, too.
**Hours:** ***12:00–20:00***

### Mandarake (1–4F)
**Hours:** ***12:00–20:00***
**mandarake.co.jp/shop/index_nkn.html**
Secondhand otaku goods chain Mandarake has a cool underground store in Shibuya and an eight-floor complex in Akihabara, but Nakano is its home base. Indeed, with 25 different shops spread on four of Nakano Broadway's five floors, it's an inescapable presence there. Luckily, each store is devoted to a different genre, so you won't lose your sanity having to go through the millions of items on offer. This is one of the few places in Tokyo that goes so far as to include people who can actually speak English and other languages among its staff. Here's a brief description of some of its 25 storefronts:

**Mon 門 (1F):** Studio Ghibli goods
**Live-kan (2F):** Ladies' *dojinshi*
**Galaxy (2F):** Video-game software and hardware
**Deep-kan (2F):** Dojinshi for men
**Infinity ∞ (3F):** Boy idol- (Johnny's) and voice actor-related goods
**Anime-kan (4F):** Anime scripts and cels, signed sketches
**Hen-ya 変や (4F):** Novelty goods, vintage and antique toys
**Mania-kan (4F):** Vintage manga magazines and books (including Tezuka Osamu's original editions), records (anime, *tokusatsu*), movie scripts
**Plastic (4F):** Dolls (Volks, Blythe, Licca-chan), doll wigs and other accessories
**Special 1-6 (2–4F):** Each store is devoted to a particular genre of figures and models

### Murakami Takashi's Galleries
Art superstar Murakami Takashi is a very media- and market-savvy guy. So it's no wonder that he opened not one but three galleries and a bar inside Nakano Broadway to showcase otaku-inspired works that he and other up-and-coming artists created, along with original anime and video game art. All the galleries (each one with a different character) are open 12:00–19:00, but only when they have an exhibition ongoing.

### Animanga Zingaro (2F)
**pixiv-zingaro.jp**

### Hidari Zingaro (3F)
**hidari-zingaro.jp**

### Oz Zingaro (4F)
**oz-zingaro.jp**

### Parabox Shop (3F)
This shop has everything you need to make your own custom doll, from bodies, heads and eyes to clothes, shoes, wigs and other accessories. They come in different sizes, from 1/6 to 1/3 scale. The staff provide advice and maintenance service as well.
**Hours:** ***12:00–19:00***
**parabox.jp/eng_new** ***(English)***

### Plabbit プラビット (1F)
Let's say you love those gorgeous Gunplas but you're too lazy to build them yourself. No problem! The good folks at Plabbit have a great selection of pre-built models on sale for 20,000 to 30,000 yen. They also excel at customization. Do you want a new paint job, or maybe you want to add some accessories or some other custom modification? Just ask. But remember that custom work takes time (between one and four months, depending on what you want), so it's not an option if you are in a hurry or just visiting Tokyo for a few days.
**Hours:** ***11:00–20:00*** **plabbit.ocnk.net**

### TACO che' (3F)
While otaku-dom has its own version of the indie world (*dojinshi* and the like), what about the off-off scene—the cutting-edge artists whom no mainstream shop dares to carry on its shelves? TACO che' is the perfect starting point for your exploration. Apparently they have more than a million publications in stock (small-press books, alternative comics, zines) plus DVDs (mostly of the weird variety), CDs (grindcore, noise, and what-the-hell-is-that music), T-shirts, badges and illustrations by such underground masters as Umezu Kazuo, Maruo Suehiro and Tawaraya Tetsunori. From time to time they even hold exhibitions and other events.
**Hours:** ***12:00–20:00*** **tacoche.com**

### Trio (3F)
You can overdose on old and new idols (both guys and girls) and J-Pop singers In Akihabara, where Trio has two more shops inside Radio Kaikan and Akiba Cultures Zone, but we prefer this store. It's filled to the brim with photos, picture fans, posters, magazine back issues and other idol-related goods.
**Hours:** ***12:00–20:00***
**trio-broadway.com/tenpo.html**

# EXPLORING WEST TOKYO

## Museums and Libraries

### 1 (3•4•5) Ghibli Museum

As stated on their website, the Ghibli Museum is a portal to a storybook world. In this sense, this place is more than just a celebration of Ghibli's animation; it's where you can understand the story-making process itself. Ideally, after walking through the five rooms that comprise this amazing house you will get a better understanding of the ideas and inspirations that go into making anime and movies in general. Miyazaki Hayao has always strived to be different from other anime people, and the museum reflects his personality. The Saturn Theater, for instance, shows original short animated features that can only be seen here; a library has been set up to give TV- and video game-obsessed children a chance to experience the pleasure of reading; and even at the café almost everything comes from organic farms. Of course, there is a shop, but besides the usual stuff you can even buy hand-painted cels and woodblock prints of scenes from Studio Ghibli films. The labyrinthine building itself looks and feels like the houses you would see in a Ghibli movie, with that typical faux-European touch that is a trademark of so many Miyazaki's films.

ABOVE AND LEFT Ome Atsuka Hall is dedicated to Akatsuka Fujio, one of Japan's most popular and beloved manga artists.

LEFT and BELOW The Ghibli Museum is the portal to a storybook world. The building and its surroundings have the faux-European touch that is typical of the works of Miyazaki Hayao.

**Admission fee:** *1,000 yen (700 yen for 13- to 18-year-olds, 400 yen for 7- to 12-year-olds, 100 yen for 4- to 6-year-olds); entrance only with advance purchase of a reserve ticket (in Japan, buy it at Lawson's; check the website for information on how to buy one from abroad)* **Hours:** *10:00–18:00; closed Tuesdays and for periodic maintenance* **Access:** *Inokashira Park West Side, 1-1-83 Shimo-Renjaku, Mitaka City (15 minutes' walk from JR Kichijoji Station)* **ghibli-museum.jp/en** *(excellent English site with plenty of information)*

### (1•2•5) Ome Akatsuka Hall

Akatsuka Fujio is one of Japan's most popular and beloved manga artists. His story is closely tied to that of other would-be famous *manga-ka*, as he was part of the gang of youngsters who lived with Tezuka Osamu at Tokiwa Mansion in the early '50s (the mansion is lovingly reproduced in this museum). During his career he created many characters, but those he is best remembered for are the proto-magical girl Secret Akko-chan (first appeared in 1962 in *Ribbon* magazine) and Bakabon (a gag manga that debuted in 1967 in *Shonen* magazine). The museum starts from the "end," as the entrance is taken up by the shop selling Akatsuka's manga and DVDs together with toys, T-shirts, food, etc. On the first floor are large reproductions and statues of Akatsuka's characters, some of their famous words and page art from his manga highlighting the author's wicked sense of humor. There is also an exclusive photo sticker machine. The museum proper is upstairs, with many colorful artworks taking up much of the space. Akatsuka had a very public persona (he became a sort of TV personality) and several photos present this side of his life. Another room is devoted to the many cute and bizarre toys and large-toothed dolls produced under his name, and at the end there is a collection of his books and weekly magazines that featured his work in the '60s and '70s.

**Admission fee:** *450 yen (children 250 yen)* **Hours:** *10:00–17:00; closed Mondays* **Access:** *66 Sumiecho, Ome-shi (five minutes' walk from JR Ome Station)* **ome-akatsukafujio-museum.com**

Suginami Animation Museum is not only one of the best museums in the Tokyo area, it's also free!

ABOVE Explore the world of manga at Tachikawa Manga Park.

### 2 (1•3) Suginami Animation Museum

This is without a doubt one of the best museums in Tokyo—and it's free! It shows, from different angles (history, entertainment, theory and practice), the unique features of anime films and how they are made. The historical and artistic sides are explained in a section devoted to the development of Japanese animation and a temporary exhibition space celebrating important works, creators and characters. On the other side, the museum offers the opportunity to experience anime production firsthand, like making your own page-flipping kind of anime (you can even save it on a CD-R or USB); using a PC to understand the process of digital animation; and trying your hand at voice recording and post-production dubbing. There is also a well-stocked library (though borrowing and photocopying are not allowed); and last but not least, you can watch anime works, either in the movie theater or by requesting a DVD from the library and enjoying it in the privacy of a booth. Did I mention all this was free?

**Hours:** *10:00–18:00; closed Mondays*
**Access:** *3F Suginami Kaikan, 3-29-5 Kami-ogi, Suginami-ku (a five-minute bus ride from JR Ogikubo Station north exit; take the Kanto Bus at the #0 or #1 stop and get off at Ogikubo Keisatsu-mae (Ogikubo Police Station)*
**sam.or.jp**

### Tachikawa Manga Park

People in Tachikawa seem to take their kids' well-being seriously. At the end of 2012 the city opened the Children's Future Center with the goal of supporting child-rearing. As manga have traditionally been regarded in Japan as learning tools, the Center decided to turn the second floor of their Good Design–awarded building into a manga paradise where, for a small fee, you are free to explore the incredibly diversified world of manga. In keeping with the Center's original goal, there are abundant educational manga on topics ranging from cooking and history to sports and science. Their target audience, though, is not just children; they offer something for every age and taste, and aside from kinky stuff, no genre is left uncovered. When the place opened, its sturdy bookshelves—each one organized by genre—carried about 30,000 volumes; their goal is to eventually reach 50,000 titles. There is also a picture-book corner with 500 volumes for younger kids. During the weekends the Center even organizes regular manga-drawing classes and flea markets. More than a library, the aptly named "manga park" invites people to get comfy while enjoying a good read. The whole area is covered with tatami mats for comfort, which means you can lounge on the floor or take your books to the café corner or out on the balcony. They even provide closet-like spaces for extra privacy. In that vein, you may want to avoid weekends and the spring and summer school breaks, as the place gets packed with kids and their parents.

**Admission fee:** *400 yen (200 yen for kids under 15, free for preschoolers)*
**Hours:** *10:00–19:00 (weekdays), 10:00–20:00 (weekends and holidays)*
**Access:** *2F Kodomo Mirai Center, 3-2-26 Nishikicho, Tachikawa (seven minutes' walk from Nishi Kunitachi Station [Nanbu Line]; 13 minutes from Tachikawa Station south exit [Chuo Line], 12 minutes from Tachikawa-Minami Station [Tama Monorail])* **mangapark.jp**

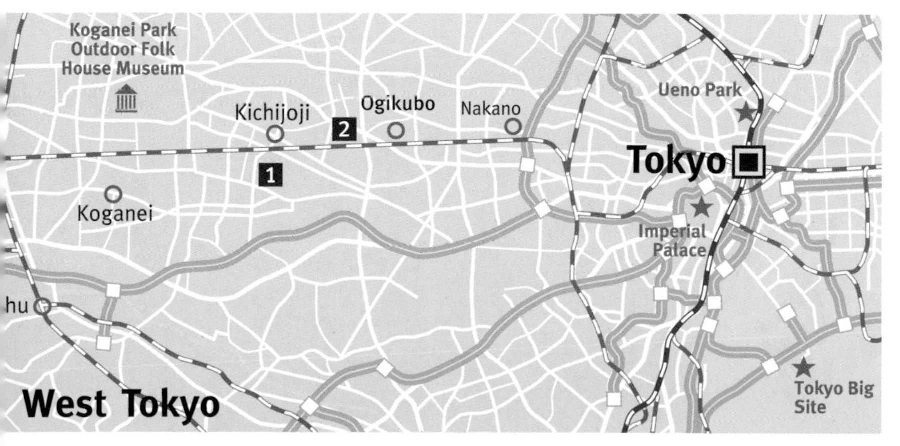

# EXPLORING IKEBUKURO

Some people can't help smirking when they talk about Ikebukuro. It could be its perceived grittier, sleazier character; or maybe the fact that the district attracts all the people from the uncool prefectures north of Tokyo. When it comes to anime and manga, though, few areas in Tokyo can boast a better pedigree than Toshima ward, where Ikebukuro is located. Since the early 1950s the ward has been home to many comic artists, including the "God of Manga" himself, Tezuka Osamu, and Yokohama Mitsuteru of Tetsujin 28 fame.

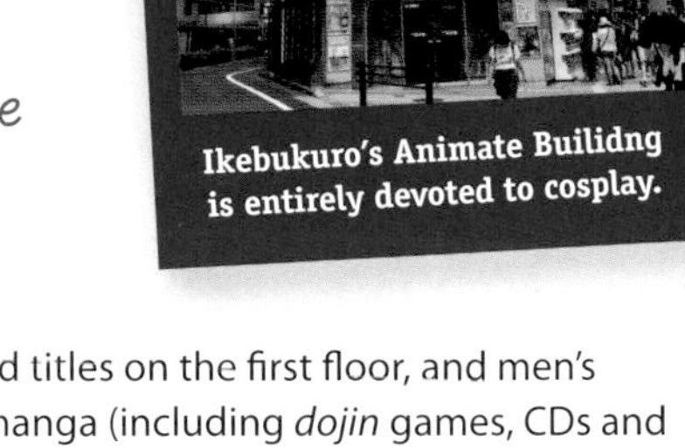

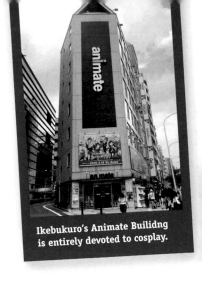

Ikebukuro's Animate Builidng is entirely devoted to cosplay.

More recently, Ikebukuro has been associated with *otome* (female otaku). Indeed, most of the local attractions are geared toward female customers. Many cafés, for instance, are manned by butlers and "high-school *bishonen*" (pretty boys) instead of maids, and many of the manga and *dojinshi* on sale are in the BL (boys' love) genre.

This guide will focus on **Otome Road**, Tokyo's new otaku center. For more detailed information on Ikebukuro, check out my *Tokyo Geek's Guide*. In any event, don't miss a chance to visit Ikebukuro. Especially after the huge success of the 2010 TV anime series *Durarara!!*, it may have finally landed on the Cool Tokyo map once and for all.

## Otome Road

### Shopping

Shops are listed in order of appearance on the road, starting with the Animate Sunshine Building.

**1 Animate Sunshine Building**
The Animate Building is devoted to cosplay. **ACOS Main Store**, on the second and third floors, sells costumes (both new and classic anime characters), wigs, cosmetics, weapons and other accessories, while on the fifth and sixth floors is **HACOSTADIUM cosset** (hacostadium.com/ikebukuro), a photo studio providing everything you need for your cosplay shoot, from different kinds of sets and props to photo gear (SL camera, tripods, reflection boards, etc.). Sandwiched between these Animate joints, secondhand chain store **Lashinbang** runs its own costume store, and sells doll costumes as well.
**Hours:** ***11:00–20:00*** **Access:** ***3-2-1 Higashi-Ikebukuro***

**2 Lashinbang Store #2**
らしんばん池袋本店　2号館
This store is all about audio and video items: anime CDs, DVDs and Blu-rays; voice-actor CDs; video-game soundtracks; BL drama CDs; video-game software and consoles; and PC games for girls.
**lashinbang.com/cont/stores.html** ***(English)***

**3 Lashinbang Main Store**
らしんばん池袋本店　本館
This "*moe* convenience store" sells comics, novels and assorted publications, with BL and other female-oriented titles on the first floor, and men's manga (including *dojin* games, CDs and other items) on the second.
**lashinbang.com/cont/stores.html** ***(English)***

**4 K-Books Anime Store アニメ館**
The closest thing to a K-Books general store, this venue sells manga, anime, video games and toys, including items for kids (lots of plushies, too!). That said, the second floor has lots of *otome* and BL games—this is Ikebukuro, after all.
**k-books.co.jp/company/shop/anime.html**

**5 K-Books VOICE StoreVOICE館**
This K-Books storefront is all about male voice actors. It has plenty of anime CDs, DVDs, and Blu-rays, of course, but also sells photos, fan magazines, concert programs and T-shirts. Many of the drama CDs are actually special editions that are hard to find elsewhere.
**k-books.co.jp/company/shop/voice.html**

BELOW and LEFT K-Books sells anime CDs, DVDs and Blu-rays, as well as photos, fan magazines, concert programs and T-shirts.

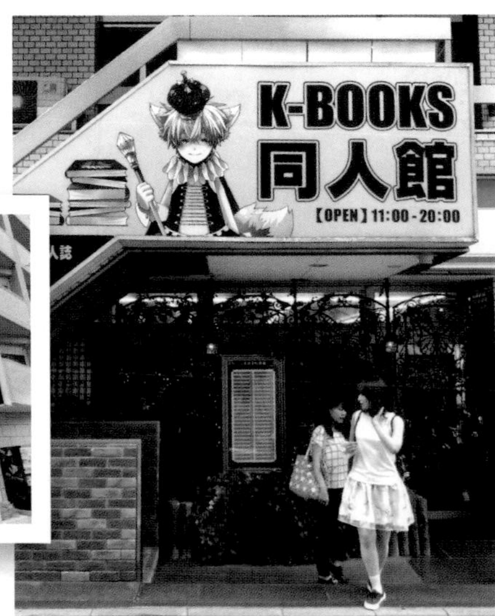

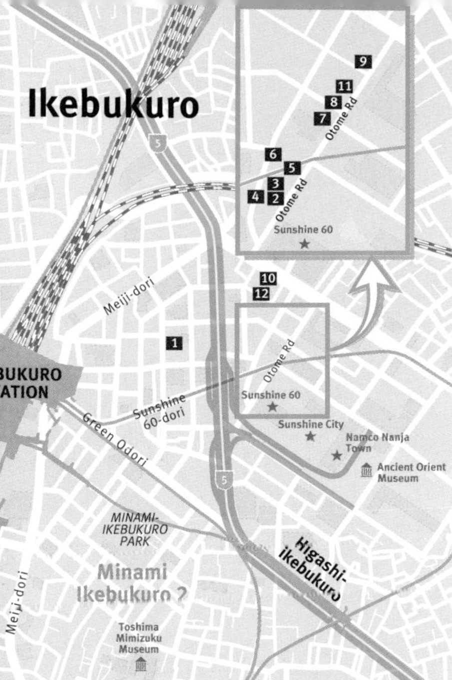


**6 K-Books Live Store ライブ館**
From CDs and DVDs to other assorted items (badges, figures, stickers, etc.), this store covers "Love Live!" "The Idolmaster," the Vocaloid genre, and other music- and idol-related anime and characters.
**k-books.co.jp/company/shop/live.html**

**7 K-Books Comic Store コミック館**
This K-Books shop is the place to find mainstream comics, light novels, magazines and picture books—many of them, of course, selected with female readers in mind.
**k-books.co.jp/company/shop/comic.html**

**8 K-Books Dojin Store 同人館**
According to some people, this is the jewel in the crown of the Tokyo K-Books chain, and if you are into BL and other female-focused manga you absolutely have to pay it a visit. The third floor sells new works, while upstairs (the second-hand shop) is where you can find the real bargains, including entire sets. On the third floor there are also independently published novels and *dojin* goods (badges, cups, cell phone straps, tote bags, etc.).
**(2F) k-books.co.jp/company/shop/doujin-2f.html**
**(3F) k-books.co.jp/company/shop/doujin-3f.html**

**9 K-Books Cosplay Store コスプレ館**
Here you can find more than 2,000 secondhand cosplay-related items, from costumes and wigs to accessories and even cosplay magazines.
**k-books.co.jp/company/shop/cosplay.html**

## Eateries

**10 Ikebukuro Danshi BL Gakuen**
The "boys' love" (BL) genre has a strong following among female fans. If you, too, are a so-called *fujoshi* "rotten girl" (note: men are welcome as well) you will enjoy this naughty Boys' BL Academy. The place looks like a schoolroom between classes, with a blackboard, school clock and staff in high school uniforms who spend the time playing around with each other and chatting up customers. You can also put them into risqué situations—for instance, if you choose the "Moso Coupling Pocky" from the game menu, for 980 yen you can pick out two students and make them eat one of those chocolate-coated biscuit sticks until they meet in the middle and kiss each other. It's either very silly or incredibly exciting, depending on your tastes.
**Hours:** *15:00–22:30 (weekdays), 12:00–5:00 (Saturdays), 12:00–22:30 (Sundays)*
**Access:** *2F, 3-9-13 Higashi-Ikebukuro*
**blcafe.jp**

**11 Swallowtail**
This is by far one of the best-looking theme cafés in Tokyo, thanks to its elegant furniture (including two massive crystal chandeliers) and the attention to detail evident in its beautiful selection of tea cups and graceful displays. You will also get the royal treatment from highly trained butlers with perfect manners and warm voices. It's the kind of place where you want to wear something smart. The menu features lunch, dinner, tea and dessert sets. Although it's especially popular with ladies, the café is open to everybody except children under five.
**Hours:** *10:30–21:20* **Access:** *B1F, Showa Bldg., 3-12-12 Higashi-Ikebukuro* **butlers-cafe.jp** *(the menu and reservation pages have an English version)*

**12 Wonder Parlour Café**
More than other maid cafés, this place aims to achieve an authentic Old England ambience, with its European-looking interior and classical background music, while the maids wear long costumes of original design. This being Ikebukuro, most of its clientele are women who are attracted by both the exotic atmosphere and the brand-name teas. Advance reservations (by telephone only, 03-3989-8224) are optional.
**Hours:** *14:00–22:00 (weekdays), 12:00–22:00 (weekends and holidays)* **Access:** *3-9-15 Higashi-Ikebukuro* **wonder-parlour.com**

Cute ketchup decorations at "boys' love" café Ikebukuro Danshi BL Gakuen.

Eating Pocky at "boy's love" café Ikebukuro Danshi BL Gakuen.

# EXPLORING ODAIBA

While Tokyo is not considered a beautiful city (at least in the traditional Western sense of the term), no one can argue that it isn't full of surprises and interesting spots. Odaiba is definitely one such place. This artificial island in Tokyo Bay didn't exist until the last century, when the metropolitan government decided to create a futuristic subcenter providing the city with a new frontier, as well as its only pedestrian access to the seashore.

Visiting Odaiba is an adventure, and the fun starts with riding the Yurikamome, the automated computer-controlled train line that crosses Tokyo Bay and connects the city center to the island via the half mile (1km) long Rainbow Bridge (a popular anime pilgrimage site for Digimon fans). The Yurikamome, by the way, must be one of the most otaku-friendly train lines in the world, as all the stations use the recorded voices of different voice actors for their announcements (you can check out the Wikipedia list at en.wikipedia.org/wiki/Yurikamome). From the train, you can even see two of the original island forts (known as *daiba* in Japanese, and from which Odaiba takes its name) that were built in 1853 by the Edo shogunate to defend the city from sea attack.

For many years Odaiba was generally viewed as an ill-considered waste of money, with only a few giant buildings dotting the otherwise deserted island. Luckily for us, a new wave of development at the turn of the twenty-first century transformed the area into one of Tokyo's major shopping and entertainment centers. Today there are plenty of things to see, starting with the iconic Fuji TV building and its stunning huge metal sphere, and a massive life-size statue of RX-0 Unicorn Gundam in front of the Diver City shopping complex that is worth a visit on its own. Speaking of remarkable architecture, Tokyo Big Sight is another important lodestone for manga and anime fans, as many of the dozen Odaiba-based otaku festivals and events take place inside this cavernous convention center.

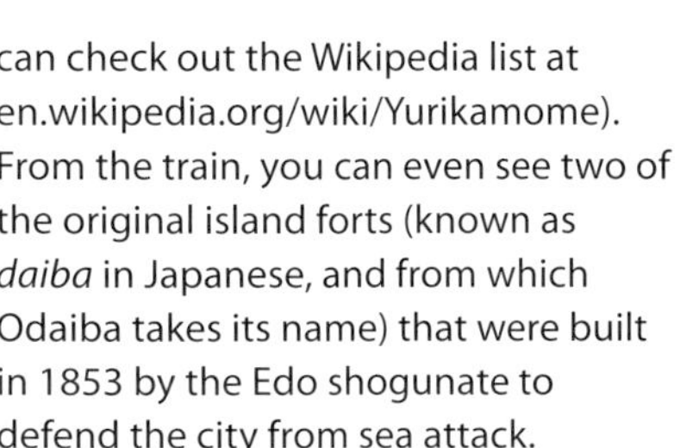

**ABOVE** Tokyo Big Sight is home to many otaku events.
**LEFT and BELOW** Daiba 1-chome Shotengai is a reproduction of an early twentieth century Tokyo shopping street, taking up the whole of the fourth floor of the DECKS building and containing a wide variety of retro-style shops.

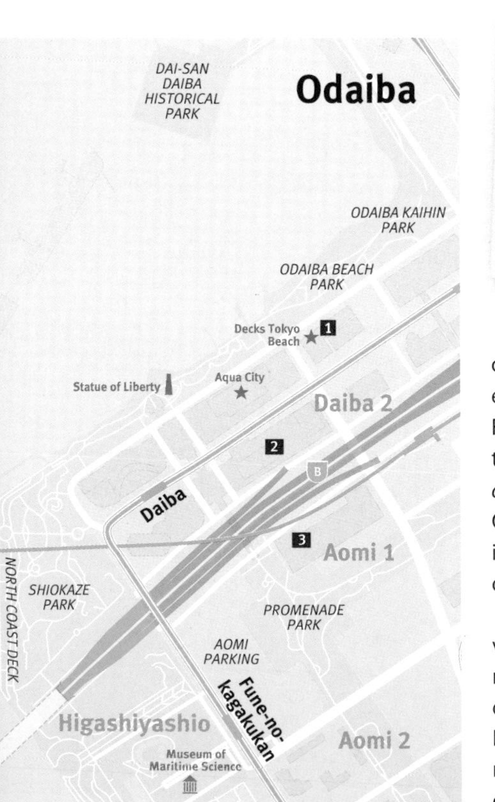

### 1 Daiba 1-chome Shotengai

When you've had enough of the 3D games and all the noise at the Tokyo Joypolis amusement park (see facing page), you can find some respite at this **Daiba 1-chome Shotengai**, a clever reproduction of a Showa-era (1926–1989) shopping street. The whole of the fourth floor of the DECKS building is completely devoted to the good old times, with retro game arcades, traditional junk food stores and assorted souvenir shops adding to the general feeling of nostalgia. Some of the best are:

#### 1-chome Play Land
一丁目プレイランド

Here you'll find a veritable treasure land of 80 to 100 retro arcade games, ranging from 10-yen-per-play old favorites like the Shinkansen Game to tabletop Space Invaders and other wonders from the '80s that have been beautifully preserved in their dedicated cabinets (Hang-On, OutRun, Tokyo Wars, etc.). Some of these games can now be found only here.

#### Daiba Yugijo 台場遊技場

Retro crane games from the '80s.

#### Daiba Kaiki Gakko 台場怪奇学校

Put a scary twist on your old (or even your current) student memories by entering this haunted school. But they won't let you in without signing an agreement relieving the "horror planner" of any responsibility in the event you wet your pants.
**obakeland.net**

#### Haikara Yokocho ハイカラ横丁

Candy, traditional junk, and toys.

#### Edoya 江戸屋

More junk food!
**Hours:** *11:00–21:00* **Access:** *4F, DECKS Tokyo Beach, 1-6-1 Daiba (next to Odaiba Kaihin Koen Station's north exit)*
**odaiba-decks.com/en/floorguide/4f.html**

Gundam Unicorn (RIGHT) and Sazae-san's family (ABOVE) welcome you to Odaiba.

### 2 Fuji TV building

Fuji TV is one of Japan's major private broadcasters. The station is famous for the Noitamina late-Thursday-night anime programming block, and it dominates Sunday's anime lineup with such heavyweights as GeGeGe no Kitaro and One Piece (9:00–10:00), and Chibi Maruko and Sazae-san (18:00–19:00). Its headquarters is also one of the most recognizable and best-looking buildings in Tokyo. Inside you will find a lot to enjoy, including the Hachitama character goods shop and Japan's only Sazae-san shop.
**Hours:** *10:00–20:00; closed Mondays*
**Access:** *2-4-8 Daiba (five minutes' walk from Daiba Station)*
**fujitv.co.jp/en/visit_fujitv.html**

### 3 The Gundam Base Tokyo

You are probably already acquainted with the towering, full-scale 65-foot (20-meter) tall Unicorn Gundam that in 2017 replaced the classic RX-78-2, but nothing really prepares you to see it with your own eyes. Inside, you'll first find a museum showcasing all the Gundam kits ever created (about 2,000, including some 20 exclusives)—and yes, each and every one of them is for sale here, from the first '80s kits to the latest models. Then there are areas where you can have your photo taken with characters from the show, a Builders' Zone where you can sit down and put together your Gundam kit under the guidance of expert builders, and even a professional booth where you can have artisans paint and style your model kits for you. And if you want to know how Gunpla are manufactured at their factory in Shizuoka, you can visit the Factory Zone. This Gundam bonanza is completed by Strict-G—a clothing and accessories shop—and the Gundam Café located on the second floor for when you need to take a rest.
**Hours:** *10:00–21:00* **Access:** *7F Diver City, 1-1-10 Aomi, Koto-ku (six minutes' walk from Daiba Station)* **gundam-base.net**

### 1 Tokyo Joypolis

If you want to upgrade your Tokyo gaming experience from a simple arcade to a full-blown amusement park, Joypolis has about 30 attractions, many of which use the latest 3-D and interactive technology. There are also a few "extreme rides," including the Initial D driving simulator and the Halfpipe Tokyo snowboarding attraction, as well as the ever-popular House of the Dead 4 SP zombie shooter. (Just remember that some of the games are Japanese-language only.)
**Fee:** *Admission is 800 yen; get an all-you-can-play passport for 3,900 yen (2,900 yen after 17:00)* **Hours:** *10:00–22:00* **Access:** *3F DECKS Tokyo Beach, 1-6-1 Daiba (next to Odaiba Kaihin Koen Station's north exit)*
**tokyo-joypolis.com/language/english**

# Odaiba Festivals and Events

Unless noted otherwise, all the events listed below take place at Tokyo Big Sight (3-11-1 Ariake, Koto-ku) which is directly accessible from Kokusai Tenjijo Seimon Station (Yurikamome Line) through a connection bridge, or with a seven-minute walk from Kokusai Tenjijo Station (Rinkai Line).

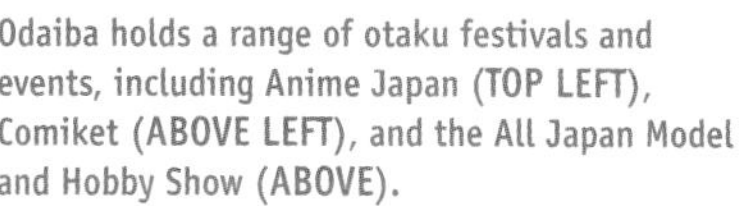

Odaiba holds a range of otaku festivals and events, including Anime Japan (TOP LEFT), Comiket (ABOVE LEFT), and the All Japan Model and Hobby Show (ABOVE).

### All-Japan Model and Hobby Show

This long-running event, which takes place annually at the end of September, began in 1963 during the Golden Age of Japanese toys; even today, after more than 50 iterations, it remains an excellent window on the local industry, with an average of 50 companies displaying over 10,000 hobby-related items. All the major manufacturers show their new and upcoming products, from plamodels and figures to radio-controlled models, trains and dolls. Among the side attractions are demonstrations of radio-controlled (*rajikon*) toys (helicopters, multicopters, cars, etc.), and Gunpla-building classes, while kids can try their hand at flying rubber-band-powered planes. The most recent shows have even featured a "junk market" where model builders dig through thousands of assorted model parts. The limited-edition model booths never fail to draw long lines. **Admission fee:** ***1,000 yen (free for junior high students and younger)*** **Dates:** ***End of Sept.*** **Hours:** ***9:00–17:00*** **hobbyshow.co.jp**

### AnimeJapan

The days between the end of March and the beginning of April signal the start of many activities in Japan, from the new business and fiscal year to the new school year. It's also the time of year when the anime industry shows off its new products and sets up new projects and collaborations at AnimeJapan. This is one of the more internationally inclined events in Japan, with the stated ambition of becoming the world's best anime event. One of the newest additions to the festival season, it began in 2014, when two competing events, the Tokyo International Anime Fair (TAF) and the Anime Contents Expo (ACE) agreed to join forces. The alliance seems to have worked out fine, as the festival regularly exceeds 100,000 visitors. The different character of the two original events is evident in AnimeJapan's hybrid character. On one side, the family-only area (with its special entrance) features activities like games and sing-alongs, and is a reminder of TAF's kid-oriented approach. On the other, the cool, hardcore side of anime fandom that ACE represented is reflected in the more adult-oriented limited-edition collaboration goods and other exclusive and preorder merchandise for sale. AnimeJapan features preview film screenings and a variety of stage events, talk shows and live performances from voice actors. Popular features are displays of original illustrations from many anime movies and their creators' signature boards. Of course, such a festival wouldn't be complete without a cosplay area. This one actually features settings from recent popular anime and even costumes that the visitors can try on. The big difference with other otaku events is that here cosplayers are free to step out of their area and walk around the booths. **Admission fee:** ***2,000 yen at the door, 1,600 yen in advance (free for elementary school students; see website for details). Only advance ticket-holders can apply to view the stage events, with the lucky ones are chosen by lottery.*** **Dates:** ***March*** **Hours:** ***10:00–17:00*** **anime-japan.jp/en**

Comiket (ABOVE) is probably Japan's largest otaku gathering, visited by more than half a million people twice a year. Another popular event is Dolls Party (TOP RIGHT and RIGHT), where people can meet and share their love of dolls.

### Comic Market

Comiket, as this event is usually called, is the world's biggest *dojinshi* (fanzine) fair and arguably Japan's largest otaku gathering, visited by more than half a million people twice a year. It is so big that even the huge Tokyo Big Sight convention center is hard put to absorb the crowds every time the *dojinshi* makers and their fans take possession of its six halls in the east wing and halls 1 and 2 in the west wing (corporate companies are relegated to halls 3 and 4), creating security problems. Unlike similar but much smaller fairs such as Super Comic City and COMITIA (see below), Comiket can only be organized twice a year, as more than 3,000 volunteers are needed to make sure that everything goes smoothly. Besides the corporate booths in the west wing (manned by PC game software makers, manga publishers, music producers, etc.) the 35,000 *dojinshi* circles, often consisting of only one person, sell everything from games, illustrations and anime to more eccentric stuff like military goods and sports items. Most fans, though, are after the zines. More than 11 million publications have been on sale in the last few iterations of the event, with nearly 9 million sold in three days. Comiket is especially famous for *niji sosaku*, publications that parody existing mainstream manga, sometimes putting together characters from different manga and anime in strange (even risqué) situations. These works, which make up the lion's share of the zines for sale, can be found in the east wing, while original publications are in halls 1 and 2 of the west wing. If you are hunting for a specific title and want to get it by any means necessary, you'll have to plan your visit carefully (get the telephone-book-sized catalog) and endure hours of waiting and very long lines. Otherwise, you'll be much better off arriving in the early afternoon after the initial charge and craziness. The first time can be quite overwhelming, so if you need help or information you can go to the International Desk on the second floor of hall 1 in the east wing. Last but absolutely not least, Comiket is famous for the huge number of cosplayers who gather in the plaza outside. Players must register in advance and pay a fee. As it is now the custom everywhere, you cannot arrive at or leave the fair already wearing your costume, and you can only change clothes in designated dressing rooms (i.e., don't do it in the toilet!).

**Admission fee:** *Free; registration fee for cosplayers 800 yen per day*
**Dates:** *Mid-August and end of December*
**Hours:** *10:00–16:00 (company booths are open until 17:00)* **comiket.co.jp**
**comiket.co.jp/index_e.html** *(English site; contains less information but is useful if you can't read Japanese)*

### COMITIA

Though smaller than the Comic Market and Comic City (see below), COMITIA has a wider geographical reach, as it is held in Tokyo, Osaka, Nagoya, Niigata and Sapporo. The other noteworthy peculiarity is that *niji sosaku* (manga parodies) are banned, so only original products can be sold—not only manga but CDs, accessories and other items as well. Following the same logic, even cosplaying is not allowed. On the other hand, professional artists can sell their works alongside the amateur circles, but only as individuals (i.e., company booths are not admitted). Traditionally at the end of COMITIA a smaller event called the "Sample Reading Club" takes place, so called because fans can read the sample *dojinshi* that were submitted to the main fair.

**Admission fee:** *No ticket required, but you need to buy the catalogue (1,000 yen)*
**Dates:** *February, May, August, November*
**Hours:** *11:00–16:00.* **comitia.co.jp**

### Dolls Party

Volks is a manufacturer of mecha and garage kits, but is particularly famous worldwide for its Dollfie, Super Dollfie and Dollfie Dream lines of dolls. In 1999 the Japan-based company began to organize an event where collectors could meet and share their love for

dolls. Dollfies (a portmanteau of "doll" and "figure") are realistic, anatomically correct ball-jointed dolls made of porcelain-like hard plastic that can be fully customized (their body parts can be easily changed, including the wigs they use for hair and even their eyes). Therefore, Dolpa—as the event is called by fans—is also an opportunity for many dealers to sell their clothes and exquisitely detailed accessories. As for the dolls themselves, other companies are featured, including fashionable Pullip and longtime fan favorite Licca-chan, but this is first and foremost a Dollfie paradise. Dolpa is currently held three times a year—twice in Tokyo and once in Kyoto, where Volks headquarters are located.
**Admission fee:** ***No ticket required, but you have to buy the Japanese-language Official Guide Book (2,000 yen). The guide can be bought on the same day, but if you want to get in line to buy limited-edition or pre-sale items, you must buy it in advance.*** **Dates:** ***Early May and December*** **Hours:** ***10:00–17:00*** **volks.co.jp/jp/dolpa_portal/index.html**

Anime Japan is a showcase for the industry's new products.

LEFT and BELOW The twice-yearly Itasha Tengoku motorshow is one of the world's largest gatherings of otaku cars. You'll even see otaku motorbikes, scooters and bicycles!

### International Tokyo Toy Show

The grand dame of otaku festivals was born in 1962 and is still going strong, with an average of 140 exhibitors and 140,000 visitors. Unsurprisingly, it's more mainstream and child-oriented than other toy shows. This is, after all, the industry's most important event, co-organized by the Japan Toy Association (JTA) and the Tokyo Metropolitan Government; it even enjoys the support of the Ministry of Economy, Trade and Industry. As the JTA states on its website, one of the show's main purposes is to "provide a venue for announcing new products to markets inside and outside of Japan and for conducting business negotiations," and indeed, access to the event in the first two days is limited to registered traders (almost 19,000 in 2014). No problem—there's plenty to see and enjoy in the last couple of days. In 2014, for instance, a grand total of 35,000 items were on display. Thirty-five of them won the Japan Toy Award that every year honors the best products in seven different categories, including boys' and girls' toys, educational and innovative toys, and even "high-target" toys, which are mainly designed for grown-up kids (i.e., adults). All the industry's heavyweights are here peddling their games, models, dolls, robots and gadgets of every kind. This being Japan, no toy show would be complete without an army of character-based "enterTOYment" (as the rather cheesy event motto says)—not only the usual suspects (Hello Kitty, Pretty Cure, Ultraman and One Piece, to mention just a few) but also the increasingly popular *yuru-chara* and even characters from Internet-based apps and games like LINE and Puzzles & Dragons. The show includes demonstrations of the latest products, Super Sentai stage shows, exhibits illustrating the history of Japanese toys and even the opportunity to take a picture with your favorite character!
**Admission fee:** ***Free*** **Dates:** ***June*** **Hours:** ***9:00–17:00*** **toys.or.jp/toyshow**

### Itasha Tengoku

In the 1980s, when Japan was threatening to become the world's number one economic power and people were more than happy to show off their newfound wealth, more and more luxury cars began to roam Tokyo's streets. The ultimate status symbol, an Italian sports car, became known as an *itasha* ("ita" for Italy; *sha* means car). The good times were rather short-lived, but otaku car fans have recently appropriated the nickname for their manga-, anime- and video-game-character-decorated vehicles. Only in this case the prefix "ita" is short for *itai* (painful) to show the amount of time, energy and money these people have spent beautifying their four-wheeled loves. Originally organized by *Ita-G* magazine, this sort of itasha motor show is probably the world's largest gathering of otaku cars, and we have no reason to doubt it (because, let's face it, such things could only happen in Japan). Itasha Tengoku attracts vehicles from all over Japan to Odaiba's open spot not far from Fuji TV's futuristic-looking building. Apart from some 1,000 heavily decorated cars—some sporting huge stereo systems pumping out *anison* from their giant speakers—there are plenty of *itansha* (motorbikes) and even a few scooters and *itachari* (bicycles). Besides the four- and two-wheeled beauties, there's a stage devoted to idol group performances and one for voice-actor talk shows and comedy performances. And yes, cosplayers are welcome here too.

**Admission fee:** *1,500 yen (5,000 yen to enter your* itasha*; 4,500 yen for a motorbike; 3,500 yen for a bicycle); cosplay event is 500 yen* **Dates:** *April (and October, inside Tokyo Motor Fes)* **Hours:** *9:30–16:00* **Access:** *Located at the big parking lot next to Fune-no-kagakukan Station (Yurikamome Line)*
**itasha-tengoku.yaesu-net.co.jp/event/2018_odaiba**

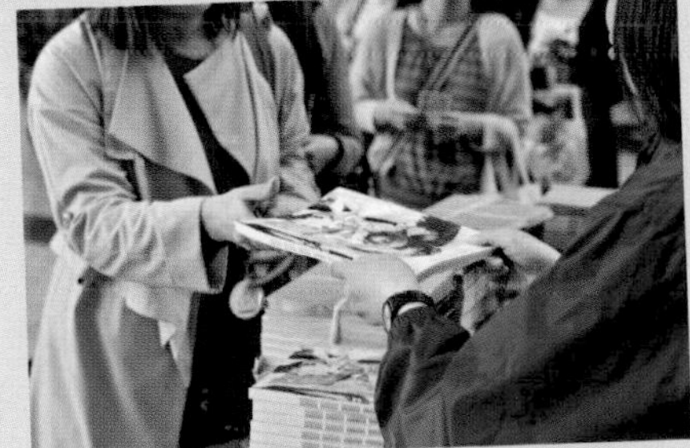

At Super Comic City you'll find independently produced comics and other goods for otaku.

## Super Comic City

Akaboo is a printing company that mainly caters to *dojinshi* makers. Every year it sponsors about 20 *dojinshi* fairs in Tokyo, Osaka and Fukuoka, the biggest of which is Tokyo's Super Comic City (SCC). Though much smaller than the two Comikets, this is still the third-largest fair in Japan. As at Comiket, you can find any sort of independently produced works here (manga, illustrations, music, games, character goods, etc.); cosplayers are allowed in certain areas. The main differences are that 1) SCC has a stronger corporate feeling; 2) it only lasts for five hours; 3) original works are less that 10 percent of the total; and, most importantly, 4) this event is predominantly oriented to female audiences. So if you are a guy you will be surrounded by thousands and thousands of girls without any male geeks in sight—which makes for a surreal, delightful and scary experience.

**Admission fee:** *Simple admission ticket (1,000 yen); event booklet (1,200 yen). Registration for cosplayers is 1,000 yen per day (cloakroom is 500 yen); registration for cosplay photographers is 1,000 yen* **Dates:** *Early May* **Hours:** *10:00–15:00*
**akaboo.jp/event/index_en.html** *(in English)*

## Tokyo Idol Festival

Japan's (and maybe the world's) biggest idol festival started in 2010, a product of the Tokyo Idol Project's tireless work to spread idol culture around the globe. This event has rapidly achieved big numbers, with the last few editions averaging over 100 idol groups and 30,000 to 40,000 fans. The good and bad thing about this festival is that it has so many concerts in just a couple of days. In 2018, for instance, 138 groups were spread around seven stages, with performances starting every few minutes, making it impossible to see all one's favorite idols. Still, it's a good opportunity to confirm that not all idols look and sound alike—there are rock and heavy metal groups and some weirder stuff. TIF is the place to witness the birth of new idol sensations. On the other hand, some groups choose this stage to perform for one last time before disbanding or morphing into different combos. All in all, there's a lot going on, including the usual talk shows and—drum roll—handshake sessions! In order to gain access to the stages, you need to exchange your ticket for a wristband (see website for details on place and time). Ticket sales start a few months before the festival, and sell out very quickly. In its drive to attract more foreign visitors, TIF is planning to make ticket purchases possible from anywhere in the world. Check the English webpage for details.

**Admission fee:** *One-day ticket 5,500 yen; two-day ticket 9,500 yen (advance tickets are 5,000 and 8,800 yen respectively)* **Dates:** *First weekend in August* **Hours:** *9:30–22:00* **Access:** *The stages are located around Odaiba and Aomi; the concert area stretches between Kokusai Tenjijo Seimon Station and Telecom Center Station (see website for map and details)* **idolfes.com**

## Tokyo International Comic Festival

This young but promising festival showcases comics by more than 50 artists from around the world. As the organization committee led by Frenchman Frederic Toutlemonde states on its home page, their hope is to eventually "become as significant as the U.S. International Comic-Con or France's Angoulême International Comics Festival" and to provide a platform "where people all around the world who have an interest in manga culture can freely exchange their opinions and ideas." For the last few years they have partnered with COMITIA (see above). This means that while the festival itself is free of charge, you must pay the entrance fee to the *dojinshi* market.

**Admission fee:** *1,000 yen (COMITIA entrance fee)* **Dates:** *November* **Hours:** *11:00–16:00*
**kaigaimangafesta.com**

# Shops Elsewhere in Tokyo

### Billiken

This gallery-cum-shop is very well regarded by local toy collectors, and with good reason: This is one of the best places to look for plastic monsters by the likes of Pico Pico, Sunguts and Yomomark, as well as the kind of indie toys you can find at such events as the Super Festival (see page 51). They have art and children's books, paintings and illustrations as well.

**Hours:** *12:00–19:00; closed Mondays*
**Access:** *5-17-6 Minami Aoyama, Minato-ku*
**billiken-shokai.co.jp**

### Manga Yado/Shirakuna シラクナ・工房

In Japan even the blandest-looking neighborhoods can hide a treasure. Take this shop: it used to sell tin toys, then in 2008 its owner began to manufacture vinyl toys under the Shirakuna brand. Today his original *kaiju* figures share space with a wide range of antique toys dating from the 1950s all the way back to the prewar years. This cluttered place functions as a studio as well. If you're lucky, when you pay it a visit you'll have a chance to watch the artists working on their new creations. You may want to call in advance (03-3659-1990) to check if it's open.

**Hours:** *13:30–19:00; closed Mondays*
**Access:** *1-10-4 Nishi Koiwa, Edogawa-ku*

### Monstock

This small shop is quite off the beaten track, but recommended if you are into indie toys. They sell figures by such makers as Toumart and Atelier G-1.

**Hours:** *16:00–20:00 (closes at random; call before going)*
**Access:** *4-13-5 Kami-Jujo, Kita-ku*
**geocities.jp/monstock_tokyo/home.html**

### Real Head 真頭玩具

For some people this is the holy grail of indie vinyl toy stores, and it's totally worth the trip. Mori Katsura has been making and selling his original takes on fighter figures and mutant monsters since 2004, and today "Real x Head" is one of the most revered and sought-after brands in the universe. The shop itself, lost in Tokyo's deep eastern suburbs, is a sort of museum. Just remember to call (03-3690-9353) before you go, as its schedule is irregular to say the least.

ABOVE and LEFT Real Head is the holy grail of indie vinyl toy stores. Real x Head figures are one of the most sought-after brands in the universe. BELOW Sofubi Cruiser Cosmo Night Alpha specializes in soft vinyl monster figures.

**Hours:** *18:00–21:00 (weekdays), 12:00–17:00 (weekends and holidays); closed irregularly*
**Access:** *3-32-9 Aoto, Katsushika-ku*
**realxhead.jp**

### Sofubi Cruiser Cosmo Night Alpha

The grannies who frequent the narrow shopping street where this store is located are regularly startled by the parade of monsters on display. Inside you'll find floor-to-ceiling soft vinyl figures and other toys (vintage items too), including the Yusei Majin figures created by the shop itself.

**Hours:** *12:00–20:00; closed Tuesdays and irregularly (call before going)*
**Access:** *25-17 Ekoda, Nerima-ku*
**sofvi.com/news**

### Third Uncle/Character Toy
さあどあんくる

Serious collectors with fat wallets can forget about the other shops in this book and head directly to Third Uncle. They'll be sure to leave the store with their hands full and much lighter pockets. From monsters, action figures and robots to mini cars, plamodels and everything in between, Third Uncle offers a huge stock, all in mint condition and beautifully displayed.

**Hours:** *13:00–21:00; closed Mondays*
**Access:** *3-34-8 Nishi Koiwa, Edogawa-ku*
**third-uncle.com**

### Tokyo Solamachi

The 2,000-foot (634-meter)-tall Sky Tree is the latest addition to the admittedly short list of internationally famous Tokyo landmarks. While you're there, take time to explore Solamachi, the huge shopping mall at the base of the tower, which has lots of character-based and toy shops (e.g., Takara Tomy's model cars and railroad toys, Studio Ghibli's Donguri Kyowakoku shop, etc.). The only downside is that, unlike Tokyo Station's compact **Character Street**, they are scattered over different floors.

**Hours:** *10:00–21:00* **Access:** *Tokyo Sky Tree, 1-1-2 Oshiage, Sumida-ku*
**tokyo-solamachi.jp/en** *(English)*

# Other Museums and Libraries in Tokyo

**Meiji University Contemporary Manga Library (Naiki Collection)**
In the first 20 years after World War II, many people in Japan didn't buy books and manga; they used to rent them the same way they would later rent videotapes and DVDs. *Kashihon* (rental) manga became popular in the early '50s and continued to flourish until the early '60s, when they were gradually replaced by weeklies like *Shonen Sunday* and *Shonen Magazine*. Naiki Toshio was a comic lover who in 1955 opened one such store in Shinjuku when he was still in high school. His passion for manga was so great that in 1978 he turned his 20,000 volume collection into a library. Currently the Gendai Manga Toshokan has grown to 180,000 books and magazines, and is part of the Meiji University manga library system. It includes many rare publications from the '50s through the early '60s, when manga culture began to spread across Japan. All this stuff can be read on site for a small fee (100 yen per item), but only members of the Tomo no Kai who pay the annual 6,000-yen membership fee have access to the publications from 1970 and earlier.
**Admission fee:** *300 yen (200 yen for junior high school students and under)*
**Hours:** *12:00–19:00; closed Tuesdays and Fridays* **Access:** *2F, 565 Waseda Tsurumakicho, Shinjuku-ku* **sites.google.com/site/naikilib**

The Hasegawa Machiko Art Museum in Setagaya-ku displays work collected by Hasegawa Machiko, the creator of mega-successful manga and anime Sazae-san.

**(1•5) Hasegawa Machiko Art Museum**
Practically no one in Japan is unaware of Hasegawa Machiko (one of the first female manga artists) and her mega-successful manga and anime *Sazae-san*. This museum, however, mainly displays paintings and other artworks collected by Hasegawa and her sister Mariko through the years. Just once a year, during the summer holidays, Fuji TV sponsors an exhibition entirely devoted to *Sazae-san*. The rest of the year, only a small space on the second floor (Machiko's Corner) is devoted to her manga art. Probably the best thing for *Sazae-san* fans is the small but well-stocked shop on the first floor selling a seemingly infinite array of original goods (toys, cups, file folders, towels, memo pads, snacks, etc.). Ironically, you have a better chance to see Hasegawa's work outside the museum, as the area features 12 statues of the Isono family besides assorted banners and wall art.
**Admission fee:** *600 yen (high school and university students 500 yen, junior high students and under 400 yen)*
**Hours:** *10:00–17:30; closed Mondays*
**Access:** *1-30-6 Sakura Shinmachi, Setagaya-ku*
**hasegawamachiko.jp**

**(1•2) Matsumoto Katsuji Gallery**
This tiny gallery in posh Setagaya ward is devoted to the work of another manga pioneer, Matsumoto Katsuji, a children's book illustrator who was mainly popular between the 1930s and 1950s and is best remembered for his American comic-inspired *shojo* manga *Kurukuru Kurumi-chan*. He was an inspiration to several future manga greats and is considered one of the original creators of the *kawaii* style. On display in this gallery are a few paintings and other works, and a collection of magazines and books featuring his illustrations.
**Admission fee:** *300 yen* **Hours:** *Visits by appointment only; call (03-3707-3503) or email (kurumifriend@gmail.com) at least 7 days beforehand* **Access:** *4-14-18 Tamagawa, Setagaya-ku* **katsudi.com/en/homepage**

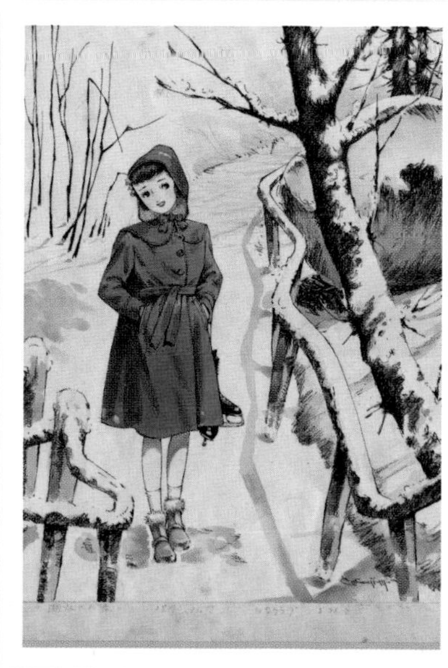

**Meiji University Yonezawa Yoshihiro Memorial Library of Manga and Subcultures**
Yonezawa Yoshihiro was a writer and manga critic who in 1975 founded **Comiket** with two college friends. He was also a collector of anything related to manga, *dojinshi* and pop culture, and when he died in 2006 his huge collection (more than 4,000 boxes and over 140,000 items) was donated to Meiji University's School of Global Japanese Studies, which opened this library in 2009. Though the place is a university facility, it's open to anyone over 18 through a membership system. One-day members can only view open-stack materials, which means they don't have access to materials published before 1979. You can photocopy many of the items in the library, but borrowing is not allowed. For details on how to use the library, read the detailed English-language page on their website. The place is highly recommended for people who are interested in manga history and rare materials. There is also a free exhibition space on the first floor. The grand plan for this institution is for it to eventually become the (temporarily named) Tokyo International Manga Library.
**Admission fee:** *One-day membership 300 yen; 1 month 2,000 yen; 1 year 6,000 yen* **Hours:** *14:00–20:00 (Mondays and Fridays), 12:00–18:00 (weekends and national holidays)* **Access:** *1-7-1 Sarugaku-cho, Chiyoda-ku* **meiji.ac.jp/manga**

**ABOVE** The Meiji University Contemporary Manga Library includes many rare manga from the 1950s and '60s. **RIGHT** An exhibit from the Nuri-e Museum.

**(1•2•4•5) Nuri-e Museum**
*Nuri-e* is Japanese for coloring book, and this museum is completely devoted to that particular children's pastime. In Japan, *nuri-e* were one of the many cultural imports from the West during the Meiji era. The practice really took off in the first 20 years of last century, but no one became as good or famous as Tsutaya Kiichi, who elevated a simple hobby into an art. His images of cute young girls (a mix of Shirley Temple and Kewpie doll) were particularly popular between 1945 and 1965, and the museum's collection, which was put together by his niece, is particularly strong for these two decades. At the entrance one finds the museum shop and the temporary exhibits, which change monthly. Another exhibition space is mainly devoted to Tsutaya's works. There is even a corner where visitors can try their coloring skills and maybe feel a little like when they were kids.
**Admission fee:** *500 yen (junior high and up), 100 yen (elementary school)* **Hours:** *12:00–18:00 (March–October), 11:00–17:00 (November–February); open only on weekends and national holidays* **Access:** *4-11-8 Machiya, Arakawa-ku* **nurie.jp**

**(1•2•5) Yayoi-Yumeji Museum**
People in search of a bargain will be happy to know that here they can see two museums with a single ticket. The Yayoi Museum mainly displays the works of illustrators from the end of the Meiji era to the postwar era (1890–1945). The Yumeji Museum is dedicated to the works of illustrator Yumeji Takehisa, one of the foremost artists and poets of the Taisho era (1912–1926), when girls' culture flourished in Japan. Indeed, he was especially famous for his portraits of beauties that he published in girls' and ladies' magazines like *Shojo no Tomo*. At the time, it was in these publications that most manga artists had a chance to hone their skill. Exhibitions are rather small but still worth a visit if you are into early 20th-century art, older comics and *shojo* manga. There's also a café and a shop selling many goods featuring Yumeji's distinct style.
**Admission fee:** *900 yen (high school and university students 800 yen, junior high and younger 400 yen)* **Hours:** *10:00–17:00; closed Mondays* **Access:** *2-4-2/3 Yayoi, Bunkyo-ku* **yayoi-yumeji-museum.jp** *(good English explanations)*

The Yayoi-Yumeji Museum is worth visiting if you are interested in early 20th-century art.

# Museums and Libraries Near Tokyo

## Kanagawa Prefecture

### (4•5) Yokohama Anpanman Children's Museum and Mall

For many years now, Anpanman has been the undisputed darling of all Japanese children. The bread-roll-headed superhero has sold over 50 million books so far, while the ubiquitous franchise has become a trillion-yen business. So it's not a surprise that this place is yet another money-making machine. To be sure, though it's called a museum, it's closer to an amusement-park-cum-shopping-mall. The rather expensive "museum" side of the impressive-looking building is divided into three floors featuring the usual kid-friendly attractions in addition to a small exhibition room and a diorama. Anpanman Square, on the other side, is a typical mall providing many chances to spend your money with nine souvenir shops, 10 eateries and even a hair salon and photo studio! *Sore ike! Anpanman!!*

**Admission fee:** *1,500 yen (over one year old)*
**Hours:** *10:00–18:00; closed on New Year's Day; shopping mall open 10:00–19:00; Anpanman & Pecos Kitchen open 10:00–20:00*
**Access:** *4-3-1 Minato Mirai, Nishi-ku, Yokohama*
**yokohama-anpanman.jp/main.html**

Yokohama Anpanman Children's Museum and Mall is full of kid-friendly attractions centered on Anpanman, beloved by all Japanese children.

### (1•4•5) Fujiko F Fujio Museum

Fujimoto Hiroshi and Abiko Motoo created many unforgettable characters under the pen name Fujiko Fujio (Perman, 21emon, Kiteretsu Daiyakka, Esper Mami, etc.), but there's no doubt that the one for which they have become world famous is Doraemon. Since the first appearance of the robot cat from the 22nd century in 1969, the stories featuring Doraemon and his young friends have sold more than 100 million copies, making him one of the most recognizable symbols of Japanese pop culture. So it's no surprise that he gets the lion's share in the museum devoted to the work of Fujiko F. Fujio (Fujimoto's adopted name after he ended his 40-year partnership with Abiko). Indeed, this place is often called the Doraemon Museum by manga fans. The facility's centerpieces are the two

**ABOVE** The Fujiko F Fujio Museum is often called the Doraemon Museum by manga fans. **FAR LEFT and LEFT** In 2002 *Time* magazine included Doraemon in its special "Asian Hero" issue.

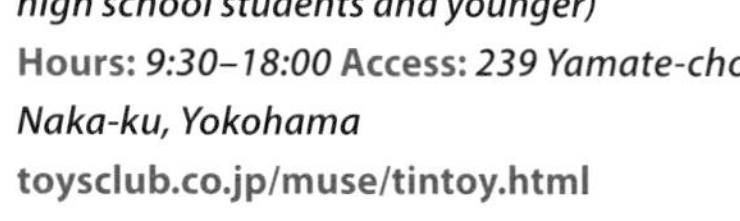

Japan used to be the world's biggest exporter of tin toys. The Tin Toys Museum packs in some 3,000 toys ranging from cars and trains to aircraft and dolls. Otaku fans will find many rarities such as '50s robots and early examples of Astro Boy.

big galleries displaying Fujimoto's original works on a rotation basis. This is one of the very few manga museums in Japan whose main purpose is to collect, preserve and display the work of a particular author. The useful English audio guide (included with admission) has a lot of commentary on his life and work. Children, on the other hand, are definitely more attracted by the playroom, manga reading room and the rooftop garden featuring "life size" statues of Doraemon & Co. together with some of the story's most recognizable places and gadgets (the playground's earthen pipes, the Dokodemo Door, etc.), while a 100-seat theater displays original short films.

If you are a fan, be sure to pack your wallet with money, because you won't be able to resist a visit to the café selling Doraemon-themed dishes and the well-stocked museum shop. Both the food and some of the goods are quite expensive (figures and dolls typically go for 4,000 to 5,000 yen).

Be aware that tickets are not sold at the museum and must be purchased in advance. The quickest and cheapest way to get them is at a Lawson convenience store through a Loppi ticket machine. A tutorial on how to do so can be found at www.tokyogig-guide.com/tickets. You will be required to make a reservation, choosing a date and time slot (10:00, 12:00, 14:00 or 16:00). If possible, try to avoid weekends and school holidays as the museum gets packed with kids.

**Admission fee:** *1,000 yen (700 yen for junior high and high school students, 500 for age four and up)* **Hours:** *10:00–18:00; closed Tuesdays (except April 29–May 5 and July 20–September 3) and 12/30–1/3* **Access:** *2-8-1 Nagao, Tama-ku, Kawasaki*
**fujiko-museum.com/english** *(excellent information in English)*

### (1•5) Tin Toys Museum

Japan used to be the world's largest exporter of tin toys. Starting in the 1910s, when they overtook Germany's output, through the mid-'60s, tin toys constituted about 60 percent of Japanese toy exports before they were gradually replaced by plastic; now, apparently, there is only one tin-toy craftman left in Japan. Kitahara Teruhisa is one of the most prolific collectors of tin toys in the world. While small, his museum packs in some 3,000 toys ranging from cars and trains to aircraft and dolls. The collection is arranged roughly by era, going all the way back to the late 1890s. It includes foreign characters like Mickey Mouse and Popeye, but otaku fans will be particularly delighted to find many Japanese examples of space rockets, Ultraman toys, rarities like those wonderful '50s robots (in mint condition!) and even early examples of Astro Boy. If you're into old tin toys, this place is a must-see.
**Admission fee:** *200 yen (100 yen for junior high school students and younger)* **Hours:** *9:30–18:00* **Access:** *239 Yamate-cho, Naka-ku, Yokohama*
**toysclub.co.jp/muse/tintoy.html**

## Saitama Prefecture

### (2•4) Saitama Manga Kaikan / Saitama Municipal Cartoon Art Museum

When debating the origins of manga, people's opinions tend to differ. However, everybody seems to agree about the role that Kitazawa Rakuten played in its development. The Saitama-born artist was in fact the first professional cartoonist in Japan, and is considered one of the founding fathers of modern manga. Now the site where he lived has been turned into a memorial museum—probably the very first manga-related institution created in Japan. The first floor features an exhibition space devoted to works by Kitazawa himself and other artists, together with a reproduction of his workroom, while the second floor is a manga library. Though it's rather off the beaten track, this museum is worth a visit, especially if you're into manga history.
**Admission fee:** *Free* **Hours:** *9:00–16:30; closed Mondays* **Access:** *150 Bonsai-cho, Kita-ku, Saitama-shi*
**city.saitama.jp/004/005/002/003/001/index.html**

# Other Festivals and Events in Tokyo

**@Jam Project**

The Tokyo Idol Festival now has a strong rival in the @Jam Project, which is behind a string of music concerts that have featured such groups as JKT48, Tokyo Girls' Style and even boy groups. Each event has a similar format but differs in size, from the more intimate monthly performances in Akiba (**@Jam Next**) to the mega-concert in Yokohama at one of the largest venues in the Kanto region (**@Jam Expo**) and the two-day festival in Odaiba. The bigger events include multiple stages, talk shows, DJing and meet-and-greet areas. Check their website for details. **at-jam.jp**

The @Jam Project is behind a string of concerts that have featured such groups as Dempagumi.inc (TOP) and JKT48 (BOTTOM). Events range from intimate performances in Akihabara to mega-concerts in Yokohama.

**Cosplay Festa TDC**

The oldest cosplay event in Japan has been held since 1997 at Tokyo Dome City, attracting an average of 6,000 people each time, from veteran cosplayers to beginners. The area devoted to cosplaying is 322,000 feet (30,000 meters) square. This is also the only event of this size which offers cloakroom service. Last but not least, all the attractions in the amusement park in the Tokyo Dome City complex are included in the entrance fee.
**Admission fee:** *2,300 yen (advance tickets 2,100 yen, available at Lawson's)*
**Dates:** *Several times a year; check the website for upcoming dates* **Hours:** *10:00–21:00*
**Access:** *Tokyo Dome City, 1-3-61 Koraku, Bunkyo-ku* **cosplayfesta.com**

**New Layers Paradise**

Basically this is like Cosplay Festa TDC (see above). You can attend even if you're not a "layer" (cosplayer) and only want to take pictures, but you need to register your camera for a fee.
**Admission fee:** *2,300 yen (advance tickets 2,100 yen, available at Lawson's); 500-yen camera registration fee for non-cosplayers*
**Dates:** *Four times a year; check the website for schedule* **Hours:** *10:00–21:00*
**Access:** *Tokyo Dome City, 1-3-61 Koraku, Bunkyo-ku* **laypara.jp**

**Super Festival**

First launched in 1992 and run by toy maker Art Storm (who owns the Fewture shop in Akihabara), this is among the favorite events of toy fans in Tokyo. Here, new and old (i.e., collectors' items) toys, models and figures are exhibited and sold by manufacturers, shops and private dealers. Established companies like Marusan and Bullmark, new emerging brands and boutique makers display a vast array of *shokugan*, alloy and tin toys, plamodels, garage kits, dolls and *bishojo* figures. There is also a special area for minicars, model trains, airplanes, etc., and a bunch of other items including T-shirts, CDs, LDs, books, magazines and cards. Equally popular with the toy-loving crowd is the Tokusatsu Archive stage, which hosts talk shows and signing events by popular creators, actors and industry veterans. This festival is very laid back and full of friendly people—stiff corporate PRs are nowhere to be seen.
**Admission fee:** *1,500 yen (800 yen for elementary-school students)*
**Dates:** *January, April and September*
**Hours:** *10:30–16:00* **Access:** *Kagaku Gijutsukan, 2-1 Kitanomaru-koen, Chiyoda-ku*
**artstorm.co.jp/sufes.html**

**Tokyo Anime Award Festival**

TAAF's stated aim is to support both the artistic and the business side of animation. Its main attraction is the international lineup of works (both feature films and shorts) shown during the five days of the event, which are divided between two sections: the Competition Grand Prize (featuring Japanese and foreign films that have not been commercially screened in Japan) and the Anime of the Year Award (films that attracted the attention of local fans during the past year). In recent years the organizers have mostly played it safe by recognizing the "usual suspects" (e.g., Disney, Studio Ghibli) that are proven winners at the box office. Let's hope they'll come up with more daring choices in the next few years. Still, for anime fans this is yet another great chance to see some good stuff.
**Admission fee:** *1,000 yen (3,000 yen for all-night screenings)* **Dates:** *March* **Hours:** *See website for schedule* **Access:** *TOHO Cinemas Nihonbashi, COREDO Muromachi 2, 3F, 2-3-1 Nihonbashi Muromachi, Chuo-ku*

**animefestival.jp/en**

### Tokyo Doll Show

Since 1998 the Tokyo Doll Show has been a chance for both manufacturers and hobbyists to show and sell their dolls and doll accessories. All the major brands (Volks, Pullip, Licca-chan, etc.) are present, along with smaller companies as well. Perhaps the most fascinating aspect of the show is seeing the care with which the dolls' "parents" prepare and proudly show their dolls, often dressing them like famous manga and anime characters. Taking pictures is usually okay, but you should always ask for permission.

**Admission fee:** *The catalog/brochure costs 1,000 yen (500 yen for junior high and high school students; free for elementary school students). If you want to be among the first to enter, you also have to buy a numbered ticket (500 yen), otherwise you have to wait in line.*
**Dates:** *Scheduled irregularly three times a year (see website for details)* **Hours:** *11:00–16:00*
**Access:** *Sunshine City Hall D, 3-1-1 Higashi Ikebukuro, Toshima-ku*
**dollshow.net** *(mostly Japanese with a detailed if rather confusing English page)*

# Other Festivals and Events Near Tokyo

## Kanagawa Prefecture

### Tales of Festival

*Tales* (known as *Tales of* in Japan) is the third-biggest role-playing video-game series in Japan, with about 20 console games plus spin-offs and mobile app games. While lacking the cultural cachet of *Final Fantasy* and *Dragon Quest*, it's so popular that it's had its own dedicated two-day festival in Yokohama for more than a decade, and the fun is screened in movie theaters across the country.

The events include live skits performed by cast members of the *Tales* games; talk shows; concerts; and announcements for upcoming products (games, manga, anime, CDs, etc.).

**Admission fee:** *7,000 to 13,500 yen*
**Dates:** *June* **Hours:** *15:00* **Access:** *Yokohama Arena Main Hall, 3-10 Shin-Yokohama, Kohoku-ku (five minutes' walk from the Shin-Yokohama subway station)*
**tof.tales-ch.jp**

## Chiba Prefecture

All the festivals in Chiba take place at Makuhari Messe (2-1 Nakase, Mihama-ku, Chiba City) which is a two-minute walk from Kaihin Makuhari Station (JR Keiyo Line). From Tokyo Station it takes 30 to 40 minutes. The Makuhari Messe site provides useful information in English: m-messe.co.jp/en/index.html

### Japan Amusement Expo

The world of Japanese arcade games is ruled by two powerful groups, the Japan Amusement Machine and Marketing Association and the All-Nippon Amusement Machine Operators' Union. They used to run two competing events, but in 2012 they decided to merge them into a giant fair, the Japan Amusement Expo. Visiting JAEPO is like stepping into a huge game center where all the machines on display are brand new. This is, in fact, where Japan's main arcade-game makers unveil their latest creations. The main exhibition area is packed with some 1,000 machines. The next-biggest area, the Prize Zone, features UFO-catcher gadgets, while the other, smaller areas are devoted to publications covering the amusement and entertainment industry and the few foreign exhibitors (usually from China). And let's not forget the ever-present army of cosplayers who descend on Makuhari Messe to show off their skin-revealing outfits, even in February's cold temperatures.

**Admission fee:** *1,000 yen (free for elementary school kids and those over 60)*
**Dates:** *February* **Hours:** *10:00–17:00*
**jaepo.jp/top_en.html** *(English)*

### Jump Festa

What sets this event apart from similar conventions is that Jump Festa is sponsored by manga publishing giant Shueisha and focuses on the content of four titles in its bestselling "Jump" series of *shonen* manga magazines. Traditionally each festival showcases new movies, games and merchandise for the upcoming season. From goods to live performances and even food, everything follows the same theme. The Jump Super Stage gives fans an

TOP LEFT These Dollfie Dream dolls are some of the many you may see at the Tokyo Doll Show. BELOW A trip to the Japan Amusement Expo is like stepping into a huge game center.

LEFT To Love-Ru at the Jump Festa. ABOVE Mario Cart at the Jump Festa. BELOW RIGHT A scene from the Tokyo Game Show. BELOW Nico Nico Chokaigi is a hodgepodge of otaku events.

opportunity to meet popular voice actors as well as current and former Jump artists, while in the Genga World they can admire original art and signed illustrations. Recent iterations have averaged nearly 150,000 visitors, many of whom are lured by the limited-edition goods on sale.

**Admission fee:** *Free* **Dates:** *Third weekend in December* **Hours:** *10:00–19:00*
**jumpfesta.com**

### Next Generation World Hobby Fair

The biggest game and hobby event in Japan is organized by publishing company Shogakukan (one of the major peddlers of manga in the country) and is held in four different cities. The Tokyo meeting takes place in nearby Chiba twice a year. Compared to other otaku events, many of the latest toys and video games showcased are geared to younger kids (elementary and junior high school) but everybody is invited to try them all day long for free. There is also a market area where you can get limited-time goods, as well as stage events devoted to the hottest items and even signing sessions where kids up to 15 years old can get an autograph from one of their favorite artists.

**Admission fee:** *Free* **Dates:** *January and June* **Hours:** *9:00–16:00*
**whobby.com**

### Nico Nico Cho-kaigi

This "super meeting" (*cho-kaigi*) is a hodgepodge of events, mixing together typical otaku favorites (anime, video games, cosplay, vocaloid, etc.) with the mildly weird (UFOs, dinosaurs, pro wrestling and . . . sumo?!) and the frankly disturbing (a Japan Self-Defense Forces booth doing some PR work for hawkish prime minister Abe Shinzo). The anime area features hands-on attractions from a number of popular works that will give you a chance to try your hand at voice acting, idol producing or replicating the characters' exploits. Festival organizer Nico Nico, Japan's answer to YouTube, has developed the biggest video community in this country. Videos uploaded on this site feature an original (shall we say "only-in-Japan"?) commenting system where comments posted by viewers appear directly on the video screen, allowing users to interact in real time. Depending on your tastes and inclinations, the effect can be cute, exhilarating or just plain annoying. The site, by the way, is particularly famous for homemade videos creatively mixing *anison* and images, and the festival indulges Nico

Nico users' interests with plenty of amateur singing, dancing and performances. Each edition largely exceeds 100,000 attendees over two days, while the online live broadcast is followed by more than 7.5 million people. Those who have some energy left can even attend the Nico Nico Cho Party in the late hours.

**Admission fee:** *2,000 yen (advance ticket 1,500 yen); two-day pass 2,500 yen (advance purchase only)* **Dates:** *Last weekend in April* **Hours:** *10:00–18:00*
**chokaigi.jp** *(limited English-language information)*

### Tokyo Game Show

In the world of supposedly "international" otaku festivals, the Tokyo Game Show (Japan's biggest video-game exhibition) seems to be one of the few events with a true global appeal: in the last few years nearly half of the 400-plus exhibitors came from outside Japan. Gaming has recently entered a new dimension, with different technological supports like smartphones, tablets and VR gadgets offering fans novel ways to play. This festival's Social Game Area showcases the hundreds of titles specifically created for iOS, Android and other such platforms. The Family Area is off-limits to "kids" older than 11 (parents excepted) and features the usual character-related events. On the other end of the spectrum, the Romance Simulation Game Area is all about the dating-simulation PC games that otaku of both sexes love so much. Other favorite areas are devoted to startups and independent developers, merchandise sales, game hardware and live music events; there's also the usual cosplay area.

**Admission fee:** *1,200 yen (advance tickets 1,000 yen), free for kids under 12* **Dates:** *September* **Hours:** *10:00–17:00 expo.* **nikkeibp.co.jp/tgs**

At the Tokyo Game Show you'll find merchandise sales, game hardware and live music events, as well as the usual cosplay area.

### Wonder Festival

Garage-kit fans and collectors are a rabid bunch who can hardly wait to see their favorite products firsthand. To help quench their thirst, figure manufacturer Kaiyodo brings all the best figures and models under one roof twice a year, making WonFes (as this festival is colloquially known) the best event in Japan for showing and selling prototype figures by both amateur and professional creators, with an average of 1,800 dealers and 50,000 fans in attendance. Many companies now showcase limited editions especially produced for this festival, and it's one of the few occasions when amateurs can show off their manga- and anime-inspired PVC and cold-cast creations without violating copyright laws, thanks to the "one-day-copyright-waiving" system. So if you're on the lookout for works by some garage-kit superstar like Bome, this is definitely the go-to place. Just be prepared to fight with thousands of other fans, as these works sell out immediately.

Since 1999, the festival has hosted a parallel event every year called Wonder Showcase, where a selected number of gifted sculptors who have been selected by the planning committee are given the royal treatment, with their works displayed in special glass booths (the works are also for sale). Wonder Showcase is the official label of WonFes and the pieces featured in that year's event are later available at the Kaiyodo Hobby Lobby Tokyo in Akihabara as well as at the Kaiyodo Online Shop.

**Admission fee:** *2,000 yen* **Dates:** *February and October* **Hours:** *10:00–17:00* **wonfes.jp**

## Saitama Prefecture

### Anime Manga Festival in Saitama

Saitama is famous for being the site of a number of popular manga and anime, and in 2013 the local authorities decided to start a festival that would help further promote the prefecture as an otaku destination. The concept seems to have been very successful, as the first two iterations have attracted about 60,000 visitors. The festival features idol stage shows, concerts by *anison* performers, talk shows, and even an *itasha* (anime-decorated car) exhibition and cosplay event.

**Admission fee:** *500–600 yen for market, café and tourism exhibitions (free for high school students and younger); concert is 6,800 yen; all other events are free*
**Dates:** *October* **Hours:** *10:00–18:00*
**Access:** *Sonic City, 1-7-5 Sakuragicho, Omiya-ku, Saitama* **anitamasai.jp**

### Animelo Summer Live

Anisama (as the Japanese call it) is the most prominent music festival for songs from anime, video games and *tokusatsu* TV shows; most performers

LEFT Wonder Festival attracts thousands of garage-kit fans. RIGHT Animelo Summer Live is a unique chance to see many of your favorite anison singers and voice actors perform on stage. FACING PAGE TOP LEFT Get ready for an overdose of cute mascots at the World Character Summit in Hanyu, Saitama prefecture.

are singers and voice actors specializing in these genres. The three-day event has more than 100 performers and is famous for its artist collaborations. It reaches its climax with a theme song (different each year) sung by all performers at the end of the concert.

**Admission fee:** *8,700 yen (see website for ticket details)* **Dates:** *End of Aug* **Hours:** *16:00–21:00* **Access:** *Saitama Super Arena, 8 Shin-Toshin, Chuo-ku, Saitama* **anisama.tv**

# Calendar of Otaku Festivals and Events in and around Tokyo

**January**
Akiba Daisuki Festival (Akihabara)
Next Generation World Hobby Fair (Chiba)
Super Festival (Kitanomaru Park, Chiyoda-ku)

**February**
Wonder Festival (Chiba)
Japan Amusement Expo (Chiba)
COMITIA (Odaiba)

**March**
AnimeJapan (Odaiba)
Tokyo Anime Award Festival (Chuo ku)

**April**
Nico Nico Chokaigi (Chiba)
Super Festival (Chiyoda-ku)

**May**
Super Comic City (Odaiba)
Dolls Party (Odaiba)
Design Festa (Odaiba)
COMITIA (Odaiba)
@ Jam (Aomi, Odaiba)

**June**
International Tokyo Toy Show (Odaiba)
Next Generation World Hobby Fair (Chiba)
Japan Media Arts Festival (Roppongi)
Tales of Festival (Kanagawa)

**July**
Wonder Festival (Chiba)

**August**
Tokyo Idol Festival (Odaiba)
Comic Market (Odaiba)
Animelo Summer Live (Saitama)
@Jam Expo (Yokohama)
Akiba Daisuki Festival (Akihabara)
Ultraman Festival (Ikebukuro)
COMITIA (Odaiba)

**September**
Tokyo Game Show (Chiba)
All Japan Model and Hobby Show (Odaiba)
Super Festival (Chiyoda-ku)

**October**
Kichijoji Anime Wonderland (Kichijoji)
Ita-G Festa (Odaiba)
Nerima Anime Carnival (Nerima, near Ikebukuro)
Anime Manga Festival in Saitama (Saitama)
Tokyo International Film Festival (Roppongi, etc.)

**November**
Animate Girls Festival (Ikebukuro)
Design Festa (Odaiba)
Tokyo International Comic Festival (Odaiba) (or end of October)
World Mascot Character Summit in Hanyu (Saitama)
COMITIA (Odaiba)

**December**
Jump Festa (Chiba)
Dolls Party (Odaiba)
Comik Market (Odaiba)

**World Character Summit in Hanyu**

*Yuru-chara* (from the English "character") are cute mascots which are mainly used as promotional tools. Most of them (the so-called *gotochi-chara*) represent cities and regions around Japan, and are employed as a way to stimulate tourism and lift sagging economies. Their popularity in Japan is due to their *yurui* ("loose" in a gentle, laid-back way) quality. Often created by amateur artists, their unsophisticated, oversimplified design and naïveté add to their *kawaii* appeal. Indeed, their popularity is such that the combined mascot army now commands character-driven sales worth 2 trillion yen.

One of the unlikely centers of *yuru-chara* activity is Hanyu, a small city in the northernmost part of Saitama prefecture where every November hundreds of mascots converge from around Japan and even a few foreign countries. The two-day event attracts more than 400,000 visitors. On each stage, the mascots take turns doing their gags and performances, while the rows of booths across the event location are subject to continuous assault by thousands of goods-hunters. All in all, it's a veritable only-in-Japan experience.

**Admission fee:** ***100 yen*** **Dates:** ***Third weekend of November*** **Hours:** ***9:00–15:30*** **Access:** ***Hanyu Suigo Park, 751-1 Mitakaya, Hanyu-shi, Saitama*** **gotouchi-chara.jp/hanyu2014/index.html**

# CHAPTER 2

# The KANSAI REGION

# Osaka, Kyoto and Kobe

# OSAKA: THE WESTERN CAPITAL OF OTAKU CULTURE

Osaka is an approachable and friendly city famous for its talkative natives and its great cuisine.

Many visitors bypass Osaka—or they used to. Until quite recently, the third-largest Japanese city was snubbed in favor of Tokyo, and even those who ventured west preferred its highbrow neighbors, Kyoto and Nara. That's a pity, because Osaka is an approachable, friendly city, and its people are famous for being open and talkative and having a great sense of humor. Then there's the food. Even Tokyoites (who like to badmouth this city) grudgingly admit that Osaka cuisine is great, starting with local soul food like *takoyaki* octopus fritters and *okonomiyaki* pancakes.

Osaka has much more to offer than a few dishes, though, and in the last few years the city's visitor statistics have soared (400 percent in the last six years), mainly thanks to travelers from other Asian countries, who can now fly cheaply to Kansai International Airport. The city was traditionally the merchant capital of Japan, and was home base for many businesses during the Edo period. Even today, one can enjoy the local merchant spirit and the tradition of bargaining (something nobody will dream of doing in uptight Tokyo), while in certain districts like Shinsaibashi you can eat while walking down the street and chat with people in shops and stalls.

If you are into manga, anime and other things otaku, you should definitely check out Osaka, starting with Nipponbashi, the local answer to Tokyo's Akihabara. Granted, some of the shops (Animate, K-Books, etc.) have branches in every major Japanese city, but everything in Osaka is cheaper than in Tokyo right now. Besides, there are local stores you'll only find here.

For many years now, manga and anime artists have set their stories here. In 1978, for instance, Haruki Etsumi created *Jarinko Chie* (Chie the Brat), whose titular character lives in Shinsekai—Osaka's poorest neighborhood—with her unemployed father. Expo 1970, one of the city's main postwar events, has been featured in a number of works, including Urasawa Naoki's *20th Century Boys* and Hara Keiichi's *Crayon Shin-chan: The Storm Called: The Adult Empire Strikes Back*. Recent additions to the list of Osaka-based stories include *Magical Shopping Arcade Abenobashi* (2001), *Love Com* (2001), *Kanon* (2002), *Clannad* (2007), the *Monogatari* series (2009), *Free! Eternal Summer* (2013) and *Hand Shakers* (2017).

First-time visitors to Osaka may find the following websites useful:
**insideosaka.com/first-time-in-osaka**
**japan-guide.com/e/e4009.html**
**japan-guide.com/e/e4001.html**

Manga and anime artists often set their stories in Osaka.

## Nanba Yasaka Shrine

If otaku tourism is what brought you to Osaka, you can probably skip more traditional sightseeing spots. However, if you happen to be in the Nanba district, I strongly suggest visiting this little-known shrine. You will find a giant lion head staring at you. That's the Shishi-den or Lion Hall, and while not extremely big at 40 feet (12 meters) tall, it's quite impressive and even a little scary. Nanba Yasaka Shrine 難波八坂神社 was originally established around the fifth century; although it has no manga or anime connections, the rather cartoony lion certainly smells of otaku spirit, and it would make for an excellent cosplay photo-shoot background. Despite its fearsome appearance, it is said to bring good luck. One of the deities enshrined, according to legend, once killed a large eight-headed, eight-legged snake.

**Access:** ***2-9-19 Motomachi, Naniwa-ku, Osaka (six minutes' walk from Nanba and Daikokucho Stations, Osaka Metro Yotsubashi and Midosuji lines)*** **nambayasaka.jp**

The cartoonlike giant lion head at Nanba Yasaka Shrine is quite impressive and even a little scary! It would make an excellent background for a cosplay photo-shoot.

## The Open-Air Museum of Old Japanese Farmhouses

Less than an hour from the hustle and bustle of downtown Osaka, you have a chance to step back in time and visit this beautiful park. The park, which is named Ryokuchi Koen, is the oldest open-air museum in Japan, featuring 12 original buildings dating from the 17th to 19th centuries, relocated from around the country.

Similar open-air museums can be found in Tokyo, too (see *nihonminkaen.jp* and *tatemonoen.jp/english*), but at this one you can have a cosplay photo shoot. Furthermore, every Tuesday from 10 am to 3 pm, during the warmer months of April to September, women can rent a summer kimono and stroll around the grounds for an hour (300 yen). The park itself is a large wooded area with ponds, fountains and winding paths, and a visit here makes for an excellent day out.

**Admission fee:** ***500 yen; 300 for high school students; 200 for junior high and elementary school students*** **Hours:** ***9:30–17:00; closed Mondays and 12/27–1/4*** **Access:** ***1-2 Hattori Ryokuchi, Toyonaka (15 or 20 minutes' walk from Ryokuchi-Koen Station, Kita-Osaka Kyuko Line)*** **occh.or.jp/minka**

# Simona Stanzani: Translating Manga is Translating Culture

With manga and anime conquering the world, more and more fans are trying their hand at translating their favorite works from Japanese. For every professional translator, there are scores of amateurs who are into the "scanlation" practice of scanning, translating and posting their work on the Internet. But what challenges do manga and anime pose? And is it easy to make a living as a translator? We asked Simona Stanzani, a veteran from Italy who recently celebrated her 25th anniversary in the business.

### When did you fall in love with Japan for the first time?

I grew up in a house that was always full of comics. I came across Japanese manga in 1978 when they first arrived in Italy and I immediately fell in love with them, and even tried to draw my own manga illustrations! There was a time when I seriously considered becoming a manga artist, and this love of manga was my motivation for studying Japanese at university.

### In 2007 you moved to Tokyo. What were the reasons behind your decision?

For everyone who loves manga and anime, Tokyo is obviously the place you want to be. And in addition to this, Tokyo offers a lot of opportunities job-wise. One way of finding out about those opportunities is by going to manga- and anime-related events where you'll have a chance to meet lots of different people working in these industries and develop important connections that may lead to a job. In my experience, when it comes to the translation market, there are lots of opportunities to work on many different types of interesting projects. If you are a translator, it's much easier to make a decent living in Japan than in other countries in the world, even though rates now are not as lucrative as they used to be. As well as my work for Japanese companies, I still work a lot for Italian publishers, particularly Planet Manga Panini; I usually translate three or four manga every month for them. I believe it's important to have multiple working relationships, because there's always an element of uncertainty when you're a freelancer, and you can never be exactly sure whether or when a new job will arrive.

### What are the main challenges when translating from Japanese into a Western language?

It can be particularly hard translating from Japanese into my native Italian. The Italian language is very specific, while Japanese can be vague and ambiguous—so that's one of the great challenges for a translator working between these two languages. Translating from Japanese into English tends to be slightly easier; the English language is less specific than the Italian language. I also find that English words and phrases are more "manga friendly" than Italian!

### Is there a title that you found especially hard to translate?

The manga *Ghost in the Shell* by Shirow Masamune was a real challenge for me, a sort of baptism by fire, you could say, as it was one of the first translations I did. One particular difficulty I encountered was that throughout the story, there were many references to "the Internet," at a time when most people didn't even know what the Internet was. I had to spend hours on the phone with a friend who was an IT expert trying to understand what the hell the author was talking about [*laughs*].

### In your opinion, what are the qualities needed to become a good manga translator?

You have to be able to identify with and understand the different characters in a story and adapt the language to suit that character accordingly. Obviously, a princess and a hooligan don't talk the same way. Another quality I think is important is that you must be incredibly curious and open-minded, and ready to tackle any kind of subject even if it's something you don't personally find very interesting. The wider your general knowledge, the better your translation is going to be. Translating manga is translating culture; it's a daily challenge, but very rewarding.

### How would you compare translating manga and anime?

I would say it's very different. When you translate for the screen you have to clearly convey the meaning, but the essential thing is to be concise because you can only fit so many words in the subtitles—usually about 40 characters per line. It can be particularly tricky when translating into Italian because it's such a wordy language. With manga, of course, you have more space to express something, and you always have the option of adding a note to explain certain things better.

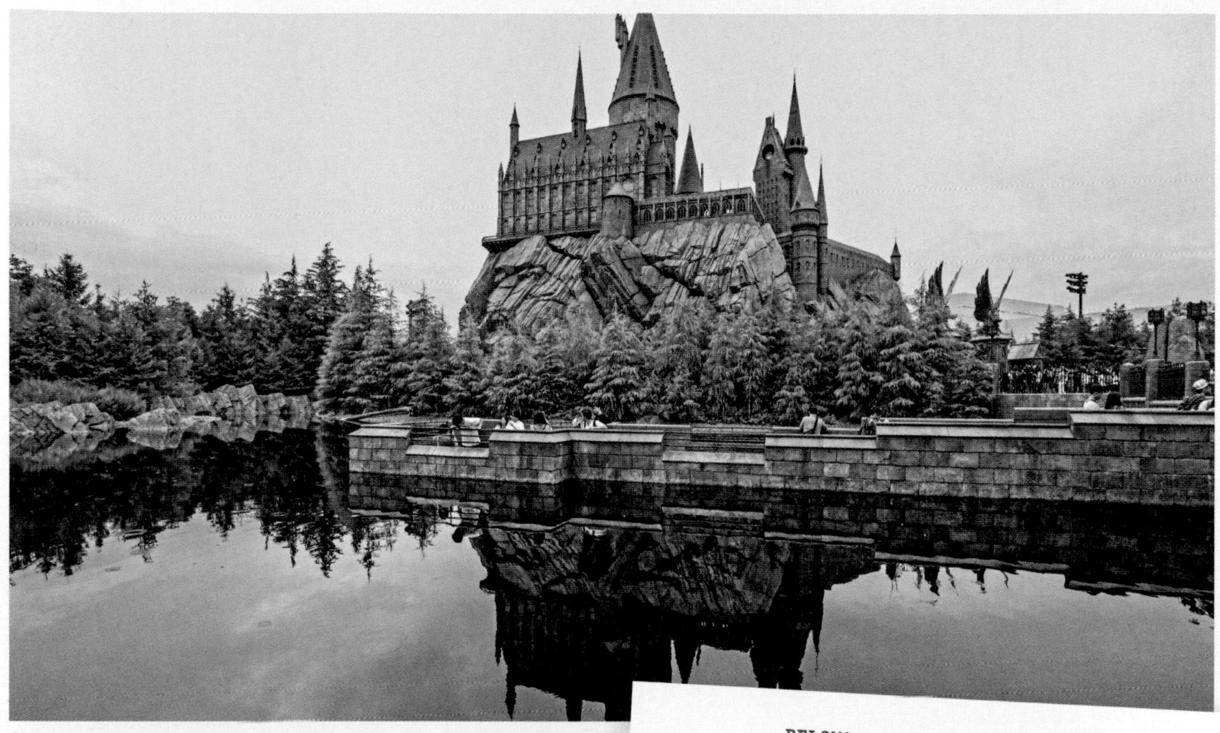

## Universal Studios Japan (USJ)

While the fun at USJ has more to do with Hollywood and American pop culture (Spider-Man, Peanuts, Sesame Street, the Terminator, Harry Potter, etc.) than with Japanese manga and anime, the popular amusement park has recently introduced a number of limited-time attractions based on such otaku powerhouses as *Neon Genesis Evangelion*, *Attack on Titan*, *Sailor Moon*, *Final Fantasy*, *Detective Conan* and *Monster Hunter* under the Universal Cool Japan banner. The really exciting news though is that USJ is planning to open a permanent new section called Super Nintendo World. Very little is known as of the time of writing, but the attractions will likely include a Mario Kart ride.

**Admission fee:** *7,900 yen (5,400 for kids age 4–11)*
**Hours:** *9:00–21:00* **Access:** *USJ is next to Universal City Station (JR Umesaki Line)*

**BELOW** A train advertises the delights of Osaka's Universal Studios.

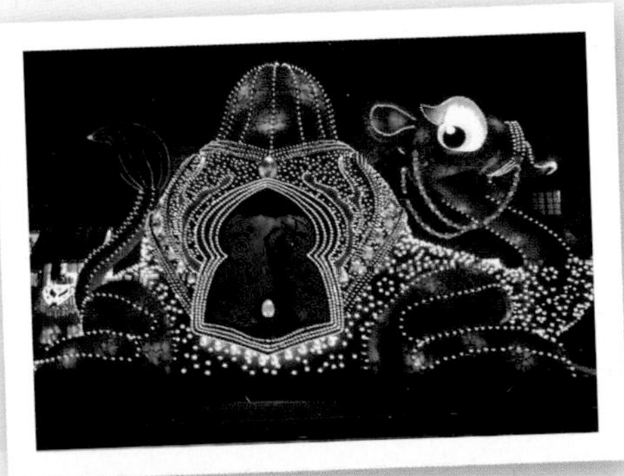

**TOP, LEFT and ABOVE** While attractions at Universal Studios Japan are largely centered on American pop culture, plans are afoot to acknowledge Japan's pop culture with the opening of a permanent new section, Super Nintendo World.

# EXPLORING NIPPONBASHI

If Akihabara is the otaku capital of eastern Japan, Nipponbashi rules the west. Indeed, it boasts the second-largest concentration of otaku shops in Japan. The similarities with Akiba don't end there: both areas, in fact, became famous after the Second World War; first, as the go-to place to buy electronic parts first, and later the consumer electronics hot spot. That's why even today Nipponbashi is known as "Den Den Town" ("den" being short for *denki*, or electricity).

The transformation into an otaku hub began in the 1990s, when the district began to attract a great number of shops selling both Japanese and American goods. Then, at the turn of the century, the large parking area on Ota Road became a sort of open-air gallery for *itasha* (anime-decorated cars).

In the last decade, more and more of the big players have opened branch stores here, often forcing the original small independent shops to close. Still, Den Den Town still retains its share of indies that you are likely to find only in Osaka.

Most of the otaku shops in Den Den Town can be found along or near two parallel roads, Sakai-suji and Nishi-dori, respectively known by the geek crowd as Den Den Street and Ota Road. The former connects the two main stations in the area—Nipponbashi in the north and Ebisucho in the south—with most of the otaku shops concentrated south of the massive Takashimaya department store. The area's center, at least from

**ABOVE** Neon-chan is the official mascot of Osaka's Nipponbashi district.

**LEFT** Osaka's Nipponbashi shares many of the same characteristics as Tokyo's Akihabara: both were originally places to buy electronic parts; both are now otaku hot spots.

**LEFT** A bird's eye view of Den Den Town.
**RIGHT** A visual *kei* band attends an in-store event at Disc Pier (see page 66).
**BELOW** Hero Gangu Kenkyujo (see page 64) is a treasure trove of toys and figures.

a visual point of view, may be the quasi-intersection with Hero Gangu Kenkyujo and Volks on the right and the attention-grabbing Gunpla mural on the left side.

The local information center (Nipponbashi Information 日本橋総合案内所, 5-9-12 Nipponbashi) is not really worth a visit (you have this book to guide you, after all) unless you want to pick up a few Neon-chan goods. Neon-chan, Den Den Town's official mascot, was created by Ito Noizi, the famous illustrator who designed characters for the *Haruhi Suzumiya* series. Quite surprisingly for a so-called information center, their sparse website has no English page.

There are three stations serving Den Den Town: Nipponbashi and Ebisucho, on the Sakaisuji subway line, are respectively the north and south limits of Sakai-suji Street, with the latter one being closer to the otaku district. Nanba Station (Nankai Line and Sennichimae subway line) is about half a mile (1 km) northwest of the area, but it could be a useful entry point if you are thinking of exploring Ota Road first or only want to check out the shops close to that station.

**Grendizer makes sure that Jungle customers don't misbehave.**

**ABOVE LEFT** Jungle (see page 64) specializes in new and secondhand figures of all kinds. **ABOVE** Comics Wonderland (see page 64) was one of the first otaku stores to open in Den Den Town, in 1994.

# Nipponbashi Shops and Museums

## Manga

**2 Comics Wonderland / COMICS**
わんだ~らんど
This store off Ota Road may look like nothing special, but it deserves a visit—let's call it a pilgrimage—as it was one of the first otaku stores to open in Den Den Town, back in 1994. Nuff respect. Even today, manga comprise 80 percent of its stock, with the remaining 20 percent light novels.
***Hours:** 11:00–20:30* ***Access:** 2-1-7 Nanba-Naka, Naniwa-ku* **wonderland1980.com**

**3 Melonbooks**
This store mainly sells *dojinshi* for men—if you're looking for Evangelion porn, say, you may find it here. You can also find CDs from Touhou Project and Vocaloid. If you live in Osaka, or visit the city often, you can get a points card and exchange those points for a discount on their original goods.
***Hours:** 11:00–21:00 (Mon-Fri), 10–21:00 (Sat, Sun and holidays)* ***Access:** Anime Bldg, 4F, 1-1-3 Nipponbashi* **melonbooks.co.jp**

Gacha House features row upon row of capsule-toy vending machines.

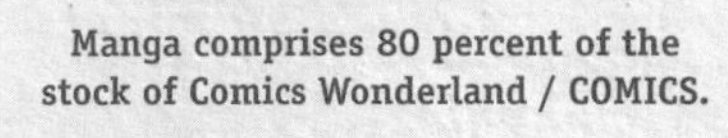
Manga comprises 80 percent of the stock of Comics Wonderland / COMICS.

## Toys

**4 Astro Zombies アストロ・ゾンビーズ**
This is a small but well-stocked old-school shop with a stylish look. It sells both Japanese and American toys, Hot Wheels minicars, cult-film T-shirts, movie props, and lots of figures (indie *sofubi*, garage kits, etc.).
***Hours:** 12:00–20:00; closed on the first and third Wednesday of every month* ***Access:** 3-6-9 Nipponbashi, Naniwa-ku* **astro-z.com**

**5 Gacha House ガチャ ハウス**
If you've caught capsule-toy fever, this is the single best place in Den Den Town to get them. It features row upon row of machines dispensing tiny toys for 200 to 500 yen each.
***Hours:** 11:00–22:00 (weekdays), 10:00–23:00 (weekends)* ***Access:** 4-16-16 Nipponbashi, Naniwa-ku* **twitter.com/gachahouse**

**6 GET'S**
In this tiny rental showcase, otaku sell their old possessions. Chances are you may find some hidden treasure. It's mainly toys (figures, plamodels, garage kits, etc.) but they welcome most otaku goods, from *dojinshi* and trading cards to DVDs, masks and other assorted collectors' items.
***Hours:** 11:00–20:00* ***Access:** 4-15-15 Nipponbashi, Naniwa-ku*
**drucya3e.wixsite.com/gets-showcase**

ABOVE The Hero Gangu Kenkyujo toy store is worth a visit for its sheer quantity and variety of products.

**7 Hero Gangu Kenkyujo**
ヒーロー玩具研究所
The Hero Toy Lab is another treasure trove of used toys and figures. It's worth a visit to see the sheer quantity and variety of products they have managed to pack into this store.
***Hours:** 12:00–19:00; closed Wednesdays*
***Access:** 4-9-21 Nipponbashi, Naniwa-ku*
**herogangu.com**

**8 Jungle**
First opened in 1995, this veteran of the local otaku scene has not only survived the fierce competition, but it has made it big, opening seven more branches nationwide (plus one in Los Angeles!) along with a model and air-gun shop in Osaka. Jungle specializes in new and secondhand figures of any kind. From *chogokin* and *gunpla* to

garage kits, Nendoroids and *tokusatsu*, they have everything. Furthermore, not content with selling them, they are now making their own line of original figures. Anything else? Ah, yes: they have two small theaters in Nipponbashi devoted to independent cinema, talk shows and live events.
**Hours:** *12:00–20:00 (weekdays), 11:00–20:00 (weekends and national holidays)* **Access:** *3-4-16 Nipponbashi, Naniwa-ku* **Independent Theater no. 1:** *5-12-4 Nipponbashi, Naniwa-ku* **Independent Theater no. 2:** *4-7-22 Nipponbashi, Naniwa-ku*
**jungle-scs.co.jp/sale_en**

### 9 Super Kids Land Main Store
スーパーキッズランド本店

With four stores along Sakai-suji, Kansai-based Joshin is one of the biggest players in Nipponbashi's otaku market, and their five-story main store is the biggest plastic-model- and hobby-related shop in the neighborhood. If you're looking for something special or for indie *sofubi*, you'll be better off checking out other places, but for mainstream products at reasonable prices, Super Kids Land is hard to beat. As soon as you enter, you'll find the specially discounted goods. The first floor is full of toys (minicars, radio-controlled models, air guns, etc.), while the others are devoted to plastic models. Famous maker Tamiya has the entire third floor to itself, but all the main brands (Bandai, Ebbro, Kyosho, Tomix, Kato, etc.) are well represented. Model-train fans can go straight to the top floor.
**Hours:** *10:00–20:00* **Access:** *4-12-4 Nipponbashi, Naniwa-ku*

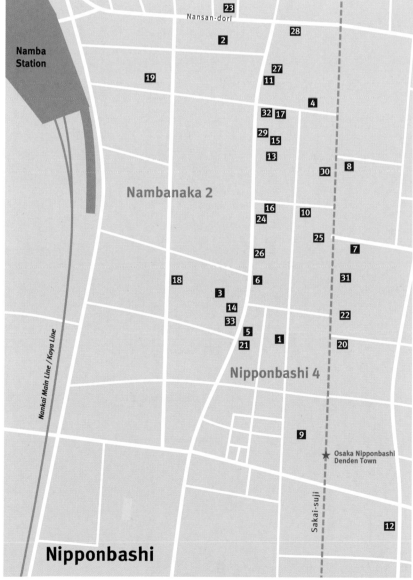

Nansan-dori
Namba Station
Nambanaka 2
Nipponbashi 4
Nankai Main Line / Koya Line
Osaka Nipponbashi Denden Town
Sakai-suji
Nipponbashi

### 10 Super Kids Land Character Store
スーパーキッズランド キャラクター館

This is one of the easiest places in the district to find—and one of the most photographed ones—thanks to the four-story-tall Gundam mural facing one of Den Den Town's main intersections. In fact, this used to be Gundam's specialty shop before it was bought by Joshin and turned into yet another

Super Kids Land branch. Don't worry, though: the Gunpla, die-cast robots, Gundam T-shirts, etc., are still there, on the second floor. The first floor is where you'll find other TV and anime character toys and figures.
**Hours:** *10:00–20:00* **Access:** *4-10-1 Nipponbashi, Naniwa-ku*

**11 Torejaras** とれじゃらす
The once-mighty Gachapon Museum, with its seven floors of capsule toys, is no more, but the company has reinvented itself as a chain store devoted to secondhand figures. A few *gachapon* machines can still be found outside the stores, but the real bonanza is inside. There's a cheap section of unboxed figures (Pokemon, Dragonball Z, Monster Hunter, One Piece, Full Metal Alchemist, etc.), while elsewhere you'll find rarer items still in their boxes at higher prices. There are two branches in Nipponbashi: the original store on Ota Road and a second shop near Animate.
**Hours:** *10:00–21:00* **Access: Ota Road shop:** *3-6-16 Nipponbashi, Naniwa-ku*
**Shop no. 2:** *4-14-1 Nipponbashi, Naniwa-ku*
**torejaras.com**

## Movies, Music & Games

**12 Disc · Pier**
The Joshin empire has two more shops, one devoted to music and movies and the other to video games. The latter faces directly on Sakai-suji and sells both new and secondhand games, consoles and manuals. There's a PlayStation Concept Shop too; the second floor is an event space. The other store is a much bigger affair: the first three floors are all music, while the upper three floors are filled with Japanese and foreign movies. Anime and *tokusatsu* DVDs, Blu-rays and CDs can be found on the top floor. Train otaku, meanwhile, should check out the fifth floor.
**Hours:** *10:00–20:00* **Access:** *5-9-5 Nipponbashi, Naniwa-ku*

## Trading Cards

**13 C-Labo** カードラボ
Card Labo is one of the major sellers of trading cards in Japan, and in Nipponbashi they have a whopping four branches. Of course, they sell all sorts of trading-card games and accessories for all the major titles (Yu-Gi-Oh!, Cardfight! Vanguard, Weiss Schwartz, Sengoku Taisen, WiXOSS, Magic: The Gathering, etc.). Each store has a "duel space" (around 50 seats) that customers can use free of charge to play with friends.
**Hours:** *11:00–20:00 (weekdays), 10:00–20:00 (weekends and national holidays)*
**Access: Ota Road main store:** *4-16-1 Nipponbashi, Naniwa-ku* **Osaka Nipponbashi store:** *5F Animate Bldg, 1-1-3 Nipponbashi-Nishi, Naniwa-ku* **Nanba store:** *B1F, 3-8-16 Nipponbashi, Naniwa-ku (inside Gamers)* **Nanba store no. 2:** *2F, 2-6-1 Nanba-Naka, Naniwa-ku*

## Cosplay

**14 Assist Wig** アシスト ウィッグ
This place may be small, but it's one of the premium cosplay shops in Den Den Town. Colorful wigs aside, you'll find everything else you need, from costumes and footwear to colored contact lenses, cosmetics and other cosplay goods and accessories.
**Hours:** *11:30–19:45 (weekdays), 11:00–20:15 (weekends)* **Access:** *1-1-4 Nipponbashi-Nishi, Naniwa-ku* **assistcosplay.com**

**15 Swallowtail**
A specialty wig shop that also sells other cosplay products such as colored contact lenses, footwear and costumes.
**Hours:** *11:00–20:00* **Access:** *4F, 3-8-18 Nipponbashi, Naniwa-ku,* **swallowtail-wig.com**

Trading-cards shop C-Labo can be found in four different locations around Nipponbashi.

# Other Osaka Shops

## General

### 21 Alice アーリス

Across the street from Animate is a unique reflexology-cum-cuddle shop. In other words, the cute staff not only offer relief from stress, but you can chat with them and buy cuddle time, too. (This is otaku-land, after all!) Prices range from 4,000 yen for a 30-minute massage to 9,000 yen for a full hour of cuddling (meaning they actually lay down with you). Extra options (500 yen each) are available, such as having staff wearing a costume (maid, nurse, Rilakkuma) or taking a walk with you around the neighborhood.

**Hours:** *15:00–22:00 (weekdays), 12:00–22:00 (weekends and national holidays)*
**Access:** *4-16-5 Nipponbashi, Naniwa-ku*
**a-l-i-c-e.net/NPB**

### 22 Taito Station

The lone game center in the district is a five-story game bonanza! **First floor**: crane games (avoid at all costs). **Second floor**: driving and shooting games plus *purikura* (photo sticker) booths. **Third floor**: card games and more shooting games (here you'll find Gunslinger Stratos). **Fourth floor**: music and rhythm games. **Fifth floor**: lots of fighting/action games belonging to the NESiCAxLive system. Also, kids' card games.

**Hours:** *10:00–24:00* **Access:** *4-9-14 Nipponbashi, Naniwa-ku*

## Chain Stores

### 33 Animate

**Hours:** *10:00–21:00*
**Access:** *1-1-3 Nipponbashi-Nishi, Naniwa-ku*

### 13 Gamers

**Hours:** *10:30–20:00 (Mon–Thu); 10:00–20:00 (Fri, Sat, Sun and national holidays)*
**Access:** *3-8-16 Nipponbashi, Naniwa-ku*

### 23 Gee! Store

**Hours:** *11:00–20:00* **Access:** *7-7 Nanba-Sen-nichi-mae, Chuo-ku*

### 24 Gee! Store Annex

**Hours:** *11:00–20:00* **Access:** *4-15-21 Nipponbashi, Naniwa-ku*

### 25 K-Books

**Hours:** *12:00–20:00* **Access:** *4-10-4 Nipponbashi, Naniwa-ku*

### 26 Kotobukiya

**Hours:** *11:00–20:00* **Access:** *4-15-18 Nipponbashi, Naniwa-ku*

### Mandarake

This store is not in Nipponbashi, but on the other side of Nanba Station.

**Hours:** *12:00–20:00* **Access:** *2-9-22 Nishi-Shinsaibashi, Chuo-ku*

### Sanrio Anime Store Nanba Marui

**Hours:** *11:00–20:30* **Access:** *7F Nanba Marui, 3-8-9 Nanba, Chuo-ku*

**BELOW** Assist Wig may be small, but it's one of the premium cosplay shops in Den Den Town.
**BELOW RIGHT** Volks is famous worldwide for its Dollfie, Super Dollfie and Dollfie Dream line of dolls.

### Sanrio Osaka Takashimaya

**Hours:** *10:00–20:00* **Access:** *5-1-5 Nanba, Chuo-ku*

### 27 Sofmap 1 ソフマップ Saurus

**Hours:** *11:00–20:00* **Access:** *3-6-18 Nipponbashi, Naniwa-ku*

### 28 Sofmap 2 ソフマップ ザウルス 2

**Hours:** *11:00–20:00* **Access:** *3-6-25 Nipponbashi, Naniwa-ku*

### 29 Super Potato Ota Road Store スーパーポテト レトロ館

**Hours:** *11:00–20:00 (weekdays); 10:30–20:00 (weekends and national holidays)*
**Access:** *3-8-18 Nipponbashi, Naniwa-ku*

### Super Potato Nanba Store スーパーポテト なんば店

**Hours:** *11:00–21:00* **Access:** *15-17 Nanba-Sennichi-mae, Chuo-ku*

### 13 30 Toranoana とらのあな

**Hours:** *11:00–21:00 (weekdays); 10:00–21:00 (Weekends and national holidays)* **Access:** **Nanba Store A:** *2-3 F, 3-8-16 Nipponbashi, Naniwa-ku* **Nanba Store B:** *3-7-6 Nipponbashi, Naniwa-ku*

### 31 Volks ボークス

**Hours:** *11:00–20:00* **Access:** *4-9-18 Nipponbashi, Naniwa-ku*

### 32 33 Yellow Submarine

**Hours:** *11:00–20:00* **Access:** *3-8-23 Nipponbashi, Naniwa-ku* **Nanba Store:** *2-1-3 Nanba-Naka, Naniwa-ku*

# Matteo Togni: An Italian Otaku in Japan

Italian-born Matteo Togni is the international sales manager for Jungle Co. Ltd. He is also in charge of the company's International Creative Department. A 16-year resident of Japan, Togni lives and works in Osaka.

**How did you end up in Japan?**
Many years ago, I studied English for one year in Dublin, Ireland. My roommate happened to be from Japan. He loved Italian soccer, while my passion was manga and anime. We quickly became friends, and when it was time to go home, he came with me and ended up spending eight months in Verona, my home town. We kept in touch even after he returned to Japan. The economic situation in Italy wasn't very good, so a few years later, in 2002, I decided to pay him a visit, and ended up staying in Japan for good. After a few months in Tokyo, I moved first to Kobe and then to Osaka, where I went through several odd jobs to pay for my Japanese-language classes. Among other things, I taught Italian to opera singers and English to elementary school kids, and worked as a narrator, interpreter, fashion model and salesperson at a department store.

**I guess living in Japan further fueled your love for all things otaku?**
Of course! Since I lived in Osaka, I would spend all my free time in Den Den Town. Being a long-time figure collector, I often visited Jungle, which at the time was just a tiny shop located in a Nipponbashi backstreet. I quickly became a regular, and spent hours talking to the shop manager about my favorite characters and TV series. Japanese animation first appeared on Italian television in the late 1970s, and many Italian fans were always looking for original models and figures. The manager couldn't believe that foreign fans were so in love with such "minor" series as *Steel Jeeg* and *Daitarn 3*.

Jungle's Nipponbashi shop **(FAR RIGHT)** and one of the many vintage figures on sale within **(RIGHT)**.

**How did you start working for Jungle?**
I guess they were impressed by my passion. Anyway, one day in 2009—seven years after I had arrived in Japan—the owner heard about this Italian otaku who was always talking his head off about obscure anime, and invited me to dinner. By that time, Jungle had already opened a small branch in Los Angeles, but I quickly realized they weren't aware of how big the foreign market was. To give you an example, they didn't have an English website, didn't know what PayPal was, and only had a faint idea about eBay. When the owner heard how much money they could make abroad, he hired me on the spot and put me in charge of international operations.

**It seems like you've done a hell of a job.**
Well, it's true that since then we've opened four more stores in Los Angeles and three in Shanghai. Currently Jungle has 200 employees (all avid figure and toy collectors), with branches in all major Japanese cities. We have a laboratory for made-in-Japan soft vinyl figures amd a factory in Manila, Philippines, and are developing a strong collaboration with Chinese businesses.

**You mentioned that Jungle has an original line of figures. Can you tell me more about that?**
The International Creative Department develops and produces original products for the foreign market. The Creative Department proper, which I supervise, is responsible for coming up with new ideas

Matteo Togni supervises Jungle's Creative Department, where he is responsible for coming up with new ideas to expand the range of products.

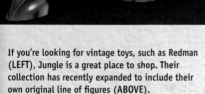

and designs. We also take care of licensing rights, promotion and distribution. The Workshop, on the other hand, is the laboratory that actually manufactures our products. Some of the classic figures we have created so far are Devilman, Mazinger Z, and Grendizer, which come in two sizes, 18 inches (45 cm), and the 6-foot (2-meter) tall "life size." This year we've added a new line of die-cast metal models.

### After living in Japan for 16 years, how would you describe the local otaku scene?

It's hard to define because it's constantly changing. In the past, character goods were mainly inspired by anime and manga, but now there's a boom in video-game-related merchandising, as popular game characters are turned into models and toys, from cheap action figures all the way to exclusive polystone statues that cost thousands of euro and weigh as much as a fridge. On the other hand, there's been a renewed interest in classic series like Tatsunoko's *Infini-T Force* and Netflix's *Devilman*, and the new *Mazinger Z: Infinity* movie.

### I guess even Den Den Town has changed during all these years?

Yes. When I first arrived, back in 2003, I was one of very few gaijin (mainly from Europe and the US) who ventured to Nipponbashi. Now the Japanese are regularly outnumbered by huge groups of Chinese, Korean and other Asian tourists who are lured by Osaka's lower prices and tax-free shops. In the last few years, all-inclusive otaku tours have become wildly popular, especially with tourists from China. They start from Tokyo, in places like Akihabara and Nakano, and then go south, with stops in Nagoya, Osaka—all the way down to Fukuoka.

In order to accommodate all the foreign tourists, a lot of hotels have recently popped up in the district. Ten years ago there were only a couple of business hotels, and they mainly catered to drunk salarymen who had missed the last train home. Now you find them everywhere, and they're always full.

If you're looking for vintage toys, such as Redman (LEFT), Jungle is a great place to shop. Their collection has recently expanded to include their own original line of figures (ABOVE).

### Matteo recommends:

**theculturetrip.com/asia/japan/articles/the-top-video-game-bars-in-osaka**

**daphne.cx**
**akibakei.info/shopinfo_b.php?shop=901**

# Nipponbashi Bars and Cafés

### 16 #78

If you walk down the side street to the right of the Super Kids Land Character Store (formerly Gundam's) you'll find a tiny bar (it seats only 10) appropriately dedicated to the famous giant robot. This is a great place to share your passion for all things Gundam. If you walk in on a quiet day, you can actually find Toshi, the English-speaking owner, working on a Gunpla. Indeed, many of the models in the bar were made by him. Beers from 500 yen, cocktails from 600; no seat charge.

**Hours:** *17:00–24:00; closed Wednesdays*
**Access:** *4-15-23 Nipponbashi, Naniwa-ku*

ABOVE #78 is for Gundam fans.

ABOVE Make your own costumes at Ataraxia Café.

### 17 Ataraxia Café

This members-only manga café / workshop / salon is only open to women, and offers a safe space for female otaku to pursue their hobbies. It's free to join, but you must be 18 or

# Princess Café 20

This collaboration café features both major and less-known manga, anime, games and light novels (*Yuri on Ice!!!, Drifters, Pop Team Epic, Idolish7, Joker Game, Eromanga Sensei,* etc.). The place is rather small, with just a few tables, and both the interior and the menu change depending on the theme (e.g., the *Yuri on Ice!!!* collaboration prominently features *katsudon* pork cutlet-over-rice). Most collaborations don't require reservations, but in certain cases you can only obtain a ticket through a lottery system. Every day on Twitter (twitter.com/princesscafeosa) they tell you whether you will need a numbered ticket, and how you can get one; be sure to check it before going. Princess Café is actually a chain with branches in Tokyo, Sapporo, Nagoya, Osaka and Fukuoka. See the website for details.

**Hours:** *11:00–19:30 (weekdays); 10:00–19:30 (weekends)* **Access:** *No. 1-2 Bldg. 2-3F, 4-8-16 Nipponbashi, Naniwa-ku, Osaka* **Shinkan:** *1-B1F, 4-9-13 Nipponbashi, Naniwa-ku, Osaka (Both branches are near Nanba Station; see detailed directions on their homepage* **pripricafe.com***)*

older, so don't forget to bring a valid ID with you. They have a large collection of manga (including BL and *dojinshi*) to read as you sip your drink. The brightly lit workspace at the back has many wide tables where members make their own costumes and style their wigs, using the sewing machines, mannequins and other tools the café provides free of charge. Laptops, printers and a long stapler are also available if you want to make your own zine.
**Admission fee:** *The premium drink plan (one drink) is 1,280 yen plus tax; the all-you-can-drink soft-drink plan is 1,580 yen plus tax* **Hours:** *12:00–23:30 (weekdays); 11:00–23:30 (weekends and national holidays); check the café's Twitter page (@ ataraxiacafe), as they sometimes close for private events* **Access:** *3F Gram Bldg., 3-8-25 Nipponbashi, Naniwa-ku, Osaka (close to Nanba Station)* **ataraxiacafe.com**

Enjoy a bistro-like atmosphere at e-maid.

### 18 Café Kissshot

This little café specializes in homemade cookies and drinks, but it's particularly worth a visit because it often hosts interesting exhibitions by otaku-inspired artists such as illustrator Eric Alien and *mansho* (manga + calligraphy) painter Hiramatsu Shinji.
**Hours:** *13:00–20:00 (Monday, Tuesday, and Thursday); 11:00–22:00 Friday and Saturday; 11:00–20:00 Sunday; closed Wednesdays*
**Access:** *1-1-14 Nipponbashi-Nishi, NanIwa-ku*

### 19 e-maid

Apart from its extensive menu, this maid café's best selling point is its first-floor location and bistro-like atmosphere. In comparison, prime mover **Cco-cha** (ccocha.com) looks more like a refectory, with its cheap-looking tables and chairs.
**Hours:** *12:00–22:30 (Monday, Wednesday, and Friday); 11:00–22:30 (weekends and national holidays); closed Thursdays*
**Access:** *2-3-6 Nanba-Naka, Naniwa-ku*
**e-maid.net**

## Cosplay in Osaka

### Nipponbashi Street Festa

日本橋ストリートフェスタ

For one day in March, Den Den Town celebrates its own otaku-ness with a big festival that attracts thousands of cosplayers every year. The festival features the usual stage performances, booths, etc., but the main events are definitely cosplay-centered, with hordes of photographers shooting scantily dressed girls, and most importantly the 1,000-people-strong parade (featuring maids from the area's cafés) that goes from Ebisucho Station to the Hero Gangu Kenkyujo store along Sakai-suji, Nipponbashi's main shopping street.

**Admission fee:** *2,000 yen (cosplayers and photographers), 2,500 yen (cosplay parade)* **Dates:** *March* **Hours:** *11:00–18:00 (Ota Rd.); 12:00–15:00 (Sakai-suji shopping street)* **Access:** *Nipponbashi is just south of Nanba Station (Osaka Metro Midosuji, Sennichimae, and Yotsubashi lines)* **nippombashi.jp/festa**

### Halloween in Triangle Park, Amemura

Amemura (short for America Mura or American Village) is a district west of Shinsaibashi Station that's often compared to Tokyo's Harajuku for the fashion-conscious people you can see roaming its streets. Amemura has more of an adult, rock'n'roll feel than Harajuku, though, with lots of bars and nightclubs. Come Halloween, the area around Sankaku Koen (Triangle Park) fills up with zombies, monsters and vampires. Truculent cosplayers aside, the park, though quite unremarkable in itself, is worth checking out for its live music and fashion shows and the colorful people who often hang out in the area.

### 1 Pollux Theater

This small theater in the heart of Nipponbashi is the go-to place to see the local grassroots idol scene in action. They have idol group concerts almost every day. Particularly worth checking out are the Idol Rush! events in the weekends, with up to 20 groups taking the small stage.

**Admission fee:** *1,000–2,000 yen plus one drink order* **Hours:** *See website for details; closed Mondays* **Access:** *4-14-3 Nipponbashi, Naniwa-ku, Osaka* **pollux-theater.com**

# Other Osaka Bars and Cafés

A-55 has a vintage feel, in both decor and menu.

### A-55

This *dagashi* (old-style junk food) bar with a nostalgic Showa-era ambiance has an interior reminiscent of a kid's room from that time: one wall is occupied by a library full of books and manga, while the other walls, the shelves, the counter and every other available space is covered with old toys and figures, posters, vintage ads and photos, Game Boy and Famicon consoles and more comics. Even the food menu consists of old and new kids' favorites—*agepan* (sweet fried dough), French fries, instant ramen, chicken nuggets, curry udon—or you can opt for the *dagashi* and ice cream all-you-can-eat plan (500 yen per hour). Drinks cost 500 yen, and the background music playing in the bar, of course, is old *anison*.

**Hours:** *19:00–1:00 (Mon–Fri and Sun), 18:00–5:00 (Fri–Sat); closed on the second and fourth Tuesday of the month* **Access:** *4F, 7-11 Taiyujicho, Kita-ku (two minutes' walk from Higashi-Umeda Station, Osaka Metro Tanimachi Line)* **after5go.com**

### Farplane ファープレーン

If you're into cosplaying with a weird twist, check out this fetish bar-cum-apparel shop. Just be warned that the overall atmosphere (including the patrons) is like Terayama Shuji's theatrical troupe playing in a Fellini movie. The darkly colorful interior, full of neon lights and penis-shaped accessories, manages to be sensual and wacky at the same time. If you're lucky, you may catch one of their burlesque shows or kinky events.

**Hours:** *20:00~; closed Wednesdays* **Access:** *3F, 2-8-19, Nishi-Shinsaibashi, Chuo-ku (six minutes' walk from Nanba Station, Osaka Metro)* **farplane.jp**

### Fire bomBAR

Fans of *Macross* definitely have to pay a visit to this small bar completely devoted to *Macross 7*, the second TV series of the anime saga, and its music (the name of the bar comes from Fire Bomber, the fictional rock band featured in the series). The owner has been a fan since he discovered *Macross* in high school. The bar is decorated with posters, figures and trading cards, while Fire Bomber's music plays nonstop. All the items on the menu (600–800 yen) take their names from

**ABOVE** and **RIGHT** The small drinking establishment Fire bomBAR is completely devoted to the Japanese anime series *Macross 7* and the music that played a central part in it.
**LEFT** Poster for fetish bar-cum-apparel shop Farplane, for anyone who's into cosplaying with a twist.

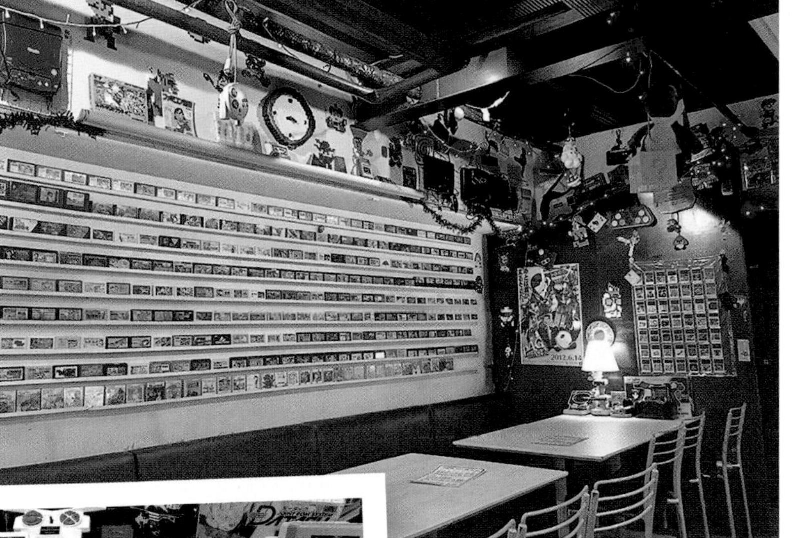

ABOVE and LEFT Game Bar Continue was the very first game bar to open in Osaka. RIGHT Having fun at Iseaki Fantasy Anime Bar.

*Macross* characters, song titles or quotes. *Macross* cosplayers and video gamers are welcome!
**Admission fee:** *1,000 cover charge includes the first drink; order at least one drink per hour or pay 300 yen per hour* **Hours:** *18:00–24:00; closed Mondays and Thursdays* **Access:** *603 1-7-13 Sonezaki, Kita-ku, Osaka (five minutes' walk from Higashi Umeda Station)* **firebombar.com**

### Game Bar Continue

The very first game bar to open in Osaka is still going strong thanks to an arsenal of countless games and 13 screens, plus a projector. The wall opposite the counter is literally covered in colorful game cartridges, but the whole place is full of memorabilia. They have board games, too, and host the occasional DJ event. There is a 500-yen cover charge; drinks from 500 yen and food from 300.
**Hours:** *18:00–5:00 (weekdays), 13:00–5:00 (weekends)* **Access:** *5F, 1-12-19 Higashi-Shinsaibashi, Chuo-ku (five minutes' walk from Shinsaibashi Station, Osaka Metro Midosuji, Nagahori Tsurumi-ryokuchi, and Yotsubashi lines)* **gamebar.jp**

### Isekai Fantasy Anime Bar real+ize
### 異世界ファンタジーアニメバー real+ize

Enter a "parallel universe" (*isekai*) where anime fans can talk all night about their favorite subject. Pay 3,000 yen (only 2,000 for gals) for one hour of unrestricted boozing and singing. "Only" 2,000 for the next hour.
**Hours:** *20:00–5:00 (closed Sundays and national holidays)* **Access:** *2F 6-1 Soemoncho, Chuo-ku* **twitter.com/real_ize_pub**

### Kinguu 宮禁

There are cute cafés and strange bars, and then there's Kinguu. Starting with the bloodied human figure on the door, this Victorian horror-themed bar embraces the macabre and bizarre like no other. Inside it's dark and crowded with taxidermied animals, including an actual stuffed camel. (It is also, by the way, one of the very few places in Japan where you can order genuine mead and absinthe.) The creatures inhabiting this bar—starting with the owner himself—seem to be straight out of a retro horror movie (check out the online pictures), and first-time visitors may find the joint a little intimidating, but don't worry; the scary-looking boss is actually very kind and even speaks quite good English.
**Hours:** *21:00–5:00; closed Tuesdays* **Access:** *5F, 1-19-8 Higashi-Shinsaibashi, Chuo-ku (five minutes' walk from Shinsaibashi Station, Osaka Metro Midosuji, Nagahori Tsurumi-ryokuchi and Yotsubashi lines)* **twitter.com/KinguuBot** **facebook.com/KinguuBar**

ABOVE and LEFT Kinguu is a Victorian horror-themed bar.

RIGHT and ABOVE Steampunk bar Shinka is partially constructed from submarine parts. BOTTOM Video Game Bar Space Station.

### Shinka 深化

If you manage to find the secret entrance to this bar (it's at the end of a narrow passage between two nondescript buildings), this promises to be one of your best discoveries. As the name Shinka ("Deepening") implies, this steampunk-inspired bar was partially constructed out of real submarine parts. Its dark interior and atmosphere notwithstanding, it's actually a pretty casual and welcoming joint. Their gin-and-tonic is particularly famous. And be sure to check out their toilet, which features a creepy-looking diving suit.

**Hours:** *19:00–3:00; closed Wednesdays* **Access:** *1-1-10 Andojimachi, Chuo-ku (seven minutes' walk from Tanimachi Rokuchome Station, Osaka Metro Tanimachi and Nagahori Tsurumi-ryokuchi lines)*

### Square Enix Café

The second Square Enix café (the original one is in Akihabara) has a different theme every month or so featuring one of the company's properties (*Final Fantasy, Kingdom Hearts, Dragon Quest, Secret of Mana, SaGa: Scarlet Grace*). Whereas the Akiba café is all-black, the interior in this one is completely white, with framed art decorating the walls. The food and drinks, of course, are loosely themed around the featured game. Guests get a free coaster (randomly chosen) every time they order a drink. As is often the case in such places, the food is generally subpar and rather expensive, but most fans come here to take in the atmosphere and buy souvenirs. The shop, by the way, sells both limited goods from the café's current collaboration and general merchandise for various Square Enix titles, including notebooks, pin badges, postcards, plushies, and capsule toys. You have to book your 90-minute slot in advance on the Japanese-language website. If you forget and you can't get in, you can buy a drink to go, and get a themed coaster.

**Hours:** *9:00–22:30* **Access:** *B1F Yodobashi Umeda, 1-1 Ofukacho, Kita-ku (next to JR Osaka Station and Osaka Metro Umeda Station)* **jp.square-enix.com/cafe/osaka/pc/index.php**

### The Hearth

This board-game bar and café boasts more than 100 games to choose from and an equally impressive food menu. Unlike similar places in Japan, this one is English speaker–friendly (chef and co-owner Jake is an Aussie) which means most of the games have English instructions. The Hearth hosts regular game nights and tournaments. You can play all day for just 500 yen.

**Hours:** *18:00–24:00 (Mon–Tue, Thu–Fri), 12:00–24:00 (weekends); closed Wednesdays* **Access:** *14-25 Nanba-Sennichimae, Chuo-ku (five minutes' walk from Nanba Station).* **thehearthosaka.com**

### Video Game Bar Space Station

At this great-looking (thanks to its stylish interior and cool lighting) bar, you can have reasonably priced drinks named after video games while playing your favorite titles, both new and retro. Though small, this place has 13 consoles, eight screens and games of all kinds, old and new. There's no cover charge—you only pay for your drinks—and you can play till you drop for free. They host events, too.

**Hours:** *20:00–2:00 (Mon–Thu and Sun), 20:00–5:00 (Fri–Sat)* **Access:** *2F, 2-13-3 Nishi-Shinsaibashi, Chuo-ku, Osaka (six minutes' walk from Nanba Station, Osaka Metro)* **facebook.com/SpaceStationOsaka**

# Osaka's Umeda Station Area

**ABOVE** Umeda Arts Theater stages its fair share of otaku-related shows. **ABOVE LEFT** Hunt for Gunplas at Hobby Land Pochi.

Another place you may want to visit when you're in Osaka is the area around Umeda Station. For instance, on the second basement floor in the massive **Yodobashi Camera** building (across from the north side of Osaka Station) you'll find a vast variety of toys, games, hobby goods and comics. On the 13th floor of **Daimaru** department store there's a fairly large **Pokemon Centre** selling Osaka-limited goods, and even a **Tomica** shop featuring a minicar assembly plant (600 yen) and monthly events. A little further away from the station is a smaller **Animate** where you can find items they don't have at the Den Den Town store.

## Shops

### Hobby Land Pochi ホビーランドぽち

Trains are the main business at this store selling secondhand model trains and toys. They also sell lots of Gunpla and other plamodels, figures, robots, garage kits, *chokogin*, etc. Sales are held both monthly and daily (from 17:00 on).
**Hours:** *11:00–20:00 (weekdays), 10:00–20:00 (weekends)* **Access:** *1F, 3-6-13 Tsukuda, Nishi Yodogawa-ku* **hobbyland-pochi.net**

### Romu

Model cars are everywhere here, floor to ceiling. They sell both Japanese and foreign models—also car parts, kits and decals, clear cases, books, DVDs, and even F1 team wear.
**Hours:** *12:00–20:00 (weekdays), 11:00–18:30 (Saturdays and national holidays); closed Sundays and the first two Mondays of the month* **Access:** *5F, 2-6-30 Shibata, Kita-ku (five minutes' walk from Umeda Station)* **romu-romu.com**

### Seifudo 清風堂書店

This basement bookstore has a sizeable comic section selling all the newest titles.
**Hours:** *10:00–22:00 (Monday through Saturday), 10:00–20:00 (Sundays and national holidays)* **Access:** *B2F, 2-11-16 Sonezaki, Kita-ku (next to Osaka Metro Tanimachi Line Higashi-Umeda Station)*

### Ultraman World M78 ウルトラマンワールドM78

Everything a hardcore Ultraman fan could ever want is here: toys, magazines, apparel, sweets, etc., including time-limited and collector's items.
**Hours:** *10:00–21:00* **Access:** *B1F, Hankyu Sanbangai North Bldg. (北館) 1-1-3 Shibata, Kita-ku (five minutes' walk from Umeda Station)* **m-78.jp/shop/ultramanworld-m78/osaka**

## Entertainment

### Legoland Discovery Center Osaka

Do you have kids who couldn't care less about your unhealthy passion for manga and Godzilla? Take them to Legoland. This is possibly the only place in the world where adults (16 and up) must be accompanied by a child (15 and under) to visit. There's a lot to do here, starting with a factory tour to see how those bricks are made. Then there are rides, a 4D cinema, a Build & Test zone where you build your original car and then test it on a race track, and another where you build and test a train. Finally ,you can admire the gorgeous Miniland, made out of more than a million bricks.
**Hours:** *10:00–19:00 (weekdays), 10:00–20:00 (weekends and national holidays)* **Access:** *3F, 11-10 Kaigan-dori, Minato-ku (seven minutes' walk from Osaka Metro Chuo Line Osakako Station)* **osaka.legolanddiscoverycenter.jp/en** *(English)*

### Monte 50

Osaka, and western Japan in general, are said to be cheaper than Tokyo, and here's a good example: all the machines in this game center only cost 50 yen. You won't find the latest titles, but there are still a lot of games (fighting, bullet hell, tabletop, sports, music) to enjoy. You can check out their lineup online.
**Hours:** *6:00–1:00* **Access:** *2–4F, 4-27 Komatsubaracho, Kita-ku (three minutes' walk from Umeda Station)* **monte50.com**

### Umeda Arts Theater 梅田芸術劇場

The Umeda Geijutsu Gekijo (also known as UgeGei) stages its fair share of manga/anime-inspired 2.5-D musicals and the occasional idol concert, so when you're in Osaka you should check out their schedule.
**Access:** *19-1 Chayamachi, Kita-ku (three minutes' walk from Hankyu Line Umeda Station)* **umegei.com**

### VR Zone Osaka

The latest addition to the VR Zone chain features all the classic VR attractions (Evangelion, Gundam, Dragon Ball, dinosaur survival, horror house, etc.) and the brand-new battle against Godzilla.
**Hours:** *11:00–21:00* **Access:** *8–9F, HEP FIVE 5-15 Kakudacho, Kita-cho (five minutes' walk from Umeda Station)* **vrzone-pic.com/osaka**

# EXPLORING KYOTO

Famous for its beautiful shrines and temples, refined traditional culture and exquisite cuisine, Kyoto may not give off a lot of otaku vibes. However, the former imperial capital has its share of dedicated shops. It's also home to the country's largest manga museum, and even hosts a couple of important events.

When shopping for otaku goods, the must-see area is Teramachi. Compared to Chuo-dori in Akihabara and Sakai-suji in Nipponbashi, this is more of a multi-purpose area where the otaku shops are mixed with more typical drugstores, diners, souvenir shops and even a movie theater. And this being Kyoto, you're sure to find shrines and stores selling items for Buddhist altars, too.

Teramachi-dori is a shopping street extending from north to south between Shijo-dori and Sanjo-dori. Most of the interesting spots covered in this chapter are on or near this street.

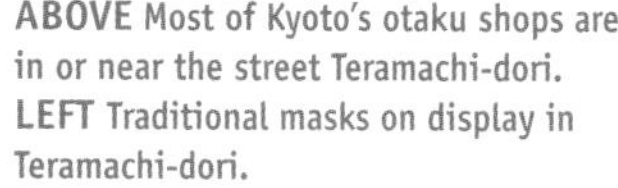

**ABOVE** Most of Kyoto's otaku shops are in or near the street Teramachi-dori.
**LEFT** Traditional masks on display in Teramachi-dori.

**ABOVE** Sign for Anime Shop Sakurasaku.
**LEFT** A dragon at a Teramachi temple.
**BELOW** Art on sale in Teramachi.
**BELOW LEFT** More otaku treasures from Anime Shop Sakurasaku.

# Exploring Teramachi

## General

Unless noted, the following shops can be reached on foot (five to eight minutes) from Hankyu Kyoto Line Kawaramachi Station.

### 2 Anime Shop Sakurasaku

アニメショップ さくらさく

Located near Nishiki Tenmangu Shrine at the intersection of Nishiki Market and the Teramachi covered shopping arcade, Sakurasaku is worth checking out, especially if you have a limited budget. They only sell old stock, so you won't find the latest items, but the upside is that everything there is inexpensive.

**Hours:** *12:00–20:00* **Access:** *2F, 537 Higashigawa-cho, Nakagyo-ku*
**sakurasaku-anime.shopinfo.jp**

### 3 Dragon Star ドラゴンスター

This trading-card specialist store sells all kinds of games. The second floor is a playing space. When they're not holding their weekly tournaments, you can engage in card battles with other patrons.

**Hours:** *12:00–21:00* **Access:** *503-16 Higashigawa-cho, Nakagyo-ku (Shin-Kyogoku-dori)*
**dragon777.jp**

### 4 Galleriapart

Even otaku sometimes get tired of their possessions. In Japan they can rent a showcase like the ones you'll find in this shop to display their goods to potential buyers. There are a whopping 232 boxes here, each one full of toys and figures, handmade works and other collectors' items. It's certainly more exciting than eBay.

**Hours:** *11:00–19:30; closed Wednesdays*
**Access:** *598 Uraderacho, Nakagyo-ku (Takoyakushi-dori)*
**galleriapart.com/english.html**

### 5 JQ Store

Located on Shijo-dori, this store is recognizable by the three life-size *Ah! My Goddess!* figures at the entrance.

**ABOVE** At Galleriapart you can rent a showcase to sell your used otaku goods.

**ABOVE** Kikuya Shoten Manga-kan sells comics and other otaku merchandise.

The place consists of three shops:

**B's Hobby (basement)**
This hobby shop sells Gunpla, Marvel figures, model parts and accessories, and model-making tools.

**Gun Good (1F and 2F)**
Gun Good is a must-visit if you make manga or are into stationery goods. From technical pens to Copic refillable markers and screentone paper, they have everything. They also sell souvenirs (keychains, fridge magnets, etc.).

**Animega (3F)**
Lots of manga, DVDs, games and character goods.

**Hours:** *10:00–22:00* **Access:** *5 Tachiuri-Higashimachi, Shimogyo-ku*

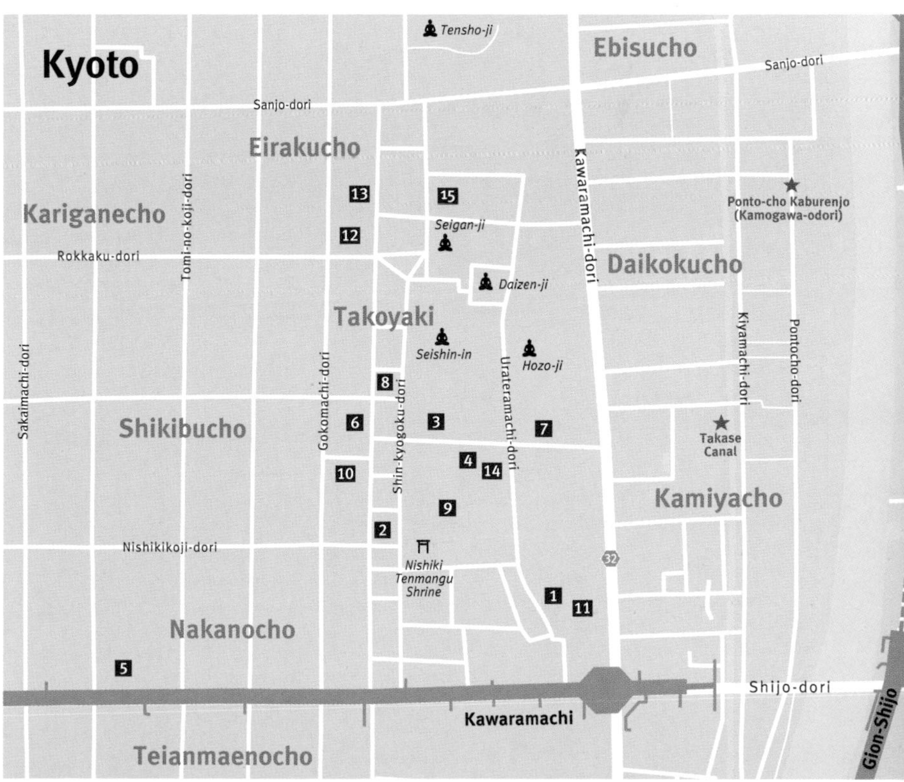

**6** **Kikuya Shoten Manga-kan**
喜久屋書店 漫画館
This Kansai-based chain store mainly sells comics, but you'll find CDs, DVDs and other otaku merchandise, too, including a corner devoted to figures.
**Hours:** *10:00–20:30* **Access:** *270 Enpukujimae-cho, Nakagyo-ku (Teramachi-dori)*

**7** **Kyoto Amanone** 京とあまのね
Amanone stands for **A**nime **MA**nga **NE**twork. This elegant shop is the official store of the **Kyoto International Manga Anime Fair**. In a departure from the typical otaku business, it specializes in products inspired by works made by Kyoto-born artists or featuring Kyoto locations. From traditional bags and purses to keyholders, fans and hand towels, all their original merchandise is made in cooperation with local factories.
**Hours:** *12:00–20:00; closed Tuesdays* **Access:** *577-14 Nakanocho, Nakagyo-ku (Shin-kyogoku-dori)* **amanone-kyoto.jp**

**8** **Ninjin Club** 人参倶楽部
Carrot Club (*ninjin* means "carrot") sells lots of figures and other anime goods, but what really makes it stand out are the 100 *gachapon* machines, with new items added every month, and its one-minute T-shirt printing service. They have more than 200 kanji-based designs, including "samurai," "ninja" and "otaku."

**Hours:** *10:30–20:00; closed from 12/31 through 1/1* **Access:** *498-3 Higashigawa-cho, Nakagyo-ku*
**kyoto-teramachi.or.jp/shop/e048**

**15** **Game Panic**
Ready to take a break from shopping? Head to this game center and get your daily dose of video games. Their lineup is particularly strong in the music and photo sticker department. They always get new *purikura* photo-sticker machines and even lend you costumes and uniforms you can put on when taking pictures. As is increasingly common these days, guys are only allowed when accompanied by one or more ladies.
**Hours:** *9:30–23:45* **Access:** *415 Sakurano-cho, Nakagyo-ku*
**www.leisurelan.co.jp/shop/kyoto.html**

## Chain Stores

**9** **Animate**
**Hours:** *10:00–20:30* **Access:** *2F, 525-1 Higashigawacho, Nakagyo-ku* **animate.co.jp/shop/kyoto**
*(click on アクセス for a photo guide)*

**10** **Animate Café Shop**
**Hours:** *11:00–20:00* **Access:** *279 Enpukujimae cho, Nakagyo-ku (Teramachi-dori)*

**11** **Book Off Plus**
**Hours:** *11:00–22:00* **Access:** *8F OPA Bldg., 4-Jo-agaru Kawaramachi-dori, Komeyacho, Nakagyo-ku*

**10** **C-Labo Kawaramachi Shop**
**Hours:** *11:30–20:30* **Access:** *5F, 279 Enpukuji-mae-cho, Nakagyo-ku (see Animate Café Shop)*

**10** **Gamers**
**Hours:** *11:00–20:00* **Access:** *4F, 279 Enpukuji-mae-cho, Nakagyo-ku (see Animate Café Labo)*

**12** **Lashinbang**
**Hours:** *11:00–21:00* **Access:** *2F, 241 Eirakucho, Nakagyo-ku (Rokkaku-dori)*
**lashinbang.com/store/kyoto**

**13** **Melonbooks**
**Hours:** *11:00–20:00 (Mon–Fri and Sun), 11:00–21:00 (Saturdays)* **Access:** *234 Eirakucho, Nakagyo-ku (Teramachi-dori)*

**14** **Yellow Submarine**
**Hours:** *12:00–21:00 (weekdays), 11:00–20:00 (weekends)* **Access:** *4F, 598 Uradera-cho, Nakagyo-ku*

## Other Shops in Kyoto

**Aeon Mall Kyoto Village Vanguard**
**Hours:** *10:00–21:00* **Access:** *4F Aeon Mall, 1 Nishikujo Toriiguchicho, Minami Ward (10 minutes' walk from Kyoto Station)*

## Near Kyoto

**Kyoani & Do Shop!**
Kyoto Animation and its associate, Animation Do (*The Melancholy of Haruhi Suzumiya, Kanon, Clannad, Lucky Star, K-On!!, Free! Eternal Summer, Sound! Euphonium, A Silent Voice*) are two respected animation studios based in the city of Uji in Kyoto prefecture. As their animators are salaried employees instead of the usual freelancers, they have been able to focus on quality

works which have made them famous worldwide. Kyoani runs a small store a 20-minute train ride away from Kyoto which sells original goods themed after their titles. This is the only store of its kind, so if you're a fan, this is a great opportunity to get some unique products, from button pins and light novels to framed art, clear files and T-shirts. They even sell goods featuring Baja, the company mascot.

**Hours:** *10:00–16:00 (Mon-Wed and Fri), 10:00–18:00 (weekends and national holidays); closed Thursdays* **Access:** *13 Higashinaka, Kohata, Uji City (a one-minute walk from JR Nara Line Kohata station)* **kyotoanimation.co.jp/en/shop**

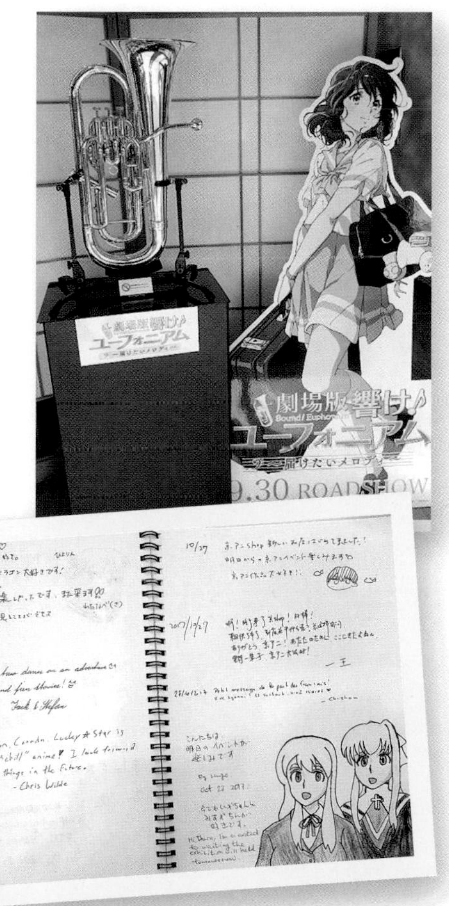


FACING PAGE, LEFT Kyoto Anamone sells otaku goods featuring Kyoto locations. CENTER Animate Café Shop. LEFT and THIS PAGE, ABOVE Buy original anime goods at Kyoani & Do Shop!

# Kyoto Otaku Eateries

### 1 Cinnamoroll Café シナモロールカフェ

One of the cutest otaku cafés in Japan is here in Kyoto, and it's devoted to Sanrio's long-eared, blue-eyed white puppy. The place is very bright and cheerful, with a simple design and lots of plushies everywhere.

The menu is particularly strong in the dessert department. Each elaborately arranged offering features Cinnamoroll's innocent-looking face staring at you—you almost feel guilty eating it! Especially recommended for the Instagram tribe.

Note: Another Cinnamoroll Café recently opened in Tokyo (see **Shinjuku Marui Annex**).

**Hours:** *11:00–21:00* **Access:** *3F Kawaramachi OPA Bldg., Agaru Shijo, Kawaramachi-dori, Nakagyo-ku, Kyoto (next to Kawaramachi Station exit 3, Hankyu Kyoto Line)* **cinnamorollcafe.com**

### Zeon Kokoku 慈恩弘国

If you're starting to get a bit tired of the usual cute cafés and boozy game bars, and you need something good to eat, why not pay a visit to this unique joint where costumed owner Nakano Rambaral—who is also the chef—dispenses kickass okonomiyaki dishes and tall tales to a motley crew of Gundam fans.

First opened in the Space Century 007 (!), it's no surprise that Zeon Kokoku is chockful of Gunplas, posters, and assorted trinkets. Once you've taken in the surroundings, you can watch a TV screen that shows nonstop videos of the Gundam saga.

**Hours:** *18:30–23:00 (only Fri–Sun)* **Access:** *3 Nishikujo Ookunicho, Minami-ku.* **ms-06zaku.com**

# Kyoto International Manga Museum

One of the biggest and most important manga museums in Japan is The Kyoto International Manga Museum 京都国際マンガ ミュージアム. Opened in 2006, it is housed in a former elementary school that was originally built in 1929, and it has a distinctive retro feeling. It's very popular with both Japanese and foreigners: currently 15 percent of its visitors come from abroad. This is one of the most ambitious manga-related projects in Japan, as it aims to introduce the public to the world of comics from a historical, artistic and sociological point of view.

The temporary exhibitions focus on particular periods (e.g., manga during the war), authors, magazines (*Margaret*) or regions (manga in Okinawa). The permanent collection includes nearly 200 portraits of *maiko* (apprentice geisha) made by manga artists; another fascinating (or slightly disturbing, depending on your tastes) exhibit features plaster casts of more than 100 artists' hands.

The museum's library has a collection of 300,000 volumes, 50,000 of which are available on open-stack shelves—the so-called Wall of Manga. The first floor is devoted to *shonen* (boys') manga, the second to *shojo* (girls') manga, and the third to the *seinen* (young adult) genre. A few specialized areas are the Manga Hall of Fame (arranged by years, 1945–2005), the MM navigation shelf focusing on a specific theme, and Manga Expo, where you can read manga in other languages (about 1,000 are in English and 1,600 are in Chinese). It is possible to access 250,000 older and rarer materials in the Research Reference Room upon registration (find all the details online). These are mainly intended for research purposes.

In the Manga Kobo (manga studio) corner, you can watch an actual manga artist at work, while in the Portrait Corner you can have a professional illustrator draw your face in standard or anime style. It takes about 30 minutes and costs 1,500 yen. If you plan to do this, be sure to arrive early, as it's very popular with visitors.

Among the other activities, two or three times a day you can watch *kami shibai* ("paper play"), a traditional form of street theater and storytelling that was very popular with kids into the mid-1950s. There are also workshops where you can learn things like how to draw manga. Some of them require a reservation and an additional fee.

**Admission fee:** *800 yen (300 yen for high school and junior high students, 100 yen for elementary school students)* **Hours:** *10:00–18:00; closed Wednesdays and on the New Year's holidays* **Access:** *Karasuma-Oike, Nakagyo-ku, Kyoto* **kyotomm.jp/en** *(English)*

ABOVE and BELOW The Kyoto International Manga Museum offers a variety of activities and a range of exhibits. BOTTOM LEFT The Wall of Manga has 50,000 volumes available for perusal.

# Toei Kyoto Studio Park

Toei Kyoto Studio Park 東映太秦映画村 is one of Japan's main TV and film production companies, and its Eiga-Mura ("film village") is a studio-cum-amusement-park where they still shoot about 200 period films and dramas every year. You can see and do a ton of things here, depending on how much money you're ready to spend.

You can see and do a ton of things at Toei Kyoto Studio Park, such as watching samurai- and ninja-related shows.

On the display side of things, the Movie Cultural Hall has both a permanent collection of famous Toei movie posters and temporary exhibitions. Recent events include original art for *Yowamushi Pedal* and a *Kamen Rider World* exhibit featuring both Ishinomori's artwork and more recent designs.

But the samurai- and ninja-related sets, shows and attractions are the best part of the experience. These are all included in the admission fee, and range from action stage plays and *chanbara* (sword-fighting) filmmaking to an Edo-period classroom and a guided park tour from a Toei actor.

The attractions do require an extra fee. Among the more interesting are the Ninja Mystery House, where you learn about some of the inner workings of this mysterious building before trying to escape through secret passages, revolving doors and other traps; the *shuriken*- (ninja star) throwing contest; the "Sword 'n' Go" ninja training camp; the "3-D Maze Ninja Fort"; and the haunted house.

You can also don period dress and be photographed; there are more than 30 different costumes to choose from, including samurai, geisha and ninja. Guests may also rent period-style costumes to wear as they enjoy the park.

Check the rather old-fashioned but informative website to discover all the park's delights.

**Admission fee:** *2,200 yen (1,300 yen for high school and junior high students, 1,100 yen for ages 3 to 11); an attraction coupon is 1,600 yen (1,200 yen), while the fee for one attraction is 500 yen (400 yen)* **Hours:** *9:00–17:00 (see the website for details); closed a few days at the end of January for maintenance (see details)* **Access:** *10 Uzumasa, Higashi Hachioka-cho, Ukyo-ku, Kyoto* **toei-eigamura.com/en** *(English)*

Toei Kyoto Studio Park has an ever-changing roster of exhibitions. Check their website to see the latest exhibiton schedule.

# Kyoto Festivals and Events

### Kyoto International Manga Anime Fair (Kyo-MAF)

京都国際マンガ・アニメフェア（京まふ）

One of the largest otaku fairs in western Japan (about 50,000 visitors) is more business-oriented (lots of booths of publishing and broadcasting companies, and even an academic institution), but can be enjoyed by everyone. The main action takes place at the Miyako Messe convention center, but the **Kyoto International Manga Museum** (see) also holds related promotional events. The Special Stage is very popular with fans who want to know about new and upcoming anime, films, etc., and hear insider stories from popular creators and voice actors. Another area is devoted to anime exhibition booths. Here you can see key frames used in anime works and other production-related information besides collaborations between anime companies and Kyoto-based traditional handicrafts. Interactive booths even offer the chance to try the latest games and VR gadgets. And then of course there are workshops, a café and the obligatory cosplay area. Remember that if you want to attend an event at the ROHM Theater you'll have to get your ticket in advance through a lottery, as all seats are reserved. Apparently foreigners with a passport get in free.

**Admission fee:** *Miyako Messe: 1,500 yen (1,200 in advance)* **Dates:** *September* **Hours:** *9:00–17:00 Saturdays; 9:00–16:00 Sundays* **Access:** *Miyako Messe: 9-1 Okazaki Seichoji-cho, Sakyo-ku, Kyoto (eight minutes' walk from Higashiyama Station, Tosai subway line)* **ROHM Theater Kyoto:** *13 Okazaki Seichoji-cho, Sakyo-ku, Kyoto* **kyomaf.kyoto/en** *(English)*

BOTTOM LEFT, LEFT, and FACING PAGE TOP Kyoto International Manga Anime Fair. ABOVE, BELOW, and FACING PAGE BOTTOM BitSummit.

BitSummit is a great opportunity for Japanese and Western developers to meet up and collaborate.

**BitSummit**
The Japanese indie game development scene is still relatively new. Though it lags well behind the US, it's gathering people's attention, especially now that Nintendo has thrown its weight behind it. And what better opportunity than checking out its premiere showcase, BitSummit. This event has steadily grown since its inception, and now attracts over 100 exhibitors, vendors and sponsors. This is a great place for Japanese and Western developers to meet up and collaborate. It also has a more intimate vibe than the bigger festival in Tokyo, giving fans a chance to interact with industry people. The two-day event features demos, live musical performances and talks by such famous developers as Final Fantasy creator Sakaguchi Hironobu and Grasshopper Manufacture founder Suda Goichi.

**Admission fee:** *2,000 yen (1,000 yen for students; free for elementary-school students and younger, but they must be accompanied by an adult)* **Dates:** *May* **Hours:** *10:00–17:00* **Access:** *Miyako Messe, 9-1 Okazaki Seichoji-cho, Sakyo-ku, Kyoto (eight minutes' walk from Higashiyama Station, Tosai subway line)* **bitsummit.jp**

## Expat Game Developers

When it comes to video games, Tokyo is where all the big publishers show off their stuff at events like the Game Show. For the indie scene, though, Kyoto is the place to be, especially if you are a foreigner.

There are more Western developers than ever in Japan, and they're working to bridge the gap between the local community and the rest of the world in their roles as game developers, localizers and organizers.

In the summer of 1990, a small British studio called Argonaut was invited to Kyoto to show Nintendo how they had managed to produce 3-D graphics on the Game Boy. Among them was an 18-year-old programmer called Dylan Cuthbert. Nintendo was impressed enough to give Argonaut a contract, and Cuthbert ended up staying in Kyoto, where he now runs Q Games.

Cuthbert was followed by other expats: Giles Goddard (another Argonaut alum who established Vitei, best known for its work on Steel Diver for the Nintendo 3DS) and Jake Kazdal, who opened a branch of 17-Bit Studios, creators of Galak-Z. These studios employ many foreigners, making Kyoto the go-to place if you hope to work in Japan.

Kyoto's big advantage over Tokyo is its tight community and the family atmosphere that prevails among local game developers, with regular get-togethers at local establishments for drinks, gossip and networking. Then there's **BitSummit**, of course, the annual event that Cuthbert and the other gaijin helped create; its main purpose is to introduce Japanese developers to Western media and facilitate a conversation between the developers—something that the Japanese are not accustomed to; traditionally, everybody does their own thing without sharing ideas and collaborating as is usual in the West.

Other companies are active in bridging the Japanese and foreign communities. Playism, for instance, is an Osaka-based digital distribution platform offering services like localization, debugging, marketing and publishing to Japanese indie developers interested in releasing their games to foreign markets. They are also actively hosting events and lectures. Going in the other direction, Dangen Entertainment was created by six game-industry veterans with the aim of helping Western developers break into the difficult-to-crack Japanese market. The company is a sort of one-stop shop for developers looking to make it in Japan: they handle everything, from publishing and localization to marketing and porting.

# EXPLORING KOBE

Kobe is often dwarfed by its more illustrious neighbors, Osaka and Kyoto, and is consequently bypassed by both Japanese and foreign travelers. The sixth-largest city in the country, Kobe is seen by many Japanese as the most elegant, refined and fashionable of the big centers in the Kansai region, and it undoubtedly has its own attractions. However, especially in the eyes of Western tourists, it's perceived as being insufficiently exotic, since trade with Europeans is such a large part of the city's history. In the end, Kobe is left to face extremely strong competition, and unless you have many days to spend in western Japan, you could probably skip it.

Kobe is often regarded as the most elegant and fashionable city in western Japan. It also has a giant Tetsujin 28 statue (TOP), symbol of Kobe's post-earthquake renaissance.

The same thing can be said about otaku Kobe: the city has only a couple of museums and events, and its main concentration of manga and anime-themed stores in the **Sannomiya** district is no match for those in Akihabara, Nipponbashi or even Kyoto's Teramachi. Besides, many of these shops are branches of big chains you can find anywhere in Japan. Considering that even the charmingly retro Motomachi Koka-dori shopping arcade is currently closed for renovations, you may as well head straight for the Tezuka Osamu Manga Museum in nearby Takarazuka.

Actually, there's one thing you shouldn't miss in Kobe: the 60-foot (18-meter) tall statue of Tetsujin 28 (Iron Man 28), one of Japan's original giant robots, better known in the West as Gigantor. Tetsujin's beautiful statue is in Shin-Nagata, the district where its creator, manga author Yokoyama Mitsuteru, was born. It was erected in 2010 as a symbol of the city's economic recovery from the 1995 disastrous Hanshin Earthquake and, unlike the giant Gundams that are taken down after a while, Tetsujin 28 is here to stay, in order to protect Kobe from further natural disasters.

Sannomiya's center of otaku action is **San Center Plaza**, next to Sannomiya Station (JR, Hankyu, Hanshin and subway lines), which is divided into three shopping complexes—San Plaza, Center Plaza and Plaza West—which are connected by walkways. There are more than 500 shops in the three plazas combined, but most of the otaku stores are on the second and third floors, with trading-card shops having a particularly strong presence. You can visit all the shops by taking one of the corridors connecting one plaza to the next (see the map at 3nomiya.net/access/accessmap).

With few exceptions, all stores are open daily between 10:00 or 11:00 and 20:00. The number after the floor shows the shop's location on the map.

## San Center Plaza

### Trading-card Shops

**Card Cult** カードカルト Plaza West 2F-05
**Card Loop** カードループ Plaza West 2F-30
**Card Square** カードスクエア Plaza West 2F-02 *(Closed Tuesdays and the first and third Mondays of every month)*
**Dragon Star** ドラゴンスター Plaza West 3F-06
**Seven Draw** セブンドロー Center Plaza 2F-39 *(Closed Tuesdays)*
**Treca Mania** トレカマニア Plaza West 2F-07
**Treca Park** トレカパーク Plaza West 3F-1

### Other Shops

**1 Honey Hart** ハニーハート
The self-appointed number-one shop

in Kobe for female otaku has in stock hundreds of PC and TV games, more than 4,000 CDs, thousands of *shojo* and BL manga and *dojinshi*, as well as DVDs.
**Access:** ***Plaza West 3F-07*** **honey-heart.jp**

**1 Ojamakan** おじゃま館
New and old video games.
**Access:** ***San Plaza 3F-37***

**1 S.d.S**
Once there was a retro game shop in Motomachi Koka-dori called AX (アくせ). The store has moved here and changed its name, but they still peddle good stuff: video games and old nostalgic toys like My Little Pony. Worth a look.
**Access:** ***Plaza West 2F-33***

**1 Suruga-ya** 駿河屋
Hyogo prefecture is the home base of this national chain store, and they have four stores in San Center Plaza alone. Each one of them is a sort of otaku mini-mart: they sell toys, video games, manga, books, CDs, DVDs and Blu-rays, stationary, apparel and even idol pictures.
**Sannomiya #1:** Center Plaza 2F-04
**Sannomiya #1** Satellite: San Plaza 3F-36
**Sannomiya #2:** San Plaza 2F-01-02
**Sannomiya #3:** Center Plaza East 2F
**suruga-ya.jp/feature/shoplist/index.html**

## Chain Stores

**Animate** Center Plaza 3F-12
**Animega** Center Plaza 2F-44
**Gamers** Plaza West 3F-14-15-16
**Lashinbang** Center Plaza 2F-06
**Melonbooks** Center Plaza B1F-07-08
**Toranoana** Plaza West 3F-21
**Volks SR** ボークス **SR** Center Plaza 3F-01-02
**Yellow Submarine** Plaza West 2F-18-20

## Bonus Shop

**7 Mosrite** モズライト
Mosrite used to be located in the Motomachi Koka-dori shopping arcade. Its new location is fairly close to Sannomiya Station but on the other side of the railway. This shop is a collector's dream come true, offering an amazing selection of vintage toys, from *chogokin* and figures (*yokai*, monsters, masked heroes, etc.) to tin toys, plamodel and Peko-chan dolls. The owner, Murata-san, has been dealing in antiques for more than 25 years, and his store looks like a toy museum. Unfortunately, the prices of many of his toys are at museum level, too. But you can still find something for a few thousand yen.

Since Murata-san is often out hunting for old toys to buy, you may want to call before you go: 078-261-2711 or 090-62427771.
**Hours:** ***13:00–19:00; closed Tuesdays***
**Access:** ***2-17-2 Naka-Yamate-dori, Chuo-ku (10 minutes' walk from Sannomiya Station)***
**kobetoy.ocnk.net**

**ABOVE and LEFT S.d.S sells all kinds of nostalgic toys. BELOW Mosrite, near Sannomiya Station, is a collector's dream come true.**

# Kobe (and Hyogo) Otaku Eateries

### Anison Karaoke Bar Seven
アニソン・カラオケバー　せぶん

The name says it all: this is a place where you can sing and get drunk. The singing is free, but the all-you-can-drink system will cost you 1,800 yen for the first 90 minutes and 600 yen for each 30-minute extension. There's also a 1,000 charge.

**Hours:** *19:00–; closed on Wednesdays* **Access:** *2F Ace Town Bldg. 1-15-7 Naka-Yamate-dori, Chuo-ku)* **anikara.7.com**

### 3 Game Bar EQULit
ゲームバー　エクルイット

Lots of board games here, from the classics to the newest titles. All-you-can-eat-and-drink is included in the time-based fee (1,500 yen for 1 hour; 2,500 yen for 2 hours; or a flat rate of 3,000 yen from 13:00 to 18:00; 3,500 yen from 18:00 to 23:00; and 3,500 yen from 23:00 to 5:00).

**Hours:** *18:00–5:00 (weekdays), 13:00–5:00 (weekends and holidays)* **Access:** *6F, 1-4-6 Kita-Nagasa-dori, Chuo-ku, Kobe (a one-minute walk from Sannomiya Station)* **twitter.com/equlit_game**

### 4 Dagashi Bar Retro Modern
駄菓子バー　レトロモダン

The interior is pretty modern, but the overall feel is retro-nostalgic, with tons of Famicon, Super Famicon and Commodore 64 software and toys that you can enjoy while feasting on *dagashi* traditional Japanese snacks and candies. All-you-can-eat is included in the 500-yen-per-hour fee.

ABOVE Café Dream. ABOVE LEFT Bar Shield.

**Hours:** *18:00–1:00 (weekdays), 16:00–1:00 (weekends and holidays)* **Access:** *1-1-5 Shimo-Yamate-dori, Chuo-ku, Kobe (near Sannomiya Station; see website for detailed photo directions)* **dagashibar-retromodern-kobe.com**

### 5 Bar Shield
The ideal place to talk about worldwide superheroes and SF (*tokusatsu*, Marvel, Star Wars, etc.). Their dishes seem to be better than those at your average otaku joint. Booze is a little overpriced. There's a 300-yen seat charge.

**Hours:** *19:00–2:00; closed Mondays* **Access:** *2F, 1-7-12 Naka-Yamate-dori, Chuo-ku, Kobe* **twitter.com/ShieldAkasi3911**

### 6 A:real ありえる
At this *anison* bar, just pay 2,980 yen for two hours and they'll let you drink and sing until you get wasted under a table. After that, it's 1,000 yen for every extra hour.

**Hours:** *18:00~* **Access:** *3F, 2-10-11 Kita-Nagasa-dori, Chuo-ku, Kobe (near Sannomiya Station)* **areal.web.fc2.com**

## Nishinomiya

### Café Dream コーヒー屋ドリーム
Fans of hit anime *The Melancholy of Haruhi Suzumiya* won't want to miss a chance to visit the place in Nishinomiya that inspired the coffeehouse frequented by Haruhi and her gang. Apparently Tanigawa Nagaru, the author of the original light novel series, lived near the café and was a regular customer. In 2017, the owner moved the café to a new, smaller location just down the road from the old one, but kept the original signboard, wooden counter and lighting. And otaku considerations aside, they make a mean house-roasted coffee.

**Hours:** *8:00–19:00* **Access:** *1-12-12 Kofuen, Nishinomiya (four minutes' walk from Nishinomiya-Kitaguchi Station, Hankyu Imazu and Kobe main lines)* **cafedream.thebase.in**

BELOW and RIGHT Dagashi Bar Retro Modern.

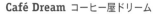

# Kobe Museums

### Kobe Tetsujin Sangokushi Gallery KOBE鉄人三国志ギャラリー

ABOVE Exhibits at the Kobe Tetsujin Sangokushi Gallery.

Fans of classic Japanese comics should pay a visit to this small but interesting gallery devoted to the work of the late Yokoyama Mitsutero, who is best known for the *Tetsujin 28-go* giant robot manga (known in America as *Gigantor*) and *Sangokushi* (the three kingdoms), a historical series based on a 14th-century Chinese novel. There's a lot to see: Yokoyama's art, original comic books, materials related to the Tetsujin 28-go monument and more. They even organize monthly card games and study-group meetups about Yokoyama's work.

**Admission fee:** *Free* **Hours:** *12:30–17:30; closed Mondays and from 12/31 to 1/4*
**Access:** *6-1-13 Futaba-cho, Nagata-ku, Kobe (nine minutes' walk from JR Shin-Nagata Station)*
**kobe-tetsujin.com/gallery**
**kobe-tetsujin.com/pdf/nagata_eng.pdf** *(English map)*

### (2•4) Osamu Tezuka Manga Museum* 手塚治虫記念館

With so many otaku museums all around Japan, it would be strange if they hadn't devoted a special place to the God of Manga himself. Indeed, when it opened in 1994, this was one of the first manga-themed museums in Japan. The building design was apparently inspired by the old European castles and other classic Western architecture Tezuka loved so much. The tower is topped by the Glass Earth—a homage to the artist's essay "Save the Glass Earth." Tezuka was famous for devising his own star system and using the same characters in different stories. The hand- and footprints of these charcters can be admired on the pavement in front of the museum, mimicking those on the Hollywood Walk of Fame. Once inside, you are welcomed by the gorgeous entrance, which is based on the royal palace featured in *Princess Knight*. The first floor is mainly devoted to Tezuka's long and remarkably active artistic career, while on the second floor there's a space for temporary exhibitions and a "search machine" where you can find information about Tezuka and his work, play video games, and watch all his short films. Speaking of films, three different works are screened in the museum

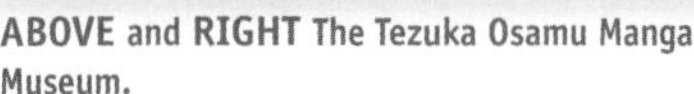

ABOVE and RIGHT The Tezuka Osamu Manga Museum.

theater every month. There's also a library with about 2,000 Tezuka-related publications (including some in English, Chinese, Korean and even Braille), while a book display full of Tezuka's rare first editions will likely give many hardcore collectors a heart attack. Finally (and probably the best part in the museum), there's an animation studio on the G-floor where you can try your hand at creating moving images—but only on weekends and national holidays.
**Admission fee:** *700 yen (300 yen for junior and senior high school students, 100 yen for elementary school students)* **Hours:** *9:30–17:00; closed Wednesdays except on national holidays and during spring and summer vacation periods; closed from 12/29 to 12/31 and 2/21 to 3/2* **Access:** *7-65 Mukogawa, Takarazuka (an eight-minute walk from Takarazuka Station (JR Fukuchiyama and Hankyu Takarazuka main lines)*
**city. takarazuka.hyogo.jp/tezuka**
**tezukaosamu.net/en** *(English)*

**Kobe Anpanman Children's Museum and Mall** (see page 49)

Anpanman is one of Japanese children's favorite characters. Several Japanese cities, including Kobe, have an Anpanman Children's Museum and Mall.

## Open-air Amusement

### Nijigen no Mori ニジゲンノモリ

Opened in 2017 on Awaji Island, Nijigen no Mori ("2-D forest") is an open-air amusement park combining technology, nature, athletic activity and, of course, otaku characters. Kids' favorite Crayon Shin-chan is present with two attractions: **Challenge! Action Kamen Air Force!** features a pair of ziplines 740 feet (225 m) and 450 feet (140 m) respectively that glide across a body of water while the rider is bombarded with giant water guns; **Bravo! Great Adventure Across the Warring States!** is an athletic course featuring characters and obstacles themed around the Shin-chan film *The Storm Called: The Battle of the Warring States*. You can actually choose one of three different courses (with different admission fees), the hardest of which reaches a height of 23 feet (7 meters). One of the park's most famous attractions is Night Walk Phoenix, a half mile (1.2 km) nighttime walk in the forest where you can enjoy a light-and-sound show based on Tezuka Osamu's *Phoenix* manga series. The area utilizes projection mapping technology in the park's natural settings. There are time-limited attractions, too (at the time of writing, for instance, there was a sort of mystery tour inspired by the popular manga and anime *Hozuki's Coolheadedness*), as well as a musical theater, event stage and other experience-based activities.

Unfortunately, the information on their website is in Japanese only, so if you can't read those bloody kanji you'll have to ask for help.

**Admission fee:** *Entering the park itself is free, but of course you'll have to shell out for the attractions, which range from 500 to 3,300 yen each. Your best option is the free-pass ticket (not available on the weekend) which gives you access to all the attractions for 4,800 yen (4,500 in advance).* **Hours:** *12:00–22:00 (weekdays), 10:00–22:00 (weekends and holidays)* **Access:** *Reaching the island is a little bit of a hassle—see the website (nijigennomori.com/access) for details.* **nijigennomori.com**

# Otaku Spots and Events in Mie Prefecture

### Shojo Mangakan TAKI 1735
### 少女まんが館 TAKI 1735

Hardcore *shojo* (girls') manga fans who live or travel in western Japan may want to undertake the long trek to this small but well-stocked library located in the Mie countryside. They have literally thousands of girls' manga books and magazines, focusing on titles from the 1980s onward. The first floor has a café and is open to everybody. The second floor is only accessible to junior high school students and older. Their hours are pretty consistent, but you may want to check their Facebook page before going, or contact them in advance (jomakan-taki@gmail.com, tel. 0598-67-4968). Consider combining this with a visit to Ise Grand Shrine, a 30- to 40-minute ride away.

**Admission fee:** *Free* **Hours:** *11:00–17:00; closed Sun–Tue and national holidays*
**Access:** *1735 Niu, Taki-cho, Taki-gun (a 12-minute car ride from Sana and Oka stations, JR Central Kisei Main Line)*
**facebook.com/jomakantaki1735**

**Note:** TAKI 1735 has an older and larger sister library (55,000 magazines and books) in Tokyo's deep western suburbs, but it's only open on Saturdays (13:00–18:00) between April and October. The address is 155-5 Ajiro, Akiruno City. **nerimadors.or.jp/~jomakan**

LEFT and BELOW The Shojo Mangakan has thousands of girls' manga and magazines.

### Ninja Museum of Igaryu
### 伊賀流 忍者博物館

Nagoya and its surrounding area played a significant role in Japanese history, particularly during the Sengoku (Warring States) period. The Japanese are endlessly fascinated by this time in history, when different feudal lords fought for control of the country. Located near Iga Ueno Castle, where the Iga school of ninjutsu (ninja fighting techniques) was based, since 1964, this museum educates and entertains about the history of ninja and ninjutsu that features so prominently in Sengoku folklore. It has an extensive collection of writings and tools, and offers visitors a chance to experience the ninja world through shows, hands-on trials, and a guided tour of the ninja clan's old residence that's full of tricks and surprises.

**Admission fee:** *756 yen (432 yen for 4- to 15-year-olds); ninja show 400 yen; shuriken-throwing experience, 200 yen for five throws*
**Hours:** *9:00-17:00; closed from 12/29 to 1/1*
**Access:** *117-13-1 Ueno-Marunouchi, Iga (10 minutes' walk from Uenoshi Station, Iga Line)*
**iganinja.jp** *(check the nice English page)*

### Ninja Festa

This festival takes place in Iga City's Ueno Park in April and May and attracts thousands of fans. Don a ninja costume (for a fee), try different weapons, and enjoy the cosplay event (2,000 yen to join). If you wear a costume, you can ride the local train for free!

**Access:** *see Ninja Museum of Igaryu (previous entry)* **Hours:** *10:00–17:00*
**iga.ne.jp/~ninjafesta**
**youtube.com/watch?v=ubdWHpN6QM**

LEFT and BELOW The Ninja Museum of Igaryu lets you experience the ninja world with shows, hands-on activities, and a guided tour of an old ninja residence.

CHAPTER 3

# Other Regions of JAPAN

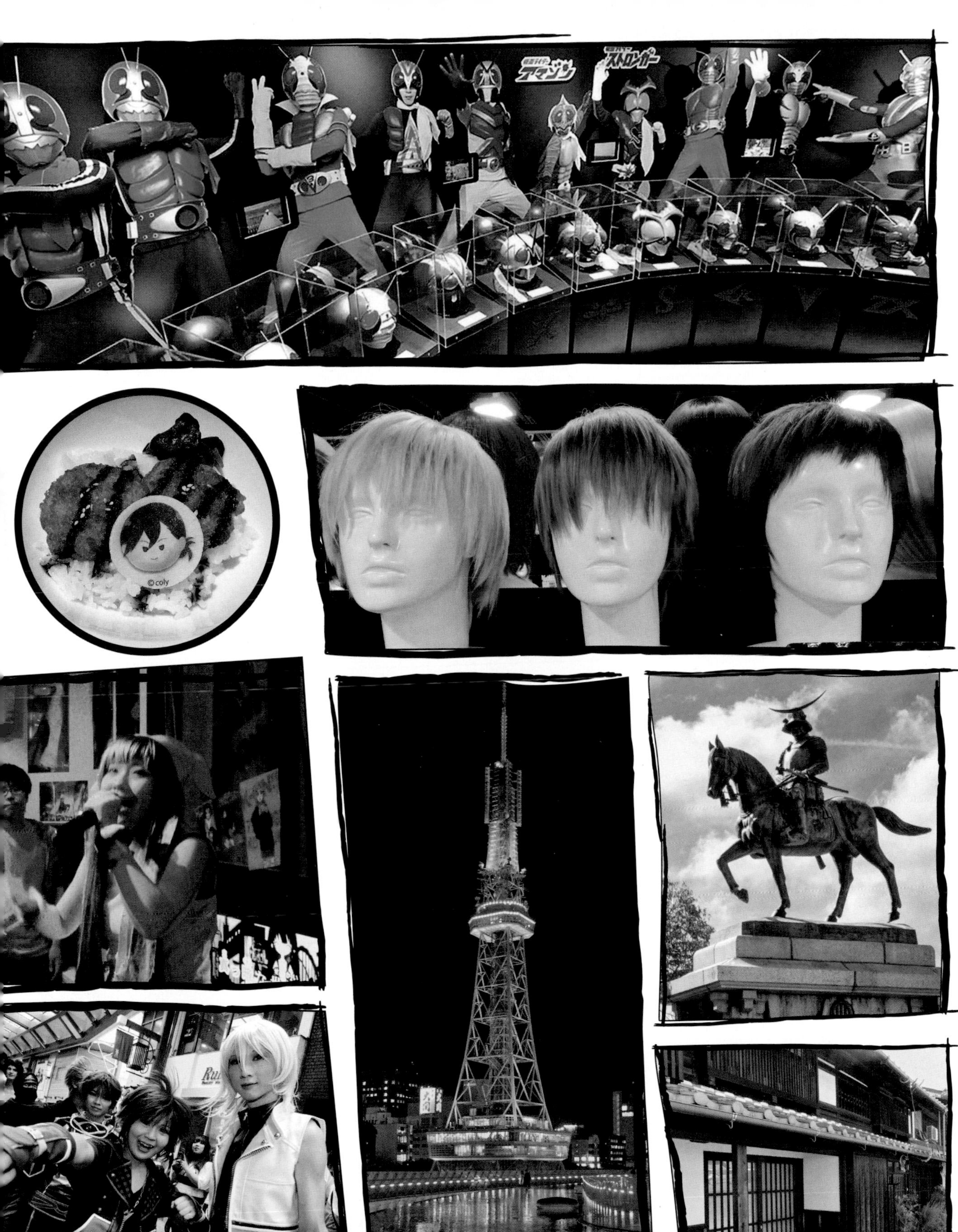
アマゾン
ストロンガー
©coly

# EXPLORING SAPPORO

Sapporo, one of the youngest cities in the world, is one of Japan's more dynamic urban centers. In some respects, it's rather un-Japanese, with its gridlike street plan, Western-style buildings, and lack of a rainy season. Travelers seldom spend much time here, as their main destination is the great Hokkaido outdoors. Though Sapporo lacks a dedicated otaku district like Akiba or Nipponbashi, several major chains are clustered near the Odori subway station, so you may want to start your hunt from there.

## General

**Aco Dolls** 亜古人形
Aco Dolls looks like a nondescript private house. But inside it's a great independent doll shop. Obitsu, Ginny, Tiny Betsy, Blythe, Misaki and Madame Alexander are all here, plus accessories, books and magazines. The store is only open three days a week.
**Hours:** *12:00–18:00 Fri, Sun; 12:00–20:00 Saturdays; closed Mon–Thurs* **Access:** *1-2-14 Kitano 3-jo, Kiyota-ku (1.5 miles [2.4 km] from Sapporo Metro Tozai Line Nango-Juhatchome Station, or 2 miles [3 km] from Toho Line Fukuzumi Station)* **acodolls.com**

**1 Excel Hobby**
Though mainly a military shop, it's not all model firearms and air guns here; there's still enough space for plastic models, Gunpla, minicars and more.
**Hours:** *11:30–20:00 (Mon–Sat), 11:30–19:00 (Sundays and national holidays)* **Access:** *3F, 1-2 Minami 1-jo-Nishi, Chuo-ku (five minutes' walk from Odori Station, Nanboku and Tozai subway lines)* **excel-hobby.com**

Animega offers manga, DVDs, games, and character goods.

**LEFT** Aco Dolls is one of the best independent doll shops in Hokkaido. **TOP** Sapporo is a young metropolis with a gridlike street plan.

**Game Shop 1983** ゲームショップ1983
In the middle of nowhere, this tiny old-school store starts showing off its retro credentials with its decrepit exterior. Inside, it's a haphazard jumble of games from every period, on metal shelves or in plastic drawers. Great atmosphere, decent prices and definitely worth checking out.
**Hours:** *12:00–22:30* **Access:** *5-1-1 Kita 35-jo-Nishi, Kita-ku (five minutes' walk from Kita-Sanjuyo-jo Station, Sapporo Nanboku subway line)* **1983.jp**

**Mandai** 万代
This recycle shop is as big as a supermarket. Indeed, they sell used clothes, consumer electronics, musical instruments and even beer! But they also have otaku goods in spades: video games, trading cards, toys, CDs, DVDs, manga, you name it. It takes time to explore, but they're open 24 hours. It's fun to have a look even if you buy nothing. Just be careful not to get lost.
**Hours:** *Open 24/7* **Access:** *2-2-8 Inaho 2-jo, Teine-ku (12 minutes' walk from Inaho Station, Hakodate Main Line)* **mandai-st.jp/shop**

**Tokyo-ya** 東京屋
*Dagashi* and toy wholesaler Tokyo-ya does retail too, in a small shop that's always busy. This may not be an otaku shop, but it sells the kind of cheap sweets and toys many manga and anime characters drool over. Apart from an endless choice of candies and

other junk food, you'll find traditional toys, kewpie dolls, trading cards, masks and character goods.
**Hours:** *April–October 9:00–18:00 (closed Sundays); November–March 9:00–17:30 (closed on weekends)* **Access:** *10-18-19 Kita 3-jo-Higashi, Chuo-ku (six minutes' walk from Naebo Station, Chitose and Hakodate main lines)* **tokyo-ya.jp**

**Yamanote Club** 山の手倶楽部
Retro dealer specializing in objects from the '50s to the '80s. They have old toys, too, including Makoto-chan dolls. You won't find much below 10,000 yen; some items (like a Wolf Boy Ken figure from the '60s or a Mirrorman from the early '70s) go for over 100,000 yen, but if you're a serious collector, you should pay them a visit.
**Hours:** *12:00–19:00; closed Mondays*
**Access:** *24-1-2 Kita 5-jo-Nishi, Chuo-ku (seven minutes' walk from Nishi-Niju-Hatchome Station, Sapporo Tozai subway line)*

## Chain Stores

The usual suspects are present in Sapporo. **Melonbooks** (B1F), **Animate** (2F), **Lashinbang** (3F), **C-Labo** (4F) and **Gamers** (5F) are located inside the Marudai (丸大) Building **2** (1-5 Minami 2-jo-Nishi, Chuo-ku) and are open 10:00–20:00. They are very close to Odori Station (Nanboku, Tozai, and Toho subway lines). **Toranoana** (10:00–21:00) is next to Marudai Bldg. **3**, on the left. **Donguri Kyowakoku** どんぐり共和国 and **Hello Kitty** (10:00–21:00) are in Sapporo Station's underground shopping mall. **Pokemon Center** (10:00–22:00) is in Daimaru department store (8F), next to Sapporo Station.

Collectors love Yamanote Club, which has goods from the '50s to the '80s.

**4 Animega**
**Hours:** *10:00–20:00* **Access:** *3-3 Minami 1-jo-Nishi, Chuo-ku (three minutes' walk from Odori Station, Nanboku, Tozai, and Toho subway lines)*

**5 Mandarake**
**Hours:** *12:00–20:00* **Access:** *2F, 5-1-1 Minami 3-jo-Nishi, Chuo-ku (two minutes' walk from Susukino Station, Nanboku subway line)*

**6 Volks** ボークス
**Hours:** *10:00–20:00* **Access:** *B2F, 9-1 Minami 1-jo-Nishi, Chuo-ku (three minutes' walk from Odori Station, Nanboku, Tozai, and Toho subway lines)*

**7 Yellow Submarine**
**Hours:** *10:30–21:00* **Access:** *6F, 4-12 Minami 3-jo-Nishi, Chuo-ku (five minutes' walk from Odori Station, Nanboku, Tozai, and Toho subway lines)*

**Snow Miku Sky Town at New Chitose Airport**
Chances are you're flying into Hokkaido, in which case you will land at the New Chitose Airport, but even if you go by train or car, don't miss a chance to check out Snow Miku Sky Town. Located on the fourth floor of the domestic terminal building, it consists of three separate areas:

The free **Snow Miku Museum**, featuring a life-sized Snow Miku statue along with various goods and artworks on display.

The **Hokkaido Gurutto Theater**, which has a 360-degree panoramic screen showing four different 15-minute programs on rotation highlighting the island's gorgeously beautiful nature.

A shop selling apparel, stationery, coin purses, plushies, figures and other items, some of them exclusive to Chitose Airport.
***Hours:** 9:00–19:00 **Access:** New Chitose Airport Station is on the JR Chitose Line, 37 minutes from Sapporo Station* **snowmiku.com/skytown/index_en.html**

# Sapporo Bars and Cafés

Hokkaido is famous for its long, cold winters, with temperatures falling well below zero in January and February. Maybe that's why there are so many otaku joints in Sapporo. What's better than meeting like-minded people indoors while the city is covered with snow and packs of wolves roam the streets?

You can rent a costume at Majori-ca, an anison cosplay bar.

## Cosplay Bars

### 8 Akibar あにこすばー
The main point of attraction of this anime cosplay bar seems to be its smooth-talking barmaids (or "cast," as they are called in otaku joints), many of whom used to work in maid cafés. The karaoke is OK too; it costs 2,000 yen per hour for guys; 1,700 for gals.
***Hours:** 20:00–3:00; closed Sundays (or on Monday when Sunday is a national holiday) **Access:** 7F, Minami 4-jo Nishi 3-chome, Chuo-ku, Sapporo* **twitter.com/akibar_squad**

### 9 Lircari-Na リルカリーナ
Sister bar to **Majori-ca** (see below) with a different fee system: 700 yen for 20 minutes.
***Hours:** 19:00–2:00 (Mon–Wed), 19:00–5:30 (Fri–Sat), 19:00–24:00 (Sun); closed Thursdays **Access:** 5F, Minami 5-jo Nishi 3-chome (a one-minute walk from Susukino Station exit 3)* **conceptbar.info/lircari-na**

### 10 Majori-ca マジョリカ
Anison cosplay bar where the clients are encouraged to join in the fun and singing action. They even rent costumes (free for girls) and have a changing room. The all-you-can-drink option is 2,000 yen per hour (1,500 for ladies).
***Hours:** 19:00–2:00 (Mon, Wed–Fri), 19:00–5:30 (weekends); closed Tuesdays **Access:** 4F, Minami 4-jo Nishi 3-1-1, Chuo-ku (a one-minute walk from Susukino Station exit 3)* **conceptbar.info/majori-ca**

### 11 Melt ボカロアニソンバー　メルト
Here the barmaids are called Melties. 1,800 yen per hour (1,200 for ladies).
***Hours:** 20:00–5:30 (Mon–Thu and Sun), 21:00–6:00 (Fri–Sat) **Access:** 3F, Minami 5-jo Nishi 3-chome, Chuo-ku (a one-minute walk from Hosui-Susukino Station exit 6, Sapporo Metro Toho Line)* **vocaloid.bar-melt.com**

### 12 Shangri-La アニメコスプレバー Shangri-La
Same concept as **Majori-ca** (see above), same building. 1,700 per hour (1,500 for gals) all-you-can-drink and all-you-can-sing system.
***Hours:** 19:00–2:00 (Tue–Thu), 19:00–3:00 (Fri–Sat); closed Sundays, Mondays and national holidays **Access:** 6F, Minami 4-jo Nishi 3-chome, Chuo-ku, Sapporo* **shangrilaxxxx.wixsite.com**

**BELOW LEFT** Licari-Na is Majorica's sister bar, with cosplay and anison. **BELOW RIGHT** At cosplay bar Melt, the barmaids are called Melties.

ABOVE LEFT Gamers Bar Lettuce. ABOVE One of the many board games at Conyotto (Game Café). RIGHT Moe Café & Bar Yurufawa

## Game Bars

### 13 Famicon Generation

ファミコン ジェネレーション

They have old Famicon and Super Famicon games to Nintendo 64, Wii, and PlayStation. The 3,000 yen-per-2-hours plan (plus 500 yen for every 30-minute extension) includes all-you-can-consume dagashi snacks. **Hours:** *20:00–3:00; closed Sundays* **Access:** *B1F, Minami 6-jo Nishi 3-chome, Chuo-ku, Sapporo (a one-minute walk from Hosui-Susukino Station exit 6, Sapporo Metro Toho Line)* **famicom-generation.com**

### 13 Gamers Bar Lettuce 702

In the same building as Famicon Generation (see above). Its main focus is fighting games, but you can bring your own stuff with you.

**Hours:** *17:30~ (Tue–Fri), 14:00–23:30 (weekends and national holidays); closed Mondays* **Access:** *4F, Minami 6-jo Nishi 3-chome, Chuo-ku, Sapporo* **lettuce702.versus.jp**

## Tokusatsu Bars

### 14 Tokusatsu Bar Marbleland

超電導まぁぶるらんど

Houses a collection of toys, figures, *chogokin* and robots, including rarities. Its main focus is *tokusatsu* (special-effects movies). The all-you-can-drink fee is 2,500 yen per 90 minutes; otherwise, there's a time system.

**Hours:** *19:00–2:00 (weekdays), 19:00–6:00 (Saturdays), 19:00–23:00 (Sundays and national holidays)* **Access:** *7F, Minami 4-jo Nishi 3-2-7, Chuo-ku, Sapporo (next to Susukino Station exit 3, Sapporo Metro Nanboku Line)* **marblel.com**

BELOW Enjoy all-you-can-drink and all-you-can-sing packages at Shangri-La.

## Board Game Cafés and Spaces

### 15 Conyotto (Game Café)

かくれがゲームカフェ こにょっと

Hundreds of board games, TRPGs (tactical role-playing games), Mafia, etc. You can bring your own food with you, but you have to buy drinks on the spot (one 300–500-yen order minimum, plus the admission fee). **Admission fee:** *700 yen (Mon–Thu), 800 yen (Fri–Sun and national holidays)* **Hours:** *17:00–23:30 (weekdays), 13:00–17:00, 17:30–23:30 (weekends and national holidays)* **Access:** *2F, Minami 3-jo Nishi 2-7, Chuo-ku (five minutes' walk from Sapporo Metro Odori Station)* **conyotto.jp**

### Friends

**Admission fee:** *500 yen (3 hours), 1,000 yen (all day)* **Hours:** *12:00–23:00* **Access:** *2F, Minami 1-jo Higashi 2-1-3 (five minutes' walk from Sapporo Metro Bus Center-mae Station; see website for detailed photo directions)* **friendsjp22061.wixsite.com/mysite**

## Maid and Butler Cafés

### 16 Romeo Giulietta

ロメオクロスジュリエッタ

**Admission fee:** *Café time table charge is 300 yen per 30 minutes; bar time (22:00~) charge is 400 yen per 30 minutes; all-you-can-drink is 2,500 yen per 90 minutes.* **Hours:** *17:00–1:00 (Mon–Thu), 17:00–3:00 (Fri–Sat), 14:00–1:00 (Sundays and national holidays)* **Access:** *3F, Minami 3-jo Nishi 4-3-4 (two minutes' walk from Susukino Station, Sapporo Metro Nanboku Line)* **www.romegiulie.com**

### 17 Moe Café & Bar Yurufuwa

萌えカフェ&バーゆるふわ

**Admission fee:** *Café time table charge: 300 yen per 30 minutes for guys; 150 yen per 30 minutes for gals; night-time table charge: 400 yen per 30 minutes for guys; 200 yen per 30 minutes for gals.* **Hours:** *16:00–3:00 (weekdays), 14:00–3:00 (Saturdays and national holidays), 14:00–21:00 (Sundays)* **Access:** *4F, Minami 4-jo Nishi 5-chome, Chuo-ku (a one-minute walk from Susukino Station, Sapporo Metro Nanboku Line)* **yurufuwa.net**

### 18 Antique Café / Steward Antique Café

On Wednesdays and Saturdays, maids are replaced by butlers, some of whom are *danso* (girls disguised as boys). **Admission fee:** *Café time (14:00–20:00) table charge: 300 yen per 30 minutes for guys, 200 yen per 30 minutes for gals; bar time (20:00–23:00) table charge: 400 yen per 30 minutes for guys, 300 yen per 30 minutes for gals.* **Hours:** *14:00–23:00* **Access:** *4F, Minami 3-jo Nishi 2-chome, Chuo-ku (five minutes' walk from Susukino Station, Sapporo Metro Nanboku Line)* **cafe-antiquecafe.com**

# Hokkaido Museums

**Manga Museum of Art (Culture Center TOM) 漫画美術館（文化センターTOM）**
This tiny but interesting museum is located in Yubari, a small town facing the frigid Sea of Okhotsk. It boasts a collection of about 500 original pictures (displayed on rotation). Hokkaido-born Monkey Punch (*Lupin III*) and Igarashi Yumiko (*Candy Candy*) are particularly well represented, but you will also find many other popular artists such as Ishinomori Shotaro, Taniguchi Jiro, Aoyama Gosho and Satonaka Machiko. Don't miss the corner where Igarashi's creation of *Candy Candy* is explained through pictures. The museum features work by local artists as well.

Not far from TOM, Furusato-kan JRY (ふるさと館JRY) is well worth a visit. This museum details the history and daily life of the *tondenhei*, the military settler colonists that defended Japan's northern frontier in the Meiji period. One such character is featured in Rurouni Kenshin.

**Admission fee:** ***Free*** **Hours:** ***9:00–17:00; closed Mondays and holidays*** **Access:** ***Nakamachi, Naka-Yubetsu, Yubetsu-cho***
**town.yubetsu.lg.jp/60kanko/03annai/tom_jry.html**

**(2•4) Monkey Punch Collection**
Monkey Punch (whose real name is Kato Kazuhiko) lived in Hamanaka, in eastern Hokkaido, until he finished high school; he then moved to Tokyo, where he would become internationally famous for his bestselling manga *Lupin III*. The town itself became the set for Lupin's 2007 TV anime special *Elusiveness of the Fog*. This museum, located inside the Hamanaka-cho Culture Center (浜中町総合文化センター), displays a wide range of manuscripts, sketches, original art, the artist's favorite drawing tools and even life-size figures of Lupin and Jigen (perfect for taking souvenir photos). Hamanaka has much more to offer Lupin fans: along Lupin the Third Street, for instance, you'll find giant billboards advertising such imaginary places as Jigen's Bar, the Kiritappu Theater, and Pub Fujiko ("only Lupin is welcome"). Also, some local buses and trains are decorated with Monkey Punch's characters. If you're going to Hamanaka through Kushiro, don't miss a chance to take the JR Hokkaido Hanasaki Line (running between Kushiro and Nemuro). You can check the timetable for the one-car Lupin train timetable at jrhokkaido.co.jp/travel/lupin. For the Lupin bus (Kushiro Bus Kiritappu Line and Hamanaka Line), see kushirobus.jp/index.html.

**Admission fee:** ***Free*** **Hours:** ***9:00–18:00; closed Mondays*** **Access:** ***1-47 3-jo Kiritappu-Nishi, Hamanaka-cho***
**hamanaka-lupin.com/mpcollection**

Exhibits at the Monkey Punch Collection, located inside the Hamanaka-cho Culture Center.

**(2) Ooba Hiroshi Memorial Space おおば比呂司記念室**
Completed in 1926, the majestic Sapporo City Museum is a Western-style building located at the edge of the elegant Oodori Park. Formerly the Sapporo Court of Appeals, it is now devoted to a number of cultural activities, and houses an exhibition space devoted to Sapporo-born manga artist and illustrator Ooba Hiroshi. About 200 original drawings are rotated regularly. You can also buy postcards and original goods and see a reproduction of his study. If you enjoy flowers, try to visit when the roses in Oodori Park are in full bloom.

**Admission fee:** ***Free*** **Hours:** ***9:00–19:00; closed Mondays and from 12/29 to 1/3*** **Access:** ***13 Oodori-Nishi, Chuo-ku, Sapporo***
**s-shiryokan.jp/floor/o-ba.htm**

**LEFT** The Manga Museum of Art in Culture Center TOM. **RIGHT** Exhibits at the Ooba Hiroshi Memorial Space.

# Hokkaido Festivals and Events

### Snow Miku Festival

Sapporo is the birthplace of Vocaloid software voicebank persona Hatsune Miku. The city didn't waste any time forging a strong relationship with the virtual idol, even going so far as to commission a winter-themed version of her image, called Snow Miku (雪ミク), for its famous Snow Festival in 2010.

Snow Miku's design is said to be based on "a pure white snow Miku sculpture," and her costumes are selected every year through an online competition.

Several Miku-related events are held for about one week in the area south of Sapporo Station: apart from the Snow Festival at Odori Park, the Sapporo beer factory hosts exhibitions, stage events, workshops, stalls selling goods and company booths, while Miku's virtual concerts take place at Zapp Sapporo; other special events are held at the Sapporo Maruyama Zoo. And if you visit Sapporo between the end of November and the end of March, don't miss the chance to ride the Snow Miku streetcar.

**Admission Fee:** *Fees depend on the event; check the Japanese website for details* **Dates:** *February* **Hours:** *10:00–20:00* **Access:** *See the locations on the event map* **snowmiku.com**

LEFT Images of Snow Miku at the Snow Miku Festival, held every February in the area south of Sapporo Station.

### Toyako Manga Anime Festa

One of Japan's major otaku festivals—it regularly attracts more than 50,000 fans—takes place on the shore of Lake Toya, which is famous for its hot springs and for hosting a G8 summit in 2008. The festival is an all-genre free-for-all featuring *anison* events, stage performances, art exhibitions, public lectures, a *dojin* market, *itasha* displays and several cosplay events, including a contest and even a disco night. Cosplayers are everywhere, using the beautiful natural environment as a background for their photo shoots. Even the staff at the local post office (kept open during the weekend of the festival) seem to participate in the cosplaying.

**Admission fee:** *1,200 yen* **Dates:** *June* **Hours:** *See website* **Access:** *Toyako Bunka Center and other venues around Toyako Onsen. Toya Station is a two-hour train ride from Sapporo. From the station, take a bus to Toyako Onsen (25 minutes). Or you can take a special shuttle bus from Sapporo; see website for details.* **tmaf.toyako-prj.net**

### Lupin III Festival in Hamanakacho

Since 2012, this festival has celebrated the eastern Hokkaido city's connection with Lupin and its creator through exhibitions, talk shows, film screenings and other live and stage events.

If you are a connoisseur of fish, don't miss the much older Kiritappu Cape Festival きりたっぷ岬まつり that's held on the same day. Here's your chance to taste such local delicacies as salmon, mackerel and sea urchin while enjoying more Lupin-related events.

**Admission fee:** *Free* **Dates:** *September* **Hours:** *10:00–17:00* **Access:** *Hamanaka-cho Sogo Bunka Center and other venues around town (check the website for details)* **hamanaka-lupin.com/festival**

The Lupin III Festival has exhibitions, talk shows, film screenings and other live events.

# EXPLORING TOHOKU

Otaku shops are scarce in this region. Sendai (Tohoku's biggest city) has several chain stores and even a few interesting independent shops. The only big company that seems to be ubiquitous in Tohoku is Animate. Same thing for events: the most you can find is some small *dojinshi* fairs. On the other hand, you'll find several unique museums that should be included in your otaku tour of Japan—a possible modest contribution to a Tohoku renaissance!

## Sendai, Miyagi Prefecture

### General

**Abe Mokei** アベ模型
Opened in 1948 as an electronics store, Abe has gradually changed its focus and now sells minicars and model trains. Nice retro atmosphere.
**Hours:** *10:00–19:30; closed Mondays* **Access:** *4-9-18 Ichibancho, Aoba-ku (three minutes' walk from Kotodai Koen Station, Nanboku subway line)* **abemokei.com**

**BELOW** Maple wig shop sells wigs exclusively. **FAR RIGHT** G Taisau Honbu specializes in Godzilla merchandise.

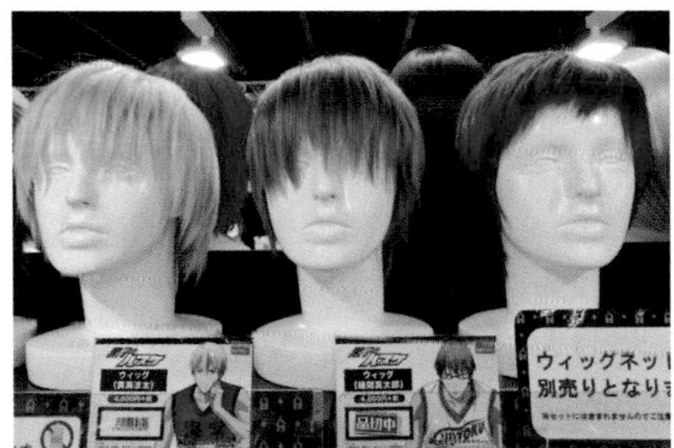

**G Taisaku Honbu** G対策本部
What's the best way to manage your fever for collecting figures? Why, open a store! That's exactly what this guy did. *Taisaku honbu* means "task force" or "emergency headquarters"; the G stands for our favorite *kaiju*. Here you'll find Gojira & co., lots of Gundams, giant robots and cute girls. The shop is a little hard to find—look for the blue COSME DECORTE sign next to the soba joint.
**Hours:** *10:30–19:30* **Access:** *4-5-18 Ichibancho, Aoba-ku (five minutes' walk from Kotodai Koen Station, Nanboku subway line)*

**Game Soft Shop SEAGULL** シーガル
Seagull has 10 branches in Miyagi (six of them in Sendai) and three in Yamagata, open 10:00 to 22:00 or 23:00. There's one in front of JR Sendai Station (3F, 3-6-7 Chuo, Aoba-ku) but it only deals in TCG. For game software, try the one near Nagamachi-Itchome Station on the Nanboku subway line (1-4-2 Nagamachi, Taihaku-ku).
**Access:** *You can get the addresses of all their stores online (Japanese only, sorry)* **seagull-jp.com/shop.htm**

**Maple** メイプル
This wig shop sells wigs exclusively—both the fashion and cosplay variety (see photo at right).
**Hours:** *10:00–20:00* **Access:** *B1F, 4-1-1 Chuo, Aoba-ku (6 minutes' walk from JR Sendai Stn)* **maple-wig.com/fas/shop/sendai.php**

**Santy**
Anime-themed souvenirs and otaku goods (video games, trading cards).
**Hours:** *10:00–19:00; closed Saturdays and Sundays* **Access:** *3-9-23 Chuo, Aoba-ku (seven minutes' walk from JR Sendai Station)* **twitter.com/santycrissroad**

### Chain Stores

The usual otaku chain stores are all represented in Sendai, including **Animate, C-Labo, Gamers, Lashinbang, Melonbooks, Toranoana, Volks.**

## Fukushima Prefecture

**10 Sukagawa,* Nebula M78's sister city**
Sukagawa is the birthplace of Tsuburaya Eiji, world-famous special-effects director, who in 1954 co-created the *Godzilla* series, and in 1966 launched the *tokusatsu* sci-fi TV series *Ultraman*.

In 2013, Sukagawa became a sister city to Nebula M78, the "Land of Light" and Ultraman's home planet, installing

a monument to the alien hero in front of Sukagawa Station, along with 11 more statues along Shin-Machi Kaido, which starts in front of the station. The statues are along a 1-mile (1.5-km) stretch of road—a long walk down an otherwise unremarkable street.

The highlight of such an outing is **SHOT M78**, an official Ultraman store run by Tsuburaya Makoto, who is the son of a cousin of Tsuburaya himself. Here you can admire various items of memorabilia (e.g., the director's 8-mm movie cameras, letters and a diorama of Tsuburaya Studios) plus the usual Ultraman merchandise.

The city is also planning to open a **Tsuburaya Eiji Museum** inside the Citizens' Culture Center (still under construction at the time of writing). One thing you can already enjoy is the **Ultra Family Great Gathering in Sukagawa**, a two-day event which attracts 5,000 fans annually.

### SHOT M78

**Hours:** *10:00–17:00; closed Tuesdays* **Access:** *14 Nakamachi (5-minute taxi ride from JR Sukagawa Station)* **m78shop.jimdo.com**

### Ultra Family Great Gathering in Sukagawa ウルトラファミリー大集合in すかがわ

**Admission fee:** *3,500 yen (free for ages two and younger)* **Dates:** *April* **Hours:** *10:30~* **Access:** *Sukagawa Culture Center (須賀川市文化センター), 11 Ushibukuro-machi (an eight-minute taxi ride from JR Sukagawa Station)* **m-78.jp/ulfami**

### Sukagawa's M78 City of Light Official Site

Anyone can register as a resident of Sukagawa's M78 City of Light. Residents can get a resident certificate with their address in the City of Light (for a fee) and enjoy the privilege of viewing original content. The city also issues Ultraman-themed license plates for cars and bikes. **m78-sukagawa.jp**

## Tohoku Festivals and Events

These are some of the main long-running otaku events in the Tohoku region. They are all *dojin* or cosplay events.

Tohoku hosts a variety of otaku events, including CRUSH (ABOVE), Carvil Sole Smak (LEFT), and Pop Cult Unfold (BELOW).

### Aomori

**Pop Cult Unfold**

**Admission fee:** *500 yen* **Dates:** *Check website* **Hours:** *11:00–15:00* **Access:** *1F Yutori ユートリー (Hachinohe Chiiki Jiba Sangyo Shinko Center 地域地場産業振興センター) 1-9-22 Ichibancho, Hachinohe (a two-minute-walk from JR Hachinohe Station east exit)* **pcus.web.fc2.com**

### Iwate

**CRUSH**

**Admission fee:** *300 yen* **Dates:** *March, July and December* **Hours:** *10:30–15:00* **Access:** *Oshu-shi Bunka Kaikan奥州市文化会館, 41 Ishibashi, Sakurakawa, Mizusawa-ku, Oshu (10 minutes' walk from JR Mizusawa Station, Tohoku Main Line)* **cmcrush.net**

### Miyagi

**Mori no Kiseki** 杜の軌跡

While the all-genre Mori no Kiseki is the headliner, there are actually two other fairs going on in the same place: the Toho Project–only Toho Tokyoso and the Kantai Collection–themed Teitoku to Zuruyasumi.

**Admission fee:** *500 yen* **Dates:** *May* **Hours:** *11:00–15:00* **Access:** *Sendai-shi Chusho Kigyou Kasseika Center 仙台市中小企業活性化センター, 1-3-1 Chuo, Aoba-ku, Sendai (two minutes from JR Sendai Station west exit)* **mori-kiseki.com**

### Yamagata

**Carvil Sole Smak**

**Admission fee:** *300 yen* **Dates:** *August* **Hours:** *11:00~* **Access:** *Sakata Kinrosha Fukushi Center 酒田勤労者福祉センター, 19-10 Midori-cho, Sakata* **carvilsole.chu.jp**

### Fukushima

**Adventures**

**Admission fee:** *500 yen* **Dates:** *Check website* **Hours:** *11:00–15:00* **Access:** *Apio Space アピオスペース Aizu Wakamatsu (a ten-minute taxi ride from JR Aizu Wakamatsu Station)* **adv-kikaku.com**

# Tohoku Museums and Libraries

## Akita Prefecture

**1 (1•2) Yokote City Masuda Manga Museum*** 横手市増田まんが美術館
This is the first manga museum ever opened in Japan. Though mainly devoted to Yokote-born Yaguchi Takao (the author of the popular fishing- and nature-themed *Tsurikichi Sanpei*), whose workspace has been recreated at the entrance, the place regularly showcases the work of other Japanese and international comic artists (see the excellent English site for a detailed event history). The permanent collection alone features original art by about 100 *mangaka*. You can also spend the whole day reading comic books and magazines in its 25,000-volume library. Amazingly, a huge tree stands in the middle of the first floor.
**Admission fee:** *Free (special exhibitions require a fee)* **Hours:** *19:00–17:00; closed Mondays* **Access:** *285 Shinmachi, Masuda-aza, Masuda-cho, Yokote-shi*
**manga-museum.com/en** *(English)*

## Yamagata Prefecture

**2 Shinjo Mogami Manga Museum**
新庄最上漫画ミュージアム
One of the newest manga museums in Japan (it opened in 2016) collects original art by a handful of artists who grew up or have some kind of relationship with the city of Shinjo. The most famous of the bunch are Togashi Yoshihiro (author of the bestselling *Hunter x Hunter*) and Umino Chika (*Honey and Clover*, *March Comes in Like a Lion*).
**Admission fee:** *Free* **Hours:** *19:00–18:00; closed the second and fourth Mondays of every month and from 12/31 to 1/1* **Access:** *1-2 Tamonmachi, Shinjo-shi* **smmm.jp**

## Miyagi Prefecture

**3 Ishinomori Mangattan Museum***
石ノ森萬画館
One of the true greats of manga, Ishinomori Shotaro has left his mark on Japanese comics, anime and *tokusatsu* with such hugely popular works as *Cyborg 009*, *Kamen Rider*, and the *Super Sentai* series. Opened in 2001 (three years after the artist's untimely death) the **Mangattan Museum** (as it's also known) was designed by Ishinomori himself to resemble a spaceship. Besides permanent and special exhibitions, the museum boasts an anime theater, manga and video libraries and a multimedia studio where visitors can experience the creation of anime. For further details, check out the excellent English website.
**Admission fee:** *800 yen (adults), 500 yen (junior and senior high school students), 200 yen (elementary school students)*
**Hours:** *(Mar–Nov) 9:00–18:00; closed the third Tuesday of every month; (Dec–Feb) 9:00–17:00; closed Tuesdays* **Access:** *2-7 Nakaze, Ishinomaki-shi*
**mangattan.jp/manga/en** *(English)*

**4 Ishinomori Shotaro Memorial Museum** 石ノ森章太郎ふるさと記念館
If you're a hardcore Ishinomori fan, you may want to combine a visit to the Mangattan (see above) with this smaller but fascinating Memorial Museum. There are two art galleries, figure displays, a video theater, and even a reproduction of Ishinomori's room at Tokiwaso in Tokyo. The house where he was born is nearby; you can visit that, too.
**Admission fee:** *500 yen (300 yen for junior and senior high school students; 100 yen for elementary school students)*
**Hours:** *9:30–17:00 (9:00–18:00 in July and August); closed Mondays and from 12/29 to 1/3* **Access:** *132 Nakada-cho Ishinomori, Tome-shi* **city.tome.miyagi.jp/kinenkan**

**LEFT** Ishinomori Shotaru Memorial Museum **BELOW** (and inset) Shinjo Mogami Manga Museum **RIGHT** (top and bottom) Ishinomori Mangattan Museum.

**ABOVE** Nagai Katsuichi Manga Museum.
**LEFT** Yokote City Masuma Manga Museum.

### 5 Nagai Katsuichi Manga Museum

長井勝一漫画美術館

One of the spaces inside the Fureai ESP culture center in the city of Shiogama celebrates the work of Nagai Katsuichi, the "god of editors." Nagai is famous for creating *Garo*, a monthly manga magazine that featured a group of wonderfully talented and original artists including Shirato Sanpei, Mizuki Shigeru, Tsuge Yoshiharu, Tatsumi Yoshihiro and Maruo Suehiro. Launched in 1964 with just 8,000 copies per issue, the magazine became so popular that its circulation quickly shot up to 80,000.

A lot of *Garo*-related items are on display, including original drawings that were used in the magazine, a wall full of *Garo* cover art, and hand-drawn New Year's cards Nagai received from his contributors. Nagai's rather modest working desk and a reading corner with several rare manga complete this small but interesting museum.

**Admission fee:** *Free* **Hours:** *10:00–18:00 (weekdays), 10:00–17:00 (weekends); closed Mondays and from 12/28 to 1/4*
**Access:** *9-1 Higashi Tamagawa-cho, Shiogama-shi*

## Fukushima Prefecture

### 6 Showa Mangakan Aomushi

昭和漫画館青虫

One of the best-kept secrets for fans of classic manga can be found in the deep Fukushima countryside, about a ten-minute walk from Tadami Station (JR Tadami Line). This white wooden building used to be a church and kindergarten, but now houses a 20,000-volume comic-book collection—mostly out-of-print jewels from the Golden Age of manga (mid-1945–1965). This is arguably the biggest open-stack manga library in Japan. Because of heavy snow from late fall to early spring, the place is only open from May through the end of October. For 500 yen per hour you can read all the manga you want (only the more delicate items are kept under glass) and check out old toys and figures. All-you-can-drink coffee and tea are included.

**Admission fee:** *500 yen per hour (adults), 300 yen per hour (under 18 years old)*
**Hours:** *12:00–17:00; only open Fri–Sun and holidays; closed November through April*
**Access:** *1085 Azatanaka, Oaza Tadami, Tadami-machi, Minami Aizu-gun*
**www16.plala.or.jp/aomusi-0064/index.html**

### 7 Tominaga Ichiro Mangaro

富永一朗・はなわ漫画廊

This small gallery shows the works that manga artist Tominaga Ichiro donated to the city of Hanawa.

**Admission fee:** *Free* **Hours:** *9:00–17:30; closed on the third Sunday of every month and from 12/31 to 1/1* **Access:** *Hanawa-machi Community Plaza, Hanawa-machi, Higashi Shirakawa-gun* **hanawa-kanko.com/spot/38**

## 8 Licca-chan Castle リカちゃんキャッスル

Licca-chan is more than 50 years old, but she certainly doesn't look her age. Born in 1967 as the local answer to Barbie, she was the doll every single little girl in Japan had—or wanted to have—back in the day. Nowadays she might not be the undisputed queen of Japanese dolls (in the last 20 years her rule has been challenged by Volks's Dollfie army), but she's still going strong. And if you're a hardcore fan or are into dolls, a visit to her kingdom is de rigueur.

First opened in 1993 on the site of a Takara factory, her castle was renovated in 2013. The factory is actually still there. It's off limits, of course, but visitors can see the dolls being made from a viewing balcony on the second floor. On the same floor there is a museum chronicling the doll's evolution and displaying all the accessories and furniture a dedicated Licca owner is supposed to have. Here you also get to meet her lesser-known family members and friends, if you're not already acquainted with her inner circle. Another area showcases her gorgeous playhouses, while in the World Travel corner, kids can have their picture taken wearing a Licca-chan dress.

For many people, the best part of the visit is the shop on the first floor. Everything Licca is on sale here. If you're a Licca fan, you'll probably have a heart attack. Be sure to bring lots of money with you.

But what if you happen to visit with a bored, cranky boy in tow? No problem: there's a corner where he can play with Takara Tomi's famous Plarail toy trains.

**Admission fee:** *800 yen (600 yen for kids 2 to 14 years old; free for those under 2)* **Hours:** *10:00–16:00; closed Mondays and at the end of the year* **Access:** *51-3 Ono-niimachi-nakadori, Ono-machi, Tamura-gun* **liccacastle.co.jp**

Note: If you can't make the trip to the Castle, you can still satisfy your Licca-related cravings at the **Licca Castle Small Shop Tokyo**. Branded as a "doll shop for adults," it's a boutique selling all sorts of clothes and accessories, including original items you can only find here. They sell Licca dolls, too.

**Hours:** *12:00–20:00; closed Mondays*
**Access:** *B1 J Square Bldg., 18-10 Nihonbashi Koami-cho, Chuo-ku, Tokyo*
**liccacastle.co.jp/lcshop**

# EXPLORING NAGOYA

*Dragon Ball* author Toriyama Akira is from Nagoya, and the original *Mobile Suit Gundam* (1979–1980) was first aired on Nagoya TV. Despite these otaku credentials, Nagoya doesn't have a great reputation with the Japanese. Although it's big (Japan's fourth-largest city), it looks anonymous and unimpressive. Mainly known for industry, it is said to lack character—there's nothing here comparable to the cultural charms of Tokyo, Yokohama, Osaka or Kyoto.

But this region played a fundamental role in Japan's history—key figures like Oda Nobunaga, Toyotomi Hideyoshi and Tokugawa Ieyasu were born in or around Nagoya. People also praise the city's livability, and visitors can appreciate the wide streets and rational layout that make the city less overwhelming than Osaka or Tokyo.

Otaku-wise, Nagoya can hold her own. The **Osu** district is not as famous as Akihabara, but has plenty to offer, and rivals Osaka's Den Den Town in terms of otaku shops. Originally a religious center sandwiched between Osu Kannon and Banshoji temples, today this area is a popular commercial district with several shopping streets selling everything from food to fashion and computer parts.

Osu's transformation into an otaku town started in the 1980s with the completion of the first **Ameyoko Building,** which sold (and still sells) audio and electronic parts. The new scene developed around Shintenchi-dori and Akamon-dori, where digital and entertainment mall **GoodWill** opened in 1989, creating a new appetite for personal computers and video games. Figure and toy stores (such as **Spanky**, **Stale** and **Volks**) came along in the late 90s, while one of Japan's first maid cafés, *M's Melody*, opened in the basement of GoodWill in 2002, pioneering the characteristic way of greeting customers, instant photo-taking, and "graduation ceremonies" for retiring maids. The café closed in July 2018, but all those features have now become standard practice in maid cafés across Japan.

Finally, in 2003, Osu became the site of the **World Cosplay Summit**, now one of Japan's biggest otaku events, which has made Nagoya the cosplay capital of the world. The Summit is so well regarded by the locals that Aichi prefecture governor Omura Hideaki often shows up in a costume (in 2018 he was Kirito from *Sword Art Online*).

Osu is not the only otaku area. There used to be many shops near Sakae Station, to the north of Osu. When the otaku boom took off in the second half of the 2000s, many of them—including **Mandarake** and **Gamers**—moved to Osu. But a few stores still remain in Sakae: **Jump Shop** (*Jump* magazine-related character goods), **Pokemon Center**, **Donguri Kyowakoku** (Ghibli

Gamestore Banesto is a must for board-game lovers.

TOP Nagoya Castle. LEFT Inside the Ameyoko Building. ABOVE and RIGHT Tamagotchi Department Store.

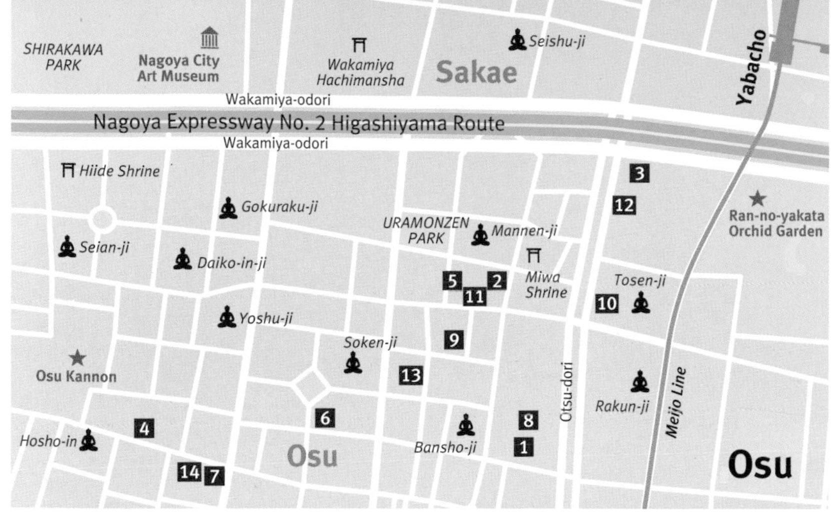


products) and **Tamagotchi Department Store** are in shopping complex Oasis 21 (1-11-1 Higashi-Sakura, Higashi-ku) next to Sakae Station (Higashiyama and Meijo subway lines): They are open from 10:00–20:00.

Last but not least, a third group of major chain stores (including Japan's biggest Toranoana branch) is located five minutes from Nagoya Station.

**Acos** *(12:00–20:00) 3F 21-2 Tsubakicho*
**Animate** *(10:00–20:30) 18-4 Tsubakicho*
**K-Books** *(12:00–20:00) 21-5 Tsubakicho*
**Melonbooks** *(10:00–21:00) 21-2 Tsubakicho*
**Toranoana** *(10:00–21:00) 22-2 Tsubakicho*

On the other side of the street there are also three maid cafés:
**Palette Maid Café** *(12:00–23:00)*

**Witches Ark** *(Mon-Fri: 17:00–23:00; weekends: 11:00–23:00)*

**Café de la Bonne** *(Mon–Tues, Thu: 18:00–23:00; Wed and Sun: 12:00–23:00; Fri–Sat: 12:00–6:00)*

# Osu Shops

## General

### 1 Amenity Dream

One of the best trading-card shops in Nagoya, with a large, well-organized selection and some of the best prices on booster packs in the city. They have a wide variety of related products such as card boxes and protectors. There's a large playing space where they hold weekly and monthly tournaments.
**Hours:** *12:00–21:00 (weekdays), 11:00–20:00 (weekends and national holidays)*
**Access:** *2F, 3-30-60 Osu, Naka-ku (five minutes' walk from Kamimaezu Station, Tsurumai subway line)*
**amenitydream.co.jp/shop/aichi-osu**

### 2 Art Jeuness

Event space holding otaku art exhibitions. Check their website for info.
**Hours:** *11:00–19:00* **Access:** *3-11-19 Osu, Naka-ku (seven minutes' walk from Kamimaezu Station, Tsurumai subway line)*
**artjeuness.net/gallery/nagoya**

### 3 Big Magic

This trading-card store has a large stock, regularly updates its selling prices, holds the biggest tournaments (high-level competition) and has the best prizes (packs, play mats, card boxes, etc). It also has a great assortment of English cards. Most of the playing is on Wednesdays.
**Hours:** *13:00–21:00 (Mon, Wed–Fri), 10:00–21:00 (weekends); closed Tuesdays*
**Access:** *2F, 4-1-3 Osu, Naka-ku (five minutes' walk from Yabacho Station, Meijo subway line)*
**bigmagic.net/nagoya.html**

### 4 Darumaya だるまや

The godfather of Osu toy stores opened in 1916, long before the otaku boom, and is still located inside the covered shopping street to the right of Osu Kannon. Before you enter, stop to admire the Kamen Rider billboard from the early 1970s. The shop sells dolls, plushies, figures, trading cards, etc., with a few traditional items, like toy swords, Japanese dolls and even the *daruma* dolls that give the shop its name.
**Hours:** *10:00–19:00; closed Wednesdays*
**Access:** *2-18-41 Osu, Naka-ku (five minutes' walk from Osu Kannon Station, Tsurumai subway line)* **darumaya-toys.com**

### 5 Hobby Station

While this trading card shop doesn't have as many cards as Amenity Dream, they almost have the same amount of playing space, and encourage you to bring your DS and PSP systems and play video games as well as trading-card games.
**Hours:** *11:00–21:00* **Access:** *4F, 3-11-34 Osu, Naka-ku (eight minutes' walk from either Osu Kannon or Kamimaezu station, Tsurumai subway line)* **hbst.net/shop/nagoya**

### 6 Spanky

A prime mover of the Osu otaku scene, Spanky started with classic US toys but now has cool indie *sofubi*, Blythe dolls, and its own original toy line.
**Hours:** *11:00–20:00; closed Wednesdays and the second and third Thursday of the month*
**Access:** *3-26-39 Osu, Naka-ku (seven minutes' walk from either Osu Kannon or Kamimaezu station, Tsurumai subway line)*
**spanky.shop-pro.jp**

Darumaya, the godfather of Osu toy stores, was established in 1916.

FAR LEFT Stale. LEFT Pokemon Center. ABOVE Spanky. BOTTOM Wondergoo.

**7** **Stale**
Don't let the fake Louis Vuitton logo and interior decor throw you: this is a great place for Japanese figures, vintage US toys, and *gachapon*.
**Hours:** *11:00–20:00* **Access:** *2-30-14 Osu, Naka-ku (seven minutes' walk from either Osu Kannon or Kamimaezu station, Tsurumai subway line)* **stale.jp**

**5** **Wondergoo**
The first floor is entirely devoted to manga; the second to anime and *anison* CDs and DVDs, and character goods; while the third has anime-related products and cosplay goods.
**Hours:** *11:00–21:00* **Access:** *3-11-34 Osu, Naka-ku (eight minutes' walk from either Osu Kannon or Kamimaezu station, Tsurumai subway line)*

## Chain Stores

**8** **Gamers**
**Hours:** *10:00–20:00* **Access:** *3-30-40 Osu, Naka-ku (four minutes' walk from Kamimaezu Station, Tsurumai subway line)*

**5** **Gee! Store**
**Hours:** *10:00–21:00* **Access:** *3-11-34 Osu, Naka-ku (eight minutes' walk from either Osu Kannon or Kamimaezu station, Tsurumai subway line)*

**9** **Mandarake**
**Hours:** *12:00–20:00* **Access:** *3-18-21 Osu, Naka-ku (seven minutes' walk from Kamimaezu station, Tsurumai subway line)*

**10** **Super Kids Land**
**Hours:** *10:00–20:00* **Access:** *4-2-48 Osu, Naka-ku (six minutes' walk from Kamimaezu Station, Tsurumai subway line)*

**11** **Super Potato**
**Hours:** *10:00-20:00* **Access:** *3-11-30 Osu, Naka-ku (seven minutes' walk from Kamimaezu Station, Tsurumai subway line)*

**12** **Volks**
**Hours:** *10:00–20:00* **Access:** *2F, 4-1-71 Osu, Naka-ku (five minutes' walk from Yabacho Station, Meijo subway line)*

**2** **Yellow Submarine**
**Hours:** *12:00–21:00 (weekdays), 11:00–20:00 (weekends and national holidays)* **Access:** *6F, 3-11-9 Osu, Naka-ku (five minutes' walk from Kamimaezu Station, Tsurumai subway line)*

## Other Shops in Nagoya

**Gamestore Banesto**
Tiny Banesto stocks some 800 board games at good prices including German and UK imports and even some games that are out of production and hard to find. The owner is a very nice guy who speaks some English.
**Hours:** *12:00–21:00 (weekdays), 12:00–18:00 (weekends and national holidays)* **Access:** *4-15 Nishishiga-cho, Kita-ku (nine minutes' walk from Kurokawa Station, Meijo subway line)*
**banesto.nagoya**

**Mishimaya Toy and Hobby** 美嶋屋
Mom-and-pop trading card shop with the best deals for single cards in Nagoya. They also sell booster packs of recent sets at competitive prices. Check their Twitter for tournament news.
**Hours:** *13:00–21:00 (weekdays except Wednesdays), 10:00–21:00 (weekends); closed Wednesdays and the first and second Thursday of every month* **Access:** *3-6-3 Ozone, Kita-ku (four minutes' walk from Ozone Station, JR Chuo and Meijo subway lines)*
**w01.tp1.jp/~sr08229403/index.htm**

## Sunshine Sakae Theater

SKE48 is one of the many sister-groups of hugely popular AKB48; their home base is Sunshine Sakae (SKE stands for Sakae). Stage shows are held weekly, but even when the girls aren't in the house, fans can see other idol groups—or dance in front of a large screen inside the theater building showing SKE48 performances. The theater itself is on the first floor, while the **SKE48 Café & Shop with AKB48** is on the fifth floor (open 11:00–23:00; on Sundays it closes at 22:00).
**Access:** *3-24-4 Nishiki, Naka-ku (next to Nagoya Metro Sakae Station exit 8, Higashiyama and Meijo lines)*
**sunshine-sakae.jp**

# World Cosplay Summit*

Nagoya has become a mecca for cosplayers, and if you want to experience the ultimate cosplay festival, you should make a point of visiting the World Cosplay Summit (WCS) at least once in your life.

Originally created in 2003 by local broadcaster TV Aichi, the WCS rapidly gained so much popularity worldwide (recent editions have attracted hundreds of thousands of fans) that even a few ministries of the Japanese government now support the event.

A team competition (the Championship) was added in 2005; the most recent contest included 36 countries from four continents. Italy and Brazil lead the cosplay nations with three wins each.

There are numerous prizes to be won at this competition, with the best overall team being awarded the title of World Cosplay Summit Grand Champion. A panel of manga and anime artists, voice actors, *anison* singers and the previous year's winners judge contestants on criteria such as costume craftsmanship and faithfulness to the original, stage performance, and overall impact.

Obviously, all costumes must be handmade, and must faithfully copy manga, anime, video-game or graphic-novel characters. Original *dojin* characters and—thank god—Disney or Star Wars costumes are not allowed. (This is Japan, after all.)

But the WCS is not only about the competition. The week-long festival includes stage performances, photo shoots, concerts, meetups, and plenty of parties.

On the first day, for instance, a big event is held at the Laguna Ten Bosch resort (a one-hour train ride from Nagoya Station; lagunatenbosch.co.jp/laguna/english/index.html) that starts at 10:00 am and goes on nonstop until 6:00 am the next day. Then the cosplay carnival moves to the Meiji Mura architectural museum (one hour by train; meijimura.com/english) and a wedding hall; on the last day the event comes to a climax with the parade in Nagoya's Osu district and the Championship at the Dolphins Arena.

**Admission fee:** *2,000 yen (Championship)* **Dates:** *July–August* **Hours:** *15:00 (Championship)* **Access:** *See website for information on all events*
**worldcosplaysummit.jp**

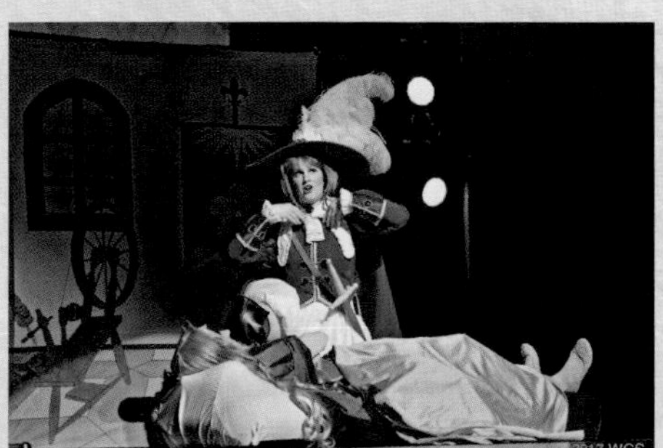

# Adam Pasion: Bringing Global Comic Culture to Japan

While many foreign comic artists dream about cracking the Japanese market and becoming the next *Shonen Jump* sensation, there are others who prefer to remain in the underground. One such creator is zine maker and Nagoya resident Adam Pasion. Pasion's comic art has been featured in such mainstream publications as the *Japan Times* and *Japanzine*, but his beginnings are firmly rooted in DIY culture.

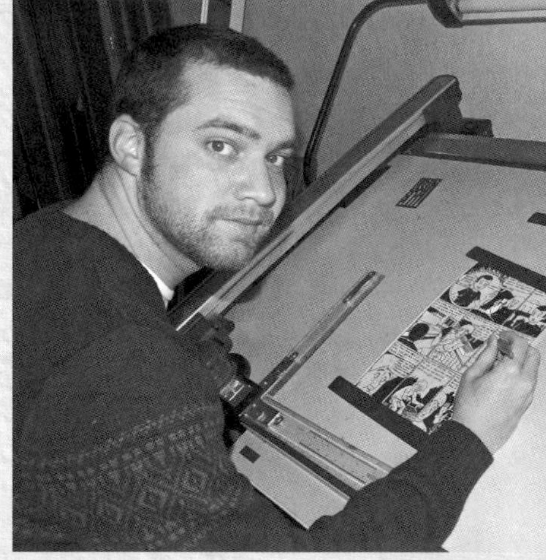

Pasion's love of the comic book medium really developed after he moved to Japan from California in 2006. "Coming from San Francisco, zines and mini-comics were so accessible that I completely took them for granted," he says. "It wasn't until moving to Japan and being cut off from that scene that I began to be more proactive about zines. I had to make new connections—real connections. I went in and actually had conversations with the zine shop owners, I searched out distros, and the apparent complete lack of zines in Japan made me really scour to find them."

Pasion admits that getting access to the local zine community was far from easy.

"I believe that Japan's zine scene is sort of divided into small parts of other subcultures. I have seen plenty of Japanese punk/hardcore zines, but they are only sold at crusty punk record stores and live houses. Other publications like art or poetry zines can be found at independent galleries and indie book stores, but these two genres never seem to mix. I think that's characteristic of Japan's scene. Without the strong history that comes along with American or European zines, the local scene is not so united.

"The hardest thing to crack into is the world of underground comics in Japan—not because they're hard to find, but because there's so much it's almost impossible to find a point of entry. There are tons of stores selling *dojinshi* fan-produced indie comics, but without exaggerating, 90 percent of it is either porno or parody (or parody-porno). As cool as it is to see Darth Vader having sex with Luke Skywalker, I really wish I could find more substantial stories. There are only so many naked Harry Potter pictures you can see before you just lose interest."

An acute observer of life in Japan, Pasion is best known in the network for his quarterly comic diary *Sundogs*, in which he chronicled his daily big and small (mis)adventures in Nagoya and all the head-scratching weirdness a foreigner encounters in Japan. More recently he has used fundraising to publish a comic anthology called *Uzomuzo*, named after a group of Nagoya-based cartoonists, illustrators and *mangaka*. "We collaborate on jam comics, 24-hour comics and all sorts of other projects with the goal of promoting more experimental and alternative-style comics in Japan," he says. "We mix styles and influences as well as our own various cultural approaches to storytelling in an attempt to bridge the gap between Western-style comics and Japanese manga."

Not content with making, selling and trading his works, in 2016 Pasion joined forces with director James Stacey (owner of Black Hook Press and the Hakusen gallery in Tokyo) and main organizer Aude Luce (a Frenchman who currently lives in Melbourne) to launch a brand new annual comic event: Comic Art Tokyo. "CAT is an

**TOP** Comic artist and Nagoya resident Adam Pasion. **LEFT** Pasion creates community-focused events with many opportunities for the public to participate.

international festival with a particular focus on the influence that Japanese comic books have on global culture," says Pasion. "The event is mostly aimed at broadening the understanding of global comic culture in Japan, and therefore the primary language is Japanese, but we have many non-Japanese speakers and artists showcasing their works, as well as interpreters for all the Japanese lectures."

When it comes to comic-book conventions, Japanese fans have been setting records for decades, starting with Tokyo's world-renowned Comiket, which attracts over half a million people twice a year. But while these events are mainly about selling and buying, and focus narrowly on *dojinshi*, CAT aspires to cover all the genres (mini-comics, art zines, indie comics, etc.) that tend to get lost in the shuffle at such large festivals. "Even in Japan, not every comic is about giant *mecha* suits and scantily clad schoolgirls," Pasion says. "That's why at CAT we're more focused on comics as an art form, and the interaction of various comic traditions such as manga, Franco-Belgian *bandes dessinées*, and North American alternative comics. Also, this is a highly community-focused event, with many opportunities for the public to participate, for example through lectures and interactive workshops. We always have panel talks with advice from industry professionals, and discussions about the history of alternative Japanese comics from publishers and well-known manga creators. Last, but certainly not least—in order to reach as many people as possible, CAT is free of charge to the public."

Though he is still based in Nagoya, Pasion's duties have actually increased. "Last year I was the coordinator, which essentially meant managing all the speakers and tables in the artists' alley and making sure they knew what to do and where to go. Now I'm taking a larger role in the planning stages. I'm planning some discussions and workshops, as well as very basic things like floor plans, layouts, budget and so on. Stacey and Luce are still doing the lion's share of the planning, but we're a tiny crew of people, so everyone is helping in whatever ways they can."

Pasion hopes to build on the event's initial success and make CAT bigger and better while keeping its originality. "Last year, for example, we had some big names, like the legendary *mangaka* Hayashi Seiichi, but more than that, I really loved the feeling of total community. Walking around and seeing people drawing portraits of each other, trading their work, getting inspiration from professionals in their field, making buttons and crafts with each other—it was a day of people just reveling in their common love of comics culture. Most of the artists had never met before, and yet they hung out and made new friends. When I see them interacting on social media or in real life it makes me so happy to think that I have been able to play a part in making that possible. I think everyone came home from that event inspired to make more art, and I couldn't ask for anything more."

**ABOVE LEFT** Lectures and panel discussions allow CAT to reach a wide audience. **ABOVE** Adam Pasion, immortalized manga-style.

**Adam Pasion: biguglyrobot.storenvy.com**
**Comic Art Tokyo: facebook.com/comicarttokyo**

# Nagoya Otaku Eateries

## Gundam Bars

Until a few years ago, Nagoya was arguably Japan's capital of Gundam fandom, with at least five bars and eateries devoted to the legendary saga. Three of them are still open today and are definitely worth a visit, especially if you are a devoted Gundam otaku.

**13 GUNDAM BAR—SIEG ZEON**
Small bar with the usual array of *gunpla*, posters and the flag of the Principality of Zeon everywhere. There's a 500-yen table charge, drinks are 500 to 600 yen; food from 800 yen.
**Hours:** *17:00–1:00; closed Mondays*
**Access:** *3F, 3-22-12 Osu, Naka-ku (seven minutes' walk from Kami-Maezu Station, Nagoya Metro Tsurumai and Meijo lines)*
**ameblo.jp/gundambar-siegzeon**

ABOVE Gundam Bar—Sieg Zeon.
RIGHT Gundam Shokudo Tamura.

**Quattro Vageena**
As its name implies, this bar is mainly devoted to the *Mobile Suit Zeta Gundam* series and one of the saga's most iconic characters, Quattro Bajeena (an alias of Char Aznable) whose bust takes pride of place on the counter. Other posters and pictures hang from the bar's red wall. A big screen behind the counter lets you enjoy videos of old Gundam anime. There's a 500-yen table charge; food is 500–1,000 yen.
**Hours:** *19:00–1:00* **Access:** *4-5-22, Sakae, Naka-ku, Nagoya-shi*

**Gundam Shokudo Tamura**
ガンダム食堂タムラ
Gunpla and other Gundam paraphernalia aside, the main reason for visiting this place is the food. This is a typical old-style *shokudo* (diner), after all. It offers delicious and hearty meals at a reasonable price.
**Hours:** *11:30–15:00, 17:30–21:00 (Tue–Sat); closed Mondays and on Sundays except for special events* **Access:** *2-7-9 Ayuchi-dori, Showaku (seven minutes' walk from Gokiso Station, Nagoya Metro Tsurumai and Sakura-dori lines)*
**facebook.com/mitocafe.nagoya**

## Other Bars

**5 Amusement Café-Bar Water 7**
Located in the heart of Osu's otaku district, this One Piece bar is chock-full of figures, comics, posters and other illustrations. Cosplayers welcome!
**Hours:** *17:00–2:00; closed Tuesdays*
**Access:** *3-11-34 Osu, Naka-ku (six minutes' walk from Kami-Maezu Station, Nagoya Metro Tsurumai and Meijo lines)*
**ameblo.jp/bar-w7**

**Critical Hit**
This small retro video-game bar is very popular with the local expat geek community. Owner Alex Fraioli has a library consisting of hundreds of retro classics that you can play on his vintage consoles. There's also a well-stocked library of old American video-game magazines and strategy guides. A 500-yen charge or one drink buys you one hour of playing.
**Hours:** *17:00–1:00* **Access:** *B1F, 1-7-4 Sakae, Naka-ku (three minutes' walk from Fushimi Station, Higashiyama and Tsurumai subway lines)* **twitter.com/criticalhitnag**

**At JoJo Bar Moriocho, you will find yourself surrounded by goods from *Jojo's Bizzare Adventure.***

**JoJo Bar Moriocho** ジョジョ BAR 杜王町
This bar is so small that you are literally surrounded by *Jojo's Bizarre Adventure* goods. Some figures even hang from the ceiling. There's a 500-yen table charge; booze is from 600 yen.
**Hours:** *18:00–2:00* **Access:** *3F, 3-9-22 Sakae, Naka-ku (eight minutes' walk from Sakae Station, Higashiyama and Meijo lines)*

**LEFT** Amusement Café-Bar Water 7 is an homage to the anime *One Piece* **BELOW LEFT** You'll find lots of cute girl figures at Bar Nerv **BELOW** Quick time has retro board and card games.

### Bar Nerv Nagoya ネルフ

Stylish Evangelion-themed bar with red furniture and lots of cute girl figures. Table charge is 500 yen, and most food and booze are around 500 yen.

**Hours:** *18:00–2:00* **Access:** *2F, 20-12 Tsubakicho, Nakamura-ku (six minutes' walk from Nagoya Station)*
**twitter.com/bar_nerv_nagoya**

### Nekketsu Seigi 大人のアニソンバー熱血正義

This bar is for nostalgic otaku who are into classic manga and anime and don't really understand the current *moe* fad. It has a nice collection of original autographed drawings that's worth a look. While on the pricey side (2,000-yen-per-hour charge for men, 1,500 for women, excluding food and drinks), it rewards long-stayers (no charge after the third hour) and loyalty (repeat customers get ever-growing discounts).

**Hours:** *19:00–1:00 (weekdays), 15:00–1:00 (Saturdays and national holidays); closed Sundays* **Access:** *4F, 4-21-23 Sakae, Naka-ku (eight minutes' walk from Sakae Station, Higashiyama and Meijo lines)*
**nekketsu-seigi.com**

### Anime no Bar Second あにめのばー セカンド

There's a 500-yen table charge (free for ladies) and almost all the food and drinks cost 500 yen. Karaoke fee: 500 yen for guys, 300 yen for gals.

**Hours:** *19:00–24:00; closed Sundays and national holidays* **Access:** *2F, 2-22-14 Higashi-Sakura, Naka-ku (four minutes' walk from Shin-Sakaemachi Station, Nagoya Metro Higashiyama Line)*
**mitinokusecond.web.fc2.com**

### Quick Time くいっくたいむ

This place calls itself a retro game cafe and bar, but judging from their Twitter page they mainly seem to be into board and card games and TRPGs. Their charge system is rather complicated; check their website for details.

Nekketsu Seigi is a bar for nostalgic otaku who are into classic manga and anime.

**Hours:** *18:00–5:00 (Mon–Wed and Fri), 14:00–5:00 (weekends and national holidays); closed Thursdays* **Access:** *4-63 Amazuka-cho, Nishi-ku (five minutes' walk from Shonai-dori Station, Nagoya Metro Tsurumai Line)*
**quick-tm.net**

### 14 Manga Kukan 漫画空間

This manga café has a space where clients can draw their own creations. It has all the necessary tools for manga production, and the staff can help you with tips and advice in order to provide a hands-on manga-drawing experience. Their reading collection is somewhat smaller than in other cafés, but features a lot of hard-to-find titles, including rare works by some of the manga greats. The first hour costs 480 yen, then it's 60 yen per 10 minutes. Or you can pay 980 yen for three hours or 1,680 for six hours.

**Hours:** *13:00–23:00 (weekdays), 11:00–23:00 (weekends and national holidays)*
**Access:** *2F 2-30-8 Osu, Naka-ku (seven minutes' walk from Osu-Kannon and Kami-Maezu stations, Nagoya Metro Tsurumai Line)* **mangakukan.com**

# Other Aichi Otaku Spots and Festivals

### Satsuki and Mei's House
サツキとメイの家

A faithful reproduction of the house featured in *My Neighbor Totoro* is located in the 200-hectare Expo Memorial Park near Nagoya. The film is set in rural Japan in the late 1950s, and a visit to the small house offers a glimpse into Japanese home life during the Showa era (1926–1989)—note, for example, the fire-heated *goemonburo* bathtub. As is typical for a project involving Studio Ghibli, the site was built with an astounding attention to detail (e.g., Mei's hand-drawn calendar and the bucket with a hole at the bottom). Particularly impressive is the father's messy studio full of books and papers. Be aware that no photography is allowed inside the house, but apart from that, you're free to explore everywhere—you're even encouraged to open drawers to find things from the movie—during your 30-minute visit. Don't forget to buy your ticket in advance and reserve the day and time of your visit, especially if you're there on a weekend. Or, if you choose a weekday, you can go early and see whether same-day tickets are still available.

The house is nestled in a small, thick forest. The Memorial Park that surrounds it is much bigger and definitely worth a visit. First opened in 2005 to host the World Expo, it still retains its popular Ferris wheel. Within the park you can take the free shuttle bus, or you can rent a bicycle for 100 yen. If possible, try to visit in autumn, when the beautiful red and yellow leaves add a magic touch.

**Note:** Studio Ghibli is currently building a much bigger theme park that is scheduled to open around 2022.

**Admission fee:** *510 yen (250 for those between 4 and 15); tickets can be purchased online (l-tike.com/event/satsukitomei) or at Lawson's convenience stores. On the 10th of each month, tickets go on sale for the next month. A limited number of tickets can be bought at the gate.*
**Hours:** *10:00–16:30 (weekdays), 9:30–16:30 (weekends and national holidays)*
**Access:** *1533-1 Ibaragabasama, Nagakute-shi (the Ai-Expo Memorial Park / Morikoro Park is a 13-minute train ride on the Linimo Line from Fujigaoka Station; Fujigaoka is the last stop on the Nagoya Metro Higashiyama Line)*
**aichi-koen.com/moricoro/shisetsu/satsukitomei**

### Next Generation World Hobby Fair (winter edition)
*(See page 53 for description)*
**Admission fee:** *Free* **Dates:** *January*
**Hours:** *9:00–16:00* **Access:** *Nagoya Dome, 1-1 Daiko-Minami, Higashi-ku (nine minutes' walk from Nagoya Dome-mae Yada Station, Nagoya Metro Meijo Line)* **whobby.com**

### (4•5) Nagoya Anpanman Children's Museum and Park
*(See page 49 for description of Yokohama Anpanman Museum)* **Admission fee:** *1,500 yen (free for children under one year old)*
**Hours:** *10:00–17:00* **Access:** *108-4 Urayasu, Nagashima-cho, Kuwana-shi, Mie prefecture (a 40-minute express bus ride from Meitetsu Bus Center in front of Nagoya Station; get off at Nagashima Spa Land)*
**nagoya-anpanman.jp**
**museum.anpanman-acm.co.jp/en** *(English)*

**TOP** World Hobby Fair. **FAR LEFT** Satsuki and Mei's house. **LEFT** Nagoya Anpanman Children's Museum and Park.

# Cosplay and Halloween

Many cosplayers have a sort of love/hate relationship with Halloween, and endlessly debate as to whether the traditional Western celebration can be considered a form of cosplay. Hardcore fans, for instance, point out the poor quality of most mass-produced Halloween costumes. Another complaint is that many participants seem to be clueless about the characters they are impersonating. To be sure, many of the people who cosplay at Halloween events have a more casual approach than otaku fans, as their main purpose is to party and have a good time. In any case, the Japanese are famous for adopting foreign traditions regardless of cultural differences

as long as they are fun, and Halloween is no exception. As a consequence, even in Tokyo, the end of October has become another opportunity to show off one's own costumes. This is also the one time of the year that Japanese girls give up the idea of looking cute and use their full arsenal of makeup, contact lenses and fake blood in order to look as ugly and scary as possible.

The first Halloween-related events took place in the late '90s at Tokyo Disneyland, and mainly targeted kids and their parents, but in the last 10 years, more and more parades and events have sprung up around the country, because both companies and local governments see them as a great way to attract people. In 2014, for instance, streaming video site Nico Nico and anime retailer Animate organized the Ikebukuro Halloween Cosplay Fest, a two-day festival featuring a parade, a free stage where anybody could perform (and be broadcast worldwide live online) and a Cosplay Gathering area divided by costume theme. The event was so successful that it attracted 52,000 visitors, including 10,000 cosplayers from Japan and 22 other countries around the world.

In Nagoya, you have not one but two chances to show off your costume: Sakae Halloween, inaugurated in 2016, is a family-friendly event featuring the ever-popular parade, street performers, a huge creators' market where 2,000 indie artists and crafts people from all over Japan sell their goods (accessories, clothes, illustrations, etc.) and even a piñata event for the kids.

On the other hand, if you are a night owl who likes loud dance music (EDM, techno, etc.), you can't miss The Absolute Halloween. This event was born in 2008 when the country had not yet caught Halloween fever, and such parties were mainly organized by and for the foreign communities in Japan. Unlike other Halloween festivals, The Absolute is an indoor event that takes place in several clubs and cafés around Nagoya. With a strong lineup of DJs, bands and assorted performers and artists, The Absolute has become the largest multi-venue Halloween party in Japan. Every year, it attracts over 3,000 club-hopping cosplayers to downtown Sakae. Once you buy your festival wristband, you are free to wander from one place to another, but it's forbidden to stand in the street or obstruct traffic outside the venues.

So if you happen to be in Japan on Halloween, check out the local media for information on events.

**Main Halloween events around Japan:**
*Ikebukuro Halloween Cosplay Festival (Tokyo)*
*Shibuhallo (Shibuya Scramble Crossing, Tokyo)*
*Halloween at Tokyo Disneyland and Disney Sea (Chiba)*
*Halloween at Universal Studios Japan (Osaka)*
*Halloween in Triangle Park, Amemura (Osaka)*
*Nagoya Cosplay Halloween (Aichi)*
*Hakata Halloween Cosplay Parade and Contest (Fukuoka)*

# Other Chubu Otaku Spots and Festivals

## Yamanashi Prefecture

### Fuji Q Highland

This amusement park located at the foot of Mount Fuji is especially famous for its extreme rides, but otaku fans should check it out for a couple different attractions: **Evangelion: World** and **Mizuki Shigeru's Ge-Ge-Ge Haunted Mansion**. The former is a sort of permanent exhibition with life-sized models (Kaworu and Mari), original artwork, and interactive installations. The highlights are a beautiful 3-D scale model of the Cyborg Evangelion Unit-01; a life-size reproduction of the Entry Plug cockpit (sorry, you can't climb into it); and the Nerv HQ with faithfully represented corridors and a replica elevator. The Haunted Mansion is not particularly scary (it's also best enjoyed if you understand the Japanese spooky narration), but it's a nice homage to Mizuki's *yokai* world and old-fashioned ghost stories. As I said, though, Fuji Q is much more than this. If you are a hardcore roller-coaster fan, you will love this place. Fuji Q has the world's steepest roller coaster (with a drop angle of 121 degrees); another one has the most spins; a third one, the highest acceleration at launch time (it can hit 107 mph [172 km/h] in only 1.8 seconds with 2.7 Gs of force); while the Fujiyama, at 79 meters (260 feet), used to be the world's tallest coaster.

**Admission fee:** *One-day pass 5,700 yen (5,200 for 12- to 18-year-olds, 4,300 for 3- to 11-year-olds); check the website for special discounts for foreign travelers* **Hours:** *9:00–17:00* **Access:** *5-6-1 Shin-Nishihara, Fujiyoshida (a 100- to 120-minute bus ride from Shinjuku, Tokyo, or Shibuya stations)* **fujiq.jp/en** *(English)*

Evangelion: World is one of the attractions at Fuji Q Highland amusement park.

## Shizuoka Prefecture

### Chibi Maruko-chan Land
ちびまる子ちゃんランド

Our favorite anime third-grader has a home near the Shizuoka city port. This theme park features reproductions of the Sakura family house, school and park. For 300 yen, you can rent the outfit of any one of six characters (including Maruko and her best friend Tama-chan), enjoy some cosplay time, and even have your picture taken in front of a typical Shizuoka scenery at the Chibi-Maru Photo Studio. Also, for 300 yen, kids can make their own sand picture of Maruko. Last, but not least, there's a gallery where you can study original drawings by Maruko-chan's creator, Sakura Momoko, as well as materials used in the creation of the anime. Sakura grew up in Shizuoka, and the original manga was based on her childhood memories. That's why the gallery features several everyday objects, toys and magazines from that specific period.

**Admission fee:** *600 yen (400 yen for ages 3 to 11)* **Hours:** *10:00–20:00* **Access:** *3F S-Pulse Dream Plaza, 13-15 Irifune-cho, Shimizu-ku, Shizuoka (a 10-minute free shuttle-bus ride from JR Shimizu Station east exit)* **chibimarukochan-land.com**

BELOW Chibi Maruko-chan Land. FACING PAGE, TOP Niigata Anime Manga Festival FACING PAGE, BOTTOM Niigata Manga Animation Museum.

The Go Nagai Wonderland Museum is devoted to Nagai Go's life and art.

## Ishikawa Prefecture

### (1•2) Go Nagai Wonderland Museum
永井豪記念館

World-famous artist Nagai Go grew up in this small seaside town in the Noto Peninsula, and the museum devoted to his life and art opened in 2009. Reaching the museum is a bit of a pain (there are no train stations in Wajima), so it's only recommended for rabid fans of *Mazinger Z*, *Devilman* and *Cutie Honey* (or my beloved *Goldrake*, aka *UFO Robot Grendizer*). The highlights include a 6-foot (2-meter) high Mazinger-Z statue shooting a rocket punch, original pages from several of Nagai's works, and a digital library of Nagai's works.

**Admission fee:** *510 yen (210 yen for kids)* **Hours:** *8:30–17:00* **Access:** *1-123 Kawai-machi, Wajima-shi (two hours by bus or car from Kanazawa; see website for details)* **go-wonderland.jp/en** *(English)*

## Niigata Prefecture

**(1•3) Niigata City Manga House*** 新潟市 マンガの家
This museum is devoted to Niigata-born manga and anime artists such as Mizushima Shinji (*Dokaben*) and Gainax studio founder Yamaga Hiroyuki (*Royal Space Force: The Wings of Honneamise*). There's a permanent exhibition space where you can take photos with life-sized figures of popular characters. Special exhibitions are also held periodically. The museum's most interesting feature is a free one-hour tour and manga basic course where you are taught the rudiments of comic-drawing. There's also a library with some 10,000 titles.
**Admission fee:** *Free* **Hours:** *11:00–19:00; closed Wednesdays and from 12/9 to 1/3* **Access:** *971-7, 6 Ban-cho, Furumachi-dori, Chuo-ku, Niigata (an eight-minute bus ride from JR Niigata Station Bandai exit; platform 0 or 1, get off at Furumachi)* **house.nmam.jp**

**(1•2•3) Niigata Manga Animation Museum*** 新潟市 マンガ・アニメ情報館
Similar to the **Manga House** on the other side of the Shinano River (see above), this museum focuses on Niigata-born or -raised artists (*Inuyasha* and *Urusei Yatsura*'s Takahashi Rumiko, *Osomatsu-san*'s Akatsuka Fujio, *Death Note*'s Obata Takeshi, *Rurouni Kenshin*'s Watsuki Nobuhiro, etc.) with plenty of permanent and temporary exhibitions. There's a corner where kids can interact with Akatsuka's characters, and elsewhere where you can test your manga-making and voice-actor skills.
**Admission fee:** *200 yen (100 yen for junior high and high school students, 50 yen for elementary school students); special exhibitions may require an extra fee* **Hours:** *11:00–19:00 (weekdays), 10:00–19:00 (weekends and national holidays); closed 1/1* **Access:** *Bandai City BP2, 2-5-7 Yachiyo, Chuo-ku, Niigata (an 11-minute walk from Niigata Station)* **museum.nmam.jp**

**Niigata Anime Manga Festival (GataFes)** にいがたアニメ・マンガフェスティバル（がたふぇす）
There used to be not one, but three otaku events in the city of Niigata. Starting from 2010, they began to be held around the same time, and were officially merged into a single big festival in 2013. The city's Bandai, Furumachi and Hakusan areas are taken over for two days by voice actors' and *anison* singers' stage performances, art exhibitions, an itasha show, a cosplay parade, and other events.
**Admission fee:** *Free (some events require a fee)* **Dates:** *October*
**niigata-animemangafes.com**

## Toyama Prefecture

**(1•2) Himi City Shiokaze Gallery (Fujiko A. Fujio Art Collection)**
氷見市潮風ギャラリー
The creative pair behind Doraemon—Abiko Motoo (aka Fujiko A. Fujio) and Fujimoto Hiroshi (aka Fujiko F. Fujio), who together adopted the pen name "Fujiko Fujio" under which the manga is written—were both born in Toyama prefecture, but while Fujiko F. Fujio's museum is located in Kawasaki, his partner has been honored in his hometown of Himi. Starting with statues of some of his more popular characters (Ninja Hattori-kun and Kaibutsu-kun), the gallery is full of exhibits and original art chronicling Motoo's career. On the first floor they

have even reproduced the room where Abiko lived at Tokiwa-so, the house he shared with Tezuka Osamu and many other young *mangaka*. On the second floor there's a display of illustrations he made of the local landscape, a small room where his anime are shown and a library with some 1,000 titles. There's actually more to see outside the gallery: many statues and illustrations are scattered along the surrounding shopping streets, while Kozenji (the temple where the artist was born) is just a couple of minutes away.
**Admission fee:** *200 yen (free for high school students and younger)* **Hours:** *10:00–17:00; closed from 12/29 to 1/3* **Access:** *3-4 Chuo-machi, Himi-shi (a five-minute taxi ride from JR Himi Station)* **himi-manga.jp**
**fujikoworld.com/road** *(area map; click on icons for details)*

**Otogi no Mori Park** おとぎの森公園
This is only for completists, but if you pass by Takaoka (Fujiko F. Fujio's hometown), and especially if you have children, you may want to check out this park. Many fans are said to come just to take pictures of the small area in the park where statues of Doraemon and friends have been installed. Other attractions include a river-based water play area, a multipurpose open area for recreation activities and events, and a forest where one can learn about nature.
**Access:** *1342 Sano, Takaoka-shi (a 15-minute walk from JR Johana Line Futatsuka Station)*
**terfel.net**

# EXPLORING HIROSHIMA

It's almost impossible to talk about Hiroshima without mentioning the atomic bomb. Every year, during the second week of August, people around Japan are reminded of the atomic bombings of Hiroshima (August 6) and Nagasaki (August 9) that contributed to the end of the Pacific War in 1945. Also, regardless of the time of the year, no one should travel to the city without visiting the Peace Memorial Park and Museum.

ABOVE The Hiroshima Peace Memorial. LEFT Nakazawa Keiji's *Barefoot Gen* is the once-controversial manga story of a boy struggling to survive after the atomic bomb.

It wasn't always like this, however: during the 1950s and 1960s, both the government and public opinion tried to sweep the subject under the carpet, treating the *hibakusha* (atomic-bomb victims) like disease-spreading untouchables while heralding the new Atomic Age and promoting the building of nuclear power plants. Memories of the bombings began to take center stage between the end of the '60s and the mid-'70s, thanks to pop culture. Toho Animation, for instance, increasingly released films featuring human mutation and other indirect references to the wartime tragedy—among them *The H-Man* (1958) and *Matango* (1963; also known as *Attack of the Mushroom People*).

Even manga and anime helped shape popular understanding of recent history—particularly Nakazawa Keiji's relentless comic work, which revealed to the general public the horrible truth about Hiroshima's destruction. An A-bomb survivor himself, Nakazawa experienced fierce discrimination. When his mother died, he wrote the fictional manga *Struck by Black Rain* out of anger, but he was told by all major magazines that the content was too radical and disturbing. Eventually it was published in 1968 by *Manga Punch*, an erotic magazine.

His major work—a memoir—is the world-famous *Barefoot Gen*, first serialized in *Weekly Shonen Jump* (a comic magazine that at the time had a circulation of 2 million) between 1973 and 1974. After all these years, the story of Gen—a nine-year-old who loses his father and two siblings on August 6 and later has to fight alongside his mother and older brother to survive hunger and discrimination in the atomic wasteland—still has the power to shock readers with its explicit images of rotting corpses and human misery. Indeed, Nakazawa was criticized because his visuals were considered

BELOW Even Hiroshima has a dedicated otaku area.

ABOVE The 10- volume set of *Barefoot Gen* can be found in most library collections. BELOW The Animate Building.

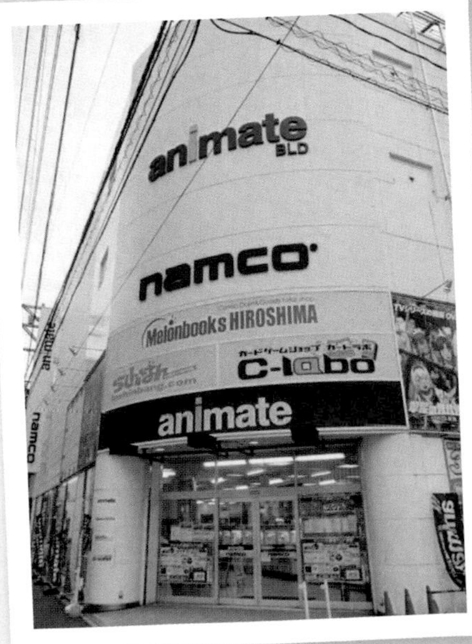

too graphic and disturbing, and *Barefoot Gen* had a troubled editorial history until its conclusion in 1985.

*Barefoot Gen* went on to become the bible of the antinuclear-weapons movement. The 10-volume series can be found in most library collections, including school libraries, and has inspired three different live-action movies (1976, 1977 and 1980), a TV drama and two animated films (1983 and 1986), all contributing to spread Nakazawa's anti-war message.

More recently, younger people who were born after the war have tackled the subject. Notable among these is Kono Fumiyo, a Hiroshima-born artist who authored a couple of manga whose female characters live in or around that city before and after the atomic bombing. Both *Town of Evening Calm, Country of Cherry Blossoms* (2003–2004) and *In This Corner of the World* (2007–2009) have enjoyed a lot of success (they were turned into a live-action film and an animated movie respectively). Her stories are faithful to the historical facts they are based on while at the same time being rather removed from the tragedy itself.

Through the years, anime creators have approached the Hiroshima bombing from different angles, often mixing facts and fiction and using time travel to create a sort of collective memory based on the intergenerational transmission of history. The short film *Natsufuku no shojotachi* (The Girls Who Wore Summer Clothes, 1988), for instance, tells the true story of 220 students from a local girls' school who were not evacuated so that they could work in the city center; they died on August 6, leaving behind their diaries where they had confessed their hopes and dreams for the future. Another short film, *On a Paper Crane* (1993), is set in the present day and tells the story of Tomoko, a student who visits the Hiroshima Peace Memorial Museum for a class assignment. When she finds herself in front of the beautiful Children's Peace Monument, the statue suddenly turns into a little girl. Tomoko learns about her tragic story, the atomic bomb and the effects of radiation. More recently, *Dr. Junod* (2010) has employed time travel to remember the eponymous Swiss doctor (whose monument can be found in the same Memorial Peace Park), the first foreign doctor to reach Hiroshima after its destruction, who delivered 15 tons of medical supplies, visited all the major hospitals, and personally administered medical care.

Speaking of manga and anime, even Hiroshima has its dedicated otaku area, though it doesn't have a name like Akiba or Den Den Town. On the indie side of business, the local scene is not terribly exciting, but many major chains have a branch here. Most shops are clustered northeast of Hiroshima Peace Memorial Park, quite close to the Atomic Bomb Dome. Several of them are located in or around the **Hondori** shopping arcade (including those inside the **Sun Mall** shopping complex) while a few others can be found in the **Animate Building** just south of the arcade.

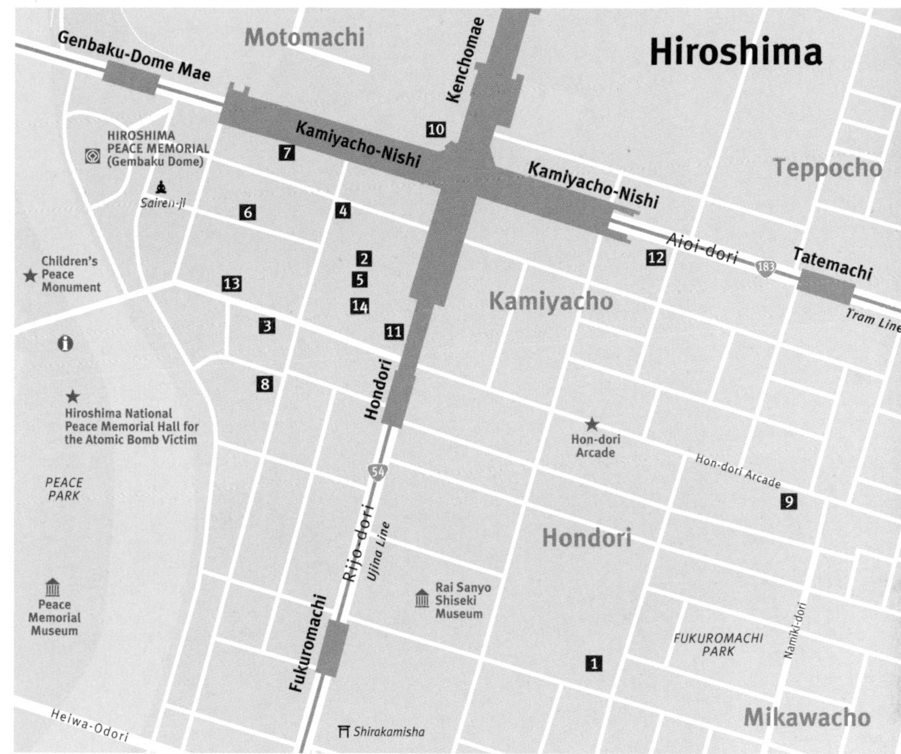


## General

### 1 Akane 茜

Collectors' shop dealing in figures, dolls, model cars and trains, *shokugan*, and lots of capsule toys.
**Hours:** *10:00–18:30* **Access:** *3F, 6-17 Fukuro-machi, Naka-ku (three minutes' walk from Fukuro-machi tram stop, Ujina Line)* **akane-shop.net**

### 2 Chuo Shoten ComiComi Studio

中央書店 コミコミスタジオ

This store focuses on comics, *dojinshi* and other goods for female otaku.
**Hours:** *11:00–20:00*
**Access:** *4F, 2-3-1 Otemachi, Naka-ku (four minutes' walk from Hondori tram stop, routes #1, 3, 7 and the Astram Line)* **chuoshoten.co.jp**

### 3 Futaba Books フタバ図書

Located inside the Hondori shopping arcade, the GIGA Hondori store stocks 400,000 new and 200,000 used books and magazines, including a fair share of manga. Also, on the fourth floor there's an **Edion** branch selling toys, figures and plamodels.

**Hours:** *10:00–22:00* **Access:** *1-8-20 Otemachi, Naka-ku (three minutes' walk from Hondori tram stop, routes #1, 3, 7 and the Astram Line)* **Note:** *Not far from here, you'll find a* **Futaba@cafe** *Internet and manga café that's open 24/7* **Access:** *2-2-34 Kamiyacho, Naka-ku* **4**

**Lepton** レプトン
This secondhand shop has almost 20 branches in and around Hiroshima, with each storefront specializing in different products (they deal in used clothes and golf clubs, too). The Itsukaichi branch is the biggest and best of the lot, selling video games, CDs, DVDs, figures and dolls, but is a little far from the city center (45 minutes from Hondori tram stop). There's a smaller shop in Jizo-dori that only sells video games.
**Hours:** *10:00–20:00* **Access:** *Itsukaichi (五日市) shop: 2-8-15 Itsukaichi-Chuo, Saeki-ku (10 minutes' walk from Rakurakuen Station, Miyajima Line) Jizo-dori (地蔵通り) shop: 1-10-4 Kokutaiji-machi, Naka-ku (eight minutes' walk from either Shiyakusho-mae or Takanobashi tram stop, Ujina Line)* **lepton.ne.jp**

**5 Sun Mall**
**1F Edion:** Video games and consoles, CDs and DVDs.
**4F Popondetta:** Everything for the model train enthusiast. Even if you're not into the toys themselves, it's worth a visit to see their giant dioramas.

LEFT Angelic Pretty sells kawaii, pastel-colored clothes. BELOW Jump Shop stocks magazine-related character goods.

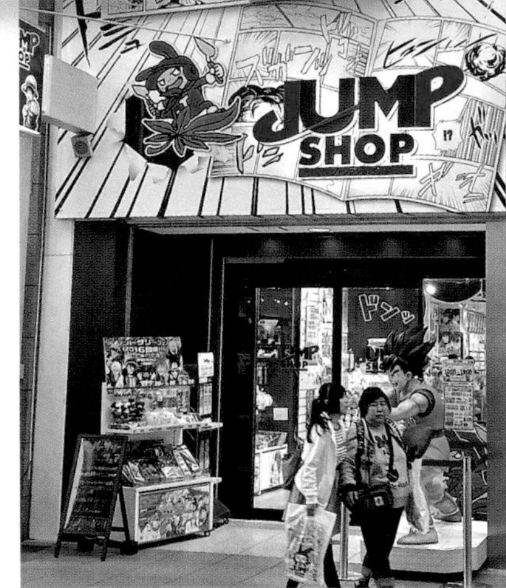


**4F Volks**
**4F Angelic Pretty:** Lolita fashion brand selling *kawaii* pastel-colored clothes full of frills and lace.
**4F Baby the Stars Shine Bright:** Similar to Angelic Pretty.
**4F chouchou ange:** Similar to Angelic Pretty, but with a somewhat darker color range.
**4F Tyche Maria:** Gothic Lolita with a punk twist.
**5F Village Vanguard**
**Hours:** *10:30–20:00* **Access:** *2-2-18 Kamiya-cho, Naka-ku (three minutes' walk from Hondori tram stop, routes #1, 3, 7 and the Astram Line)* **sunmall.co.jp/eng**

**6 Tougou** トウゴウ
The store itself is not particularly big, but it's filled with about 200 showcases of different sizes that people rent to sell their unwanted goods. Most boxes contain figures and dolls, but you will also find video games, DVDs, trading cards, idol photos and much more. You can actually see what each box currently contains by checking out their website.
**Hours:** *11:30–20:00 (weekdays), 10:30–20:00 (weekends); closed Tuesdays and the second Wednesday of every month* **Access:** *3F, 1-4-14 Otemachi, Naka-ku* **tougou.net**

**Tougou is filled with about 200 showcases that people rent to sell their unwanted goods.**

**7 Visco**
Secondhand shop selling console and PC video games, DVDs, and smartphones.
**Hours:** *10:00–23:00* **Access:** *1-1-26 Otemachi, Naka-ku (in front of Kamiyacho-Nishi tram stop, routes #2, 3, 6, 7 and 9)*

## Chain Stores

**8 Animate**
**Hours:** *11:00–20:00 (weekdays), 10:00–20:00 (weekends and national holidays)* **Access:** *1F Animate Bldg., 2-3-1 Otemachi, Naka-ku (four minutes' walk from Hondori tram stop, routes #1, 3, 7 and the Astram Line)*

**8 C-Labo**
**Hours:** *11:00–20:00 (weekdays), 10:00–20:00 (weekends and national holidays)*
**Access:** *3F Animate Bldg., 2-3-1 Otemachi, Naka-ku (four minutes' walk from Hondori tram stop, routes #1, 3, 7 and the Astram Line)*

**9 Jump Shop**
**Hours:** *10:00–19:00* **Access:** *2-5 Hondori, Naka-ku (four minutes' walk from Hatchobori tram stop, routes #1, 2, 6 and 9)*

**8 Lashinbang**
**Hours:** *11:00–20:00 (weekdays), 10:00–20:00 (weekends and national holidays)*
**Access:** *4F Animate Bldg., 2-3-1 Otemachi, Naka-ku (four minutes' walk from Hondori tram stop, routes #1, 3, 7 and the Astram Line)*

**8 Melonbooks**
**Hours:** *11:00–20:00 (weekdays), 10:00–20:00 (weekends and national holidays)*
**Access:** *3F Animate Bldg., 2-3-1 Otemachi, Naka-ku (four minutes' walk from Hondori tram stop, routes #1, 3, 7 and the Astram Line)*

**10 Pokemon Center**
**Hours:** *10:00–20:00*
**Access:** *6F Sogo Main Bldg. (Hon-kan), 6-27 Motomachi, Naka-ku (in front of Kamiyacho-Nishi tram stop, routes #2, 3, 6, 7 and 9)*

**11 Sofmap**
**Hours:** *11:00–20:00* **Access:** *2-2-12 Kamiya-cho, Naka-ku (in front of Hondori tram stop, routes #1, 3, 7 and the Astram Line)*

**12 Toranoana**
**Hours:** *11:00–21:00 (weekdays), 10:00–21:00 (weekends and national holidays)*
**Access:** *3–4F, 1-1-1 Kamiyacho, Naka-ku (two minutes' walk from Kamiyacho-Higashi tram stop, routes #1, 2, 6 and 9)*

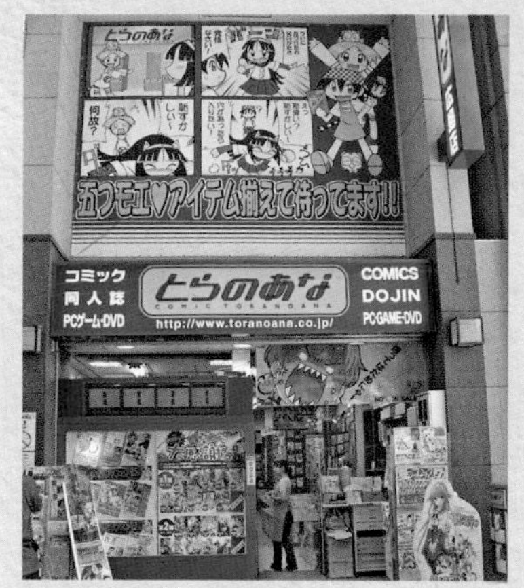


Otaku chain Toranoana is the place to stock up on indie comics and dojinshi.

**14 Volks**
**Hours:** *10:30–20:00* **Access:** *4F Sun Mall, 2-2-18 Kamiyacho, Naka-ku (three minutes' walk from Hondori tram stop, routes #1, 3, 7 and the Astram Line)*

**13 Yellow Submarine**
**Hours:** *11:00–20:00*
**Access:** *1-5-15 Otemachi, Naka-ku (four minutes' walk from Hondori tram stop, routes #1, 3, 7 and the Astram Line)*

## Other Attractions and Events

### Hiroshima City Manga Library

広島市まんが図書館

Located on the 230-foot (70-meter) high Hijiyama, a beautiful hill in central Hiroshima overlooking the Enko River, this city-run library collects and preserves manga and comic-related materials and organizes events, lectures and exhibitions. As of March 2018, they had about 151,000 volumes, including a section devoted to manga translated into other languages and another focusing on Hiroshima-related authors and themes. If you apply at the second-floor reference desk, you can even take manga outside and read them outdoors under the trees in the surrounding park.

**Hours:** *10:00–17:00; closed Mondays, from 12/29 to 1/4, and on inventory days*
**Access:** *1-4 Hijiyama Koen, Minami-ku (eight minutes' walk from either Hijiyama-shita or Danbara Itchome tram stops, Hijiyama Line)*
**library.city.hiroshima.jp/manga**
**library.city.hiroshima.jp/manga/en/index.html** *(English)*

### A-Crash!!

Monthly *anison* club event where resident and guest DJs and VJs spin their *anison*, game song and vocaloid tunes. Cosplaying is not only allowed (and they provide changing rooms), you even get a 1,000-yen discount for doing so!

**Entrance fee:** *2,000 yen (1,500 for students)*
**Date:** *Fourth Saturday of every month*
**Hours:** *18:30~* **Access:** *4F, 7-9 Yagenbori, Naka-ku (six minutes' walk from either Ebisu-cho or Kanayama-cho tram stops, Hiroden Route 1, 2 and 6)*
**twitter.com/a___crash**

The usual otaku chain stores can be found in Hiroshima, including Pokemon Center (INSET, ABOVE) and figure and doll stockist Volks (ABOVE). After shopping, why not hang out at the monthly *anison* club event A-Crash!! (RIGHT).

# In This Corner of the World: The Making of the Movie

After six difficult years in production, the animated wartime drama movie *In This Corner of the World* finally came out in 2016 to positive reviews and a good performance at the box office, winning multiple prizes and even being nominated best film of the year by respected film magazine *Kinema Junpo*. We talked with director Katabuchi Sunao about the film.

**Why did you decide to turn this Kono Fumiyo manga into a movie?**
I guess what I love the most about this story is that it shows the characters' ordinary, everyday lives in great detail. When I read the manga, it made me feel as though I had just met a distant relative whose life I knew nothing about. You can definitely feel the amount of research that went into making this story. This is exactly the same way I like to work on a project.

**The city of Hiroshima as we see it in the film was completely obliterated by the atomic bombing. How did you manage to recreate the prewar cityscape?**
Apart from the A Bomb Dome—which is now known as the Hiroshima Peace Memorial—there's only one single building still standing from the wartime years (you get to see it in the movie), so it took a long time and a great deal of effort. We found reproductions of telephone books from back then in a secondhand bookstore in Hiroshima. From these we were able to get a clear idea of the shops that existed at the time and their location. But this information was not enough, so we also looked for some visual materials in the National Archive and that's where we found some aerial photos of the port of Hiroshima taken by the Japanese air force.

We also came across some sketches that had been drawn by someone at the time. Probably because Hiroshima was completely destroyed, many people have felt the need to preserve as many records of the pre-bomb city as possible. In this sense we have been very lucky to find a lot of information. The problem was finding the information we needed about the town of Kure. Before the bombing of Hiroshima, this was an important military port, so taking photographs was severely restricted. But we managed to get hold of some, and then painstakingly checked each single building against all the other information we had managed to gather. This process continued all through the movie's production, even after we had made the storyboard.

**How would you describe Suzu-san, the film's protagonist?**
She is a very shy and pure girl with little knowledge of the world around her. She's a very reserved person. The only way she has to express herself is through her drawings. It's only when she loses her right hand—her writing hand—that she is forced to get out of her shell and speak her mind.

**Suzu-san's world is very different from now. Japanese society has changed a lot since the war. Do you think Japanese families have changed as well?**
I don't think the family itself has changed. What has changed is the legal system surrounding the family as an institution. During Suzu's times, for example, women didn't have a right to vote and couldn't really take part in political activity. They couldn't even serve in the military, which was probably good. In other words, they were discriminated against by a male-ruled society. However, I think that inside the family (at least in some families), things were a little different. Japanese society had actually changed in many ways before the war, especially in the big cities where nuclear families were becoming the norm compared to multi-generational households in the countryside. Unfortunately, the war put a stop to these social changes and imposed a more traditional and conservative system.

**It took about six years to complete this film, mostly because of lack of funds. How did you feel at the time?**
It was quite frustrating. Obviously, the sponsors are always thinking about the bottom line. No matter how good a story is, they want to be sure that there is actually an audience for that story before the film is completed. They want to see hard data, and we were finally able to do that when we resorted to crowdfunding and showed them how many people were backing the film. Over time, this film has proved to be a long seller, thanks to word of mouth. Also, it's the kind of story that attracts people in their 70s and 80s; i.e., people who usually don't go to the movies.

**What makes you particularly happy about this movie?**
The fact that these 70- and 80-year-olds praised the movie for being so accurate in its depiction of wartime Japan. Those words made me and my team very proud. We felt that all the long hours we had put into making the film were very worthwhile.

## Yamato Museum

*In This Corner of the World* is mainly located in Kure, a small port town that can be reached from Hiroshima in about 30 or 40 minutes. After getting married, the film's young protagonist moves there to live with her husband's family.

Even before the film's surprising success, Kure was famous for its Maritime Museum, better known as the Yamato Museum because its centerpiece is a one-tenth-scale model of the battleship *Yamato*, the heaviest and most powerful armed battleship ever built. The *Yamato* was designed and built in Kure, and the city's port and shipyard are shown more than once in the movie. Though the *Yamato* fired her main guns only once before being sunk in 1945, and was largely ineffective during the war, she still holds a special place in Japanese culture. Indeed, the 85-foot (26-meter)-long model is the main reason millions of people have visited the museum since it opened in 2005.

Besides technical information about the battleship and photographs and letters written by the soldiers who lost their lives in battle, the museum's collection features a ZERO Fighter, a *kaiten* manned torpedo and other weapons.

Kure used to be Japan's most important military port, and the museum shows the city's history from the Meiji era on. Among other activities, you can also try a simulated navigation of a ferry boat or a high-speed vessel, and watch some films.

**Entrance fee:** *500 yen (300 yen for high school students, 200 yen for elementary and junior high students)* **Hours:** *9:00–18:00; closed Tuesdays*
**Access:** *5-20 Takaramachi, Kure-shi (five minutes' walk from JR Kure Station)*
**yamato-museum.com**

# EXPLORING SAKAIMINATO

Sometimes the most unimpressive-looking places hide a treasure trove of historically and culturally important spots. For manga and anime otaku, Sakaiminato is one such place. This small seaside town in Tottori prefecture, in the Chugoku region is inextricably connected to Mizuki Shigeru, one of the few artists whose work inspires the same kind of respect and awe as that of Tezuka Osamu. Mizuki was born in Osaka, but he was raised in Sakaminato, and it's here that, from an early age, he not only developed his great artistic talent, but first heard the ghost stories that would later inspire so much of his work.

**ABOVE** Local trains are decorated inside and out with characters from the manga of Mizuki Shigeru. **BOTTOM** You might even ride into Sakaiminato aboard a Nekomusume Train!

The full immersion into Mizuki's unique world starts even before you reach Sakaiminato, as the train taking you to the town is decorated inside and out with characters from the master's best-known manga, *GeGeGe no Kitaro*. A statue of Mizuki himself (working at his desk, as he tirelessly did for so many years) welcomes you as soon as you step out of the station building, and signals your entrance into his parallel world.

In order to go to the **Mizuki Shigeru Memorial Museum** you have to take the street just in front of the station. That's **Mizuki Shigeru Road**, a half-mile (1 km) long shopping street lined with more than 170 bronze statues of *yokai*, the weirdly scary-but-funny creatures that inhabit Japanese folklore and are treated by the locals with a mix of reverence and affection. It only takes about 10 minutes to reach the museum, but I suggest you spend some time admiring the statues, and maybe check out the many shops along the street—which, naturally, sell tons of *yokai-* and Kitaro-related goods and souvenirs.

**1 (1•2•4) Mizuki Shigeru Memorial Museum** 水木しげる記念館

This place contains everything you always wanted to know about Mizuki sensei. In addition to the striking monster artwork and dioramas, his early works and some of the many *yokai-* and ghost-related materials he collected throughout his life are displayed here. There's also a corner devoted to his relationship with Nononba (her real name was Kageyama Fusa), the local woman who first introduced him to the world of ghosts and monsters. **Admission fee:** *700 yen (500 yen for junior high and high school students, 300 yen for elementary school students); foreigners in the same categories pay 300, 200 and 100 yen, respectively* **Hours:** *9:30–17:00 (open until 18:00 during the summer school holidays)* **mizuki.sakaiminato.net** *(some bilingual pages)*

The Yokai Pleasure Garden is a space with games for children and benches to sit on.

While Mizuki Road and the museum are Sakaiminato's main otaku spots, a few other places are worth a look.

**2 Yokai Shrine** 妖怪神社

Located on Mizuki Shigeru Road about halfway between the station and the museum, this tiny shrine is easily overlooked. Mizuki was personally involved in its creation and design. It features a 300-year-old *keyaki* tree and a stone ball shaped like Medama Oyaji (Kitaro's father, who happens to be an eyeball).

**3 Kitaro Yokai Soko** 鬼太郎妖怪倉庫

If you turn left at the first big intersection on Mizuki Road and head toward the sea, you'll find **Kitaro's Yokai Warehouse**. This is a sort of power spot guaranteed to heal any spiritual

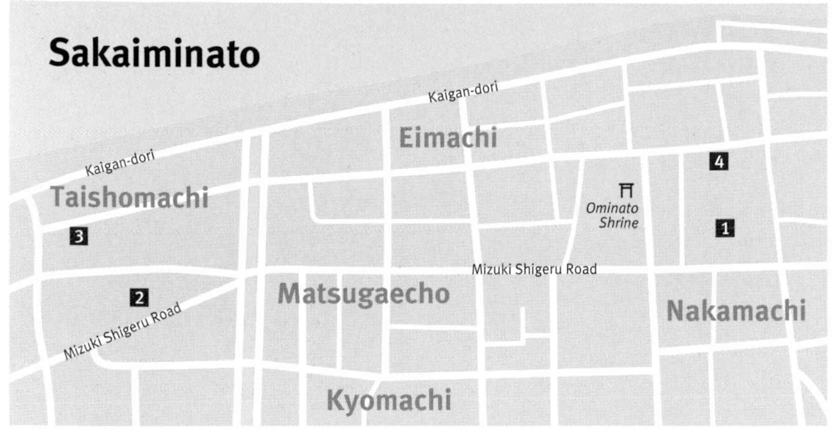


problem you might have. It's worth a visit even if you don't believe in such things, because the outside of the building is decorated with beautiful illustrations, and once you step inside, you get to walk a 330-foot (100-meter) corridor that takes you through a lineup of 30 *yokai* statues. It's almost a reverse haunted house.

**4 GeGeGe no Yokai Rakuen**
Located behind the museum, the **Yokai Pleasure Garden** may not be as gorgeous as its name suggests, but it's a free space with games for children and benches painted with Mizuki's characters. It's the ideal spot to take a break if you are tired.

**Aoyama Gosho Manga Factory***
青山剛昌ふるさと館
Twenty-five years have passed since Aoyama Gosho began to serialize *Detective Conan* in the Weekly Shonen Sunday magazine. Today, Conan is one of the best-known manga characters worldwide, and his stories have been published in some 20 countries. Opened in 2007, this museum, an hour's drive from Sakaiminato, offers a full immersion in Aoyama's world. As well as an impressive display of original drawings, film posters, and information about Aoyama's work, there is a popular experience section featuring tricks from Conan. You can even try some of the gadgets that Dr. Agasa invented for Conan, like the Voice-Changing-Bowtie and the Turbo-Engined Skateboard. For 200 yen, you can make your own original character badge, or rent a museum bike and explore the mile (1.4 km)-long Conan St. in search of Aoyama-related spots.
**Admission fee:** *700 yen (500 yen for junior and senior high school students; 300 yen for elementary school students; free if you visit on your birthday)* **Hours:** *9:30–17:30 year-round* **Access:** *1414 Yurashuku, Hokuei-cho, Tohaku-gun, Tottori* **gamf.jp/english** *(English)*

The Aoyama Gosho Manga Factory is a museum dedicated to the work of Aoyama Gosho, author of *Detective Conan*.

## Chugoku Museums

**(2) Igarashi Yumiko Museum**
いがらしゆみこ美術館
While *shojo* manga author Igarashi Yumiko is mainly known for *Candy Candy*, the famous heroine is nowhere to be found in this museum due to the legal battle Igarashi lost with writer Mizuki Kyoko over character and merchandise rights. What you'll find in the three-story building are about 50 original drawings she made for different stories, character goods (postcards, fans, etc.), a *purikura* sticker photo booth and—the main attraction for many visitors—the chance (for an extra fee) to wear a "princess dress" and get your photo taken. There are some 150 dresses to choose from.
**Admission fee:** *600 yen (400 yen for junior and senior high school students; 300 yen for children)* **Hours:** *10:00–17:00 year-round* **Access:** *9-30 Honmachi, Kurashiki, Okayama* **aska-planning-design.co.jp/museum/english.html** *(English)*

**(2) Kibi Kawakami Manga Museum**
吉備川上ふれあい漫画美術館
Part of a project to revitalize the area (there are many manga-inspired statues and billboards around the town), this is more a library than a museum, as it boasts a collection of 120,000 comics, half of them in open- stack shelves. That said, there's a small gallery devoted to the art of honorary director Tominaga Ichiro that you may want to check out.

**Admission fee:** *400 yen (300 yen for university and high school students; 200 yen for junior high and elementary students)* **Hours:** *9:00–17:00; closed Fridays and from 12/29 to 1/3* **Access:** *1834 Joto, Kawakami-cho, Takahashi, Okayama* **city.takahashi.okayama.jp/site/manga**

# EXPLORING SHIKOKU

Shikoku is the smallest of Japan's four main islands, with a warm and temperate climate. The island is famous for its ancient 88-temple Buddhist pilgrimage, its udon noodles and its mandarin oranges, but doesn't particularly stand out as an otaku destination. If you happen to be in the region, however, the towns of Takamatsu, Kochi and Kawaga all have something to offer fans of anime and manga, especially if you're a train otaku too!

Shikoku boasts the Kaiyodo Hobby train (ABOVE) and the Anpanman train (FACING PAGE).

## Tokushima

### 1 Nankai Books

One of Japan's oldest otaku stores is located in the Poppo Shopping Street next to Tokushima Station, focusing on comic books, magazines and trading cards. But they have many other genres in stock: light novels, *dojinshi*, video-game guides, CDs and even a few figures. The main store is on the first floor while the #2 store is upstairs.
**Hours:** *10:00–19:00* **Access:** *1-61-4 Terashima Honcho-Nishi (two minutes' walk from JR Tokushima Station)*
*Main store:* **nankaibooks.com**
*#2 store:* **nankaibooks.com/2**

You can enjoy anison karaoke at Anime Bar Ani-Labo.

ABOVE Nankai Books is one of Japan's oldest otaku stores, stocking comics, magazines, trading cards, *dojinshi* and even a few figures.

### 1 Animate

**Hours:** *10:00–19:30* **Access:** *1-5-1 Higashi-Shinmachi (seven minutes' walk from JR Tokushima Station)*

### 1 Anime Bar Ani-Labo

アニメバー あにらぼ

Tokushima is far from the usual otaku routes, but they sure know how to have fun. In this anime bar, you can do whatever you want: cosplay, *anison* karaoke (200 yen per song), and even show off your best *wotagei* (idol-appreciation) moves. The place is large by anime bar standards, with big windows and white furniture. There's a 500-yen seat charge. Food from 300 yen. Soft drinks cost 500 yen while booze starts from 650. Or you can opt for a 90-minute all-you-can-drink plan for 3,000 to 3,500 yen (charge included). You can also rent a costume for 1,000 yen or take a picture with a cosplaying staff for 500 yen.
**Hours:** *20:00–3:00* **Access:** *2F, 2-16-1 Kagoyamachi (twelve minutes' walk from either JR Tokushima or Awa-Tomida Station)*
**ani-labo.com/top.html**

## Kochi and Kagawa

### 3 Otaku Labo Royal おらく Laboロワイヤル

While this chain of DJ bars has branches in Kansai and other parts of Japan (including Okinawa), its home base seems to be Shikoku—particularly the cities of Takamatsu (Kagawa prefecture) and Kochi (Kochi prefecture). They often organize DJ events such as the monthly Anibeats (2,000 yen plus one drink for guys; 1,000 yen for gals).

### 3 Kochi labo

**Access:** *B1F, 2-1-36 Obiyamachi, Kochi (three minutes' walk from Horizume tram stop)*
**Hours:** *19:00–1:00*
**otaku-labo-royal.com/kochi**

### 4 Takamatsu labo

**Access:** *5F, 13-25 Furubabacho, Takamatsu (five minutes' walk from Kawaramachi Station)*
**Hours:** *18:00–1:00*
**ameblo.jp/takamatsuroyal**

### Kochi Anime Trains

The island of Shikoku is your perfect destination if you happen to be both an anime and train otaku. In fact, the smallest and most rural of Japan's four main islands has two such trains: the **Anpanman** and **Kaiyodo Hobby** trains.

### Shikoku Anpanman Trains

Anpanman was a natural choice for a Shikoku-based train since its creator, Yanase Takashi, was born in Kochi prefecture (see below for the museum in Kami devoted to his work). These colorful trains pass through many scenic areas on the Yosan, Dosan and

Kotoku train lines. A couple of them actually start from Okayama Station (Okayama prefecture). The others connect Takamatsu, Tokushima, Kochi, and other cities in Shikoku (see schedule).

The interiors are colorfully decorated, and some have a playroom. Some of the announcements are even made with the voice of Anpanman. You can order a special *ekiben* boxed lunch for 1,500 yen.

**Fee:** ***2,490 yen (one way)***
**jr-shikoku.co.jp/01_trainbus/event_train**
**jr-eki.com/aptrain/index.html** ***(schedule)***

### Kaiyodo Hobby Train

First launched in 2011, this train showcases legendary figure maker Kaiyodo's artistry and manufacturing excellence. The third version of the train, themed after the world of the *kappa* (a water *yokai*), debuted in 2016; it shows a stylized version of the mythical creature on a green or red background. Inside, a showcase was installed containing about 200 Kaiyodo figures, including a *kappa* diorama, animals and other assorted figures.

The train travels on the JR Yodo Line—a two-hour ride between Kubokawa Station in Kochi prefecture and Uwajima Station in Ehime prefecture.

**Fee:** ***1,850 yen (one way)***
**jr-shikoku.co.jp/yodo3bros/hobbytrain/index.htm** ***(schedule)***

**Shikoku**

## Anime-themed Trains in Japan

Anime-character trains are incredibly popular in Japan, and are often used to revitalize certain areas. The Evangelion Train, for instance, was originally scheduled to run between 2015 and 2017, but was extended to May 2018 due to its popularity.

Besides the **GeGeGe no Kitaro Train** (Tottori prefecture) and **Hatsune Miku Streetcar** (Sapporo) mentioned earlier in this book, there are a few other otaku trains in Japan:

### Tohoku

**Pokemon with YOU Train**
Connects Ichinoseki (Iwate prefecture) and Kesennuma (Miyagi prefecture).
**jreast.co.jp/e/joyful/pokemon.html**

### Kansai-Chugoku-Kyushu

**Hello Kitty Train**
Connects Shin-Osaka and Hakata (Fukuoka prefecture).
**jr-hellokittyshinkansen.jp/en**

### Chubu/Hokuriku

**Doraemon Streetcar**
Runs in the city of Takaoka, Toyama prefecture (birthplace of Fujimoto Hiroshi, one of Doraemon's two creators).

# Kochi Museums

**2 (1•2) Kami City Yanase Takashi Memorial Museum***
香美市立やなせたかし記念館
While Yanase Takashi owes his worldwide fame to his most famous creation, Anpanman, he was a truly multitalented and indefatigable artist, and this museum explores his work as a comic artist, illustrator and poet, as well as his lifelong support for popular culture. The museum is actually a sprawling complex divided into several facilities. The Anpanman Museum has a gallery displaying Yanase's art, a theater showing past TV anime, a room where all the merchandise is collected, and a diorama of Anpanman's town. The smaller Poem and Märchen Gallery, on the other hand, showcases the artworks that Yanase produced for his magazine of the same name. Other facilities include an annex for temporary exhibitions, a memorial park, and a playground. Check out the detailed English website for more information.
**Admission fee:** *700 yen (500 yen for junior and senior high school students, 300 yen ages three to eleven; kids under three are free)*
**Hours:** *9:30–17:00; closed Tuesdays, with a few exceptions (see website for details)*
**Access:** *1224-2 Birahu, Kahoku-cho, Kami*
**anpanman-museum.net/en** *(English)*

Kaiyodo Shimanto Museum Village celebrates the history of the world-famous figure maker.

**5 (1•4) Kaiyodo Shimanto Museum Village**
海洋堂シマント ミュージアム ビレッジ
Revered figure-maker Kaiyodo's museum is a must-see for every collector and toy fan.

The visit starts with the permanent collection tracing the company history, including Wonder Festival–related works and garage-kit artist Bome's masterpieces. There's even a booth recreating the tiny original shop in Osaka where it all started. However, the building's most striking feature is the giant model of a Spanish galleon, inside which you'll find display after display of Kaiyodo's famed *shokugan* (candy toys) and capsule figures. You can also participate in a diorama-making class (1,000 yen, apply at the front desk).

The **Kappa Museum**, on the other hand, preserves the entries from a figure-making contest organized to celebrate these mythical creatures who were said to live in the Shimanto River. Reaching these museums is quite a hassle, but definitely worth the effort. It helps that there's a shuttle service connecting them to the station.
**Admission fee:** *Kaiyodo Hobby Museum*

**BELOW** The Anpanman Museum is part of the Kami City Yanase Takashi Memorial Museum. **BELOW RIGHT** Yokoyama Memorial Manga Museum.

*Shimanto: 800 yen (400 yen for elementary and junior high school students); Kaiyodo Kappa Museum: 500 yen (300 yen); combined ticket: 1,200 yen (600 yen)* **Hours:** *10:00-18:00 (10-17 from Nov to the end of Feb); closed Tuesdays and from 12/28 to 1/1*
**Access:** *Utsuigawa, Shimanto, Takaoka-gun*
**ksmv.jp**

**(1•2) Yokoyama Memorial Manga Museum** 横山隆一記念まんが館
This museum was opened in 2002 in memory of Yokoyama Ryuichi, the first *mangaka* to be selected (in 1994) as a Person of Cultural Merit. Drawing on archival material donated by Yokoyama himself, this museum showcases his life, works and youthful spirit. His fans will particularly enjoy Fuku-chan Lane, an interactive area devoted to his most famous character, whose four-panel cartoon was serialized in a Japanese newspaper from 1956 to 1971. The Otogi Pro corner is about Yokoyama's anime studio; it features nonstop showings of works created there. Exact replicas of his workshop and even the bar that was in a corner of his house have been reproduced here. The facility includes a library with a sizeable manga collection.
**Admission fee:** *410 yen (200 yen for those over 64, and free for those under 18)*
**Hours:** *9:00–18:00; closed Mondays and from 12/28 to 1/4* **Access:** *2-1 Kutanda, Kochi*
**kfca.jp/mangakan**

The Yokoyama Memorial Manga Museum features fan-favorite Fuku-chan Lane.

# Shikoku Festivals and Events

## Tokushima

**Machi★Asobi**
Held in Tokushima City twice a year and organized by anime studio ufotable (*Fate/Zero* and *Fate/Stay Night*), this is one of Japan's most popular otaku festivals (82,000 people participated in 2017), attracting many industry people and cosplayers from abroad. It focuses mainly on popular and up-and-coming anime, but you can also enjoy art exhibitions, autograph sessions, live painting, voice-actor concerts, *itasha* displays and cosplay fashion shows. One of its highlights (in the May festival only) is the Anime Art Gallery Under the Bridge, a round-trip river cruise where you can admire giant posters placed under the bridges while listening to anime songs. The events are held in different places at the same time, so plan your visit carefully.
**Admission fee:** *Free* **Dates:** *May and September* **Hours:** *10:00–20:00*
**machiasobi.com**

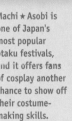

**Puchi★Asobi**
This Machi★Asobi offshoot has been held in Tokushima City since 2013. While the main event targets hardcore otaku in their 20s and 30s, this shorter version is a more inclusive, family-friendly affair that tries to attract children as well as adults.
**Admission fee:** *Free* **Dates:** *February/March*
**machiasobi.com/events/index.html**

**COMI-ESS**
Biannual *dojinshi* fair.
**Dates:** *July and December* **Hours:** *10:30–15:00*
**Access:** *Tokushima-ken JA Kaikan Bekkan徳島県JA会館別館, 5-12 Ichiban-cho, Kita Sako, Tokushima (two to three minutes' walk from Sako Station (next to Tokushima) on the JR Kotoku Line* **comiess.jp**

Machi★Asobi is one of Japan's most popular otaku festivals, and it offers fans of cosplay another chance to show off their costume-making skills.

## Kochi

**Tsurukame Zakka** つるかめざっか **/ Kuroshio Convenience** 黒潮コンビニエンス
These two *dojin* fairs, held in alternate years, are also known as "adult culture festivals" (they sell booze, too!). Check out the website for detailed schedules.
**Admission fee:** *400 yen* **Dates:** *February and August* **Hours:** *10:30–16:00* **Access:** *3–4F Kochi Shoko Kaikan 高知商工会館, 1-6-24 Honmachi, Kochi (15 minutes' walk from JR Kochi Station)*
**ww82.tiki.ne.jp/~kurocon**

# EXPLORING FUKUOKA

Japan's youngest major city is also one of the country's most dynamic, with the fastest-growing population—it recently overtook both Kyoto and Kobe. Being Asia's gateway to Japan (it's closer to Seoul than Tokyo), in the last few years Fukuoka has experienced a large increase in both tourism and trade, mainly from its Asian neighbors. Fukuoka as we know it today was created in 1889 with the merger of two cities, Hakata and Fukuoka. Interestingly, the two main otaku areas are located in these districts, even though old Fukuoka is known today as Tenjin. The Tenjin shops are distributed to the north and south of Tenjin Station; the Hakata shops are near Hakata Station.

**ABOVE** Fukuoka is one of Japan's most dynamic cities. **BELOW** Craft House Tenjin specializes in hobby robots.

## Fukuoka Shops

### General

**Card Shop Chanploo**

This shop has a simple design and clear display system. They even have a huge card database (10 volumes devoted to *Yu-Gi-Oh!* alone) and a touch-panel display where you can perform product searches and get estimates on always-changing market prices (some cards fetch more than 10,000 yen). ***Hours:*** *10:00–20:00* ***Access:*** *2-6-1-1104 Akasaka, Chuo-ku (12 minutes' walk from Akasaka Station, Kuko subway line)* **chanploo.com**

**4 Craft House Tenjin**

クラフトハウス天神

Born as a traditional craft shop selling materials and running workshops, this DIY store later added hobby robots (particularly humanoids) to its offerings, selling both exterior and interior parts and helping customers with assembling and programming them. Basic sets cost around 120,000

**RIGHT and INSET** Card Shop Chanploo has automated systems to help you search for the cards you need.

yen, the most popular items being Kondo Kagaku's KHR series (ideal for beginners) and Kyosho Corporation's MANOI series.

**Hours:** *10:00–18:00; closed Sundays and national holidays* **Access:** *2F, 2-3-10 Tenjin, Chuo-ku (five minutes' walk from Nishitetsu Fukuoka [Tenjin] Station)* **crafthouse.jp**

**Note:** *If you're based in Kyushu and you're into robots, you should check out the* **Kyushu Robot Renshu-kai** *(facebook.com/kyu.ren.robot), a "practice group" whose members meet once a month to exchange information, share ideas and train their robots for competitions.*

### 5 Henshin Zakka Shop Parfait

In this cosplay store you can not only buy wigs and other props, but you'll even find secondhand costumes (they look like new), trade in your used goods, and order custom-made outfits, wigs and even shoes. Getting a costume made usually takes two months and costs 20,000 to 30,000 yen.

**Hours:** *11:00–20:00; closed Mondays* **Access:** *2F, 3-2-18 Tenjin, Chuo-ku (five minutes' walk from Tenjin Station, Kuko subway line)* **cos-parfait.com**

### Minicar Gallery Pit Hakata

If as a child you were into *Yoroshiku Mechadoc*, *F* or *Initial D* and played with Choro-Q, you may want to trek all the way to this off-the-beaten-track shop boasting a collection of more than 3,000 model cars (the biggest in western Japan) from all over the world. The store is located on the second floor

of an actual automobile company. Be warned, these are high-quality die-cast models (made by pouring melted metal into highly accurate casts, allowing for great detail), and they certainly don't come cheap. But if you are a collector, or you're looking for a Lamborghini Countach LP 400, Ferrari 512 Berlinetta Boxer, Toyota 2000 GT or other models featured in the groundbreaking 1977 manga *Circuit no okami* (The Circuit Wolf), this is the place for you.

**Hours:** *10:00–19:00; closed Mondays and Tuesdays, New Year's and summer holidays, Golden Week and other national holidays* **Access:** *2F Hikari Jidosha, 2-4-80 Enokida, Hakata-ku (10 minutes' walk from Higashi-Hie Station, Kuko subway line)*



### 6 Mint Fukuoka

Mint first opened in Chiba in March 1995, when the TCG scene in Japan was virtually nonexistent (the world's first game, Magic: The Gathering, was created in 1993). The shop's simple and stylish layout (the shelves come up to about chest height) was modeled after American stores. They sell both TCG and sports cards.

**Hours:** *10:00–20:30* **Access:** *6F Tenjin ViVRE, 1-11-1 Tenjin, Chuo-ku (four minutes' walk from Tenjin Station, Kuko subway line)* **mint-web.jp**

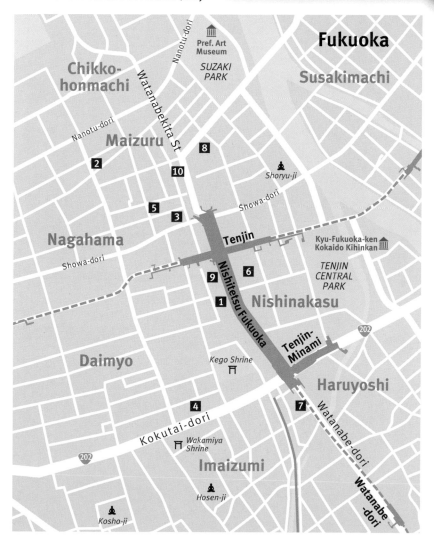

**UPPER and LOWER LEFT** Tom Sawyer has a wide range of figures and dolls. **RIGHT** Animate can always be relied on for otaku merchandise and art supplies.

**LEFT** At Toy Collector you may find unusual items that are not stocked by larger shops.

**BELOW** Animega is an otaku staple chain store selling manga, DVDs, games and character goods.

### Radio Amateurs' Shop Apollo Denshi
アポロ電子

Apollo Denshi is a paradise of *rajikon* (remote-controlled cars). In Japan, Tamiya was the first to enter the market, back in 1974, with its M4 Sherman tank. *Rajikon* generally come in 1/8, 1/10 and 1/12-scale sizes, and are far from cheap, but in 1999 the Kyosho Corporation revolutionized the market with a more affordable 1/24-scale car, the Mini-Z Racer, which can fit in the palm of your hand. All these models can be found at Apollo Denshi, together with an in-store circuit for Mini-Z cars that takes up more than half of the space. You can race your car all day for 500 yen (300 yen for children); once a month they hold their own race meet.
***Hours:** 9:00–18:30; closed around New Year's* ***Access:** 2-11 Ropponmatsu, Chuo-ku (three minutes' walk from Ropponmatsu Station, Nanakuma subway line)*

### 7 Tom Sawyer トム・ソーヤ

Though not very large, this shop has a wide range of products (figures, plamodel, garage kits, dolls, etc.) both new and old—lots of '80s jewels such as Dr. Slump, Spaceship Yamato and Armored Troopers VOTOMS. The Gunpla and Tamiya Mini 4WDs are particularly noteworthy: there are more than 300 minicars on sale, while the Gunpla include several rare items sold at regular prices. Last but not least, the shop provides artists with showcases to display their work (monsters, figures, Showa-era retro-style illustrations, etc.).
***Hours:** 10:00–20:00* ***Access:** B1F Tenjin Loft, 4-9-25 Watanabe-dori, Chuo-ku (three minutes' walk from Tenjin-Minami Station, Nanakuma subway line)*
**tomsawyer.ocnk.net**

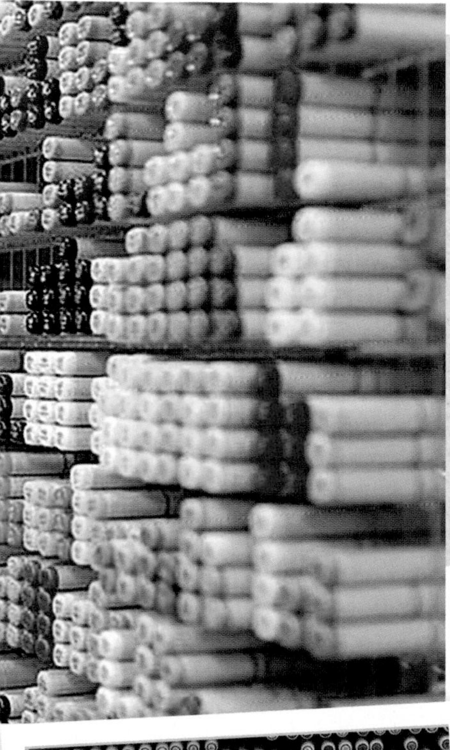

LEFT Art supplies at Animate. RIGHT and BELOW Gee! Store is the place for character goods and anime costumes.

**8** **Toy Collector**

This shop sells collector's toys (prize toys, *shokugan*, etc.), *gachapon* capsule toys, figures, trading cards and more. The owner and manager—a collector himself—used to make garage kits, and even owns a fully functional real-life replica of the red motorcycle that Kaneda rides in *Akira*. His aim is to sell items that bigger shops don't. Inside the store there's even a trading-card battle space.

**Hours:** *9:00–21:00* **Access:** *6F AEON Shoppers Fukuoka, 4-4-11 Tenjin, Chuo-ku (five minutes' walk from Tenjin Station, Kuko subway line)*

## Chain Stores

**6** **Animate Fukuoka Tenjin**

**Hours:** *10:00–20:30* **Access:** *6F Tenjin ViVRE, 1-11-1 Tenjin, Chuo-ku (four minutes' walk from Tenjin Station, Kuko subway line)*

**9** **Animega / Bunkyodo JOY**

**Hours:** *10:00–20:30* **Access:** *7F PARCO, 2-11-1 Tenjin, Chuo-ku (four minutes' walk from Tenjin Station, Kuko subway line)*

**Gamers**

**Hours:** *10:00–21:00* **Access:** *7F Hakata Bus Terminal, 2-1 Hakata Chuo-gai, Hakata-ku (next to JR Hakata Station)*

**10** **Gee! Store Fukuoka**

**Hours:** *11:00–20:00* **Access:** *2F, 3-16-21 Tenjin, Chuo-ku (four minutes' walk from Tenjin Station, Kuko subway line)*

**9** **One Piece Mugiwara Store Fukuoka**

**Hours:** *10:00–20:30* **Access:** *7F PARCO, 2-11-1 Tenjin, Chuo-ku (four minutes' walk from Tenjin Station, Kuko subway line)*

**Pokemon Center Fukuoka**

**Hours:** *10:00–21:00* **Access:** *8F, JR Hakata City (inside JR Hakata Station)*

**Ultraman World M78 Canal City Hakata Shop**
**Hours:** *10:00–21:00* **Access:** *B1F, 1-2-22 Sumiyoshi, Hakata-ku (10 minutes' walk from Gion Station, Kuko subway line)*

**8 Volks**
**Hours:** *10:00–20:00* **Access:** *6F AEON Shoppers Fukuoka, 4-4-11 Tenjin, Chuo-ku (five minutes' walk from Tenjin Station, Kuko subway line)*

ABOVE, LEFT and RIGHT Shopping mall Canal City is home to Ultraman World M78.

ABOVE Doll and figure specialist Volks is also represented in Fukuoka.

## Other Attractions

**(4•5) Anpanman Children's Museum and Mall**
See page 49 for description of the Yokohama branch.
**Entrance fee:** *1,500 yen (free for children under one)* **Hours:** *10:00–18:00*
**Access:** *5–6F Shimo-Kawabata, Hakata-ku (next to Nakasu-Kawabata subway station)*

**Next Generation World Hobby Fair**
次世代ワールドホビーフェア
See page 53 for description.
**Entrance fee:** *Free* **Date:** *February*
**Hours:** *9:00–16:00* **Access:** *Yafuoku! Domu, 2-2-2 Jigyohama, Chuo-ku (a 15-minute walk from Tojinmachi subway station)*

## HKT48 Theater 1

HKT48 (Hakata 48) is one of the more popular groups in the AKB48 family, and their theater (officially called Nishitetsu Hall) is the largest one in the AKB48 group, with a capacity of 300. As soon as you enter you are welcomed by huge panels featuring the faces of the group members. In the theater lobby there are coin lockers and a cloakroom (luggage and bags are not allowed inside), and a shop selling original merchandise.

As mentioned in the Tokyo chapter, attending a concert is not easy; you can't buy tickets on the day of the performance, but have to apply via an online lottery. Here's what you have to do:

• Register (free of charge) as a member with the AKB48 Group Ticket Center (global-ticket.akb48-group.com/en/home/top.php). Click the "Register" button in the upper right-hand corner and follow the instructions. You will be issued a membership registration ID and a password.

• Click the login button in the upper right-hand corner.

• Apply for the performance you want to see. In general, the application for general-category tickets is open from midnight to 20:00 for three days before the performance.

• Register the names of the people who will be attending.

• Confirm your application by checking the My Page section of your account.

The lottery selection usually takes place two days before the performance. If selected, you will receive a notification by mail, or you can check the results on the My Page section of your account.

On the day of the show, you should arrive at the venue 30 minutes before the start. Tickets are issued at the venue. Be sure to bring identification documents with you.

**Admission fee:** *3,100 yen for men; 2,100 yen for women and students; free for preschool kids* **Access:** *Nishitetsu Hall Solaria Stage (6F), 2-11-3 Tenjin, Chuo-ku (three minutes' walk from either Tenjin Station on the Kuko subway line or Nishitetsu Fukuoka [Tenjin] Station on the Tenjin Omuta line)* **hkt48.jp**

# Fukuoka Eateries

The Hakata branch of Anion Station has a relaxed, adult-oriented vibe.

**Anion Station アニON STATION**
This *anison* café chain has shops in Akihabara, Nanba (Osaka), Nagoya, Sapporo and Hakata (Fukuoka). Being a collaboration café, themes change every month or two. At the time of writing, for instance, Akiba's branch featured *The Idolmaster Million Live!* while the other shops hosted the smartphone game *Stand My Heroes*.

Among other things, you can put in requests from a song menu, and a DJ will play them on the spot. Apparently, this is a new feature that's recently become very popular. Each table even comes equipped with penlights!

The Hakata branch is a rather generous space, seating 54. The interior and atmosphere change every time, depending on the anime or game featured, but it's said to have a more relaxed, adult-oriented vibe than the other shops.

Of course, the menu for food (1,000–1,200 yen) and drinks (700–850 yen) features story-inspired offerings. For each 500-yen order, you'll receive a card that lets you request a song or a scene from an anime that's played on a giant screen. If you understand Japanese, you can enjoy the DJ explaining key points from the story. The DJs who work here, by the way, are students and graduates from an acting school for voice artists.

There's a 90-minute time limit, but the 500-yen cover charge includes a souvenir and one request card. You can reserve a table online or try your luck at the door.

**Hours:** ***11:00–23:00*** **Access:** ***Hakata Bus Terminal 7F, 2-1 Hakataekichuogai, Hakata-ku (next to Hakata Station, JR and subway lines)*** **bandainamco.co.jp/cafe_and_bar/anionstation/stations/hakata-bus.html**

**2 Tenjin Style 天神Style**
Believed to be the oldest maid café in Fukuoka (some say in all of Kyushu), this has all the typical trappings of a classic maid café, with *omuraisu* omelette over rice, decorated drinks and the chance to take a picture of—or with—a maid. Of the food offerings, their Ganso! Tonkotsu Pasta (Original Pork Bone Pasta) is particularly popular.

If you become a VIP member (for a fee), you are entitled to a special service and other privileges (e.g., sitting at the counter close to the maids, or attending invitation-only events). There's a 500-yen table charge, and you're expected to order a minimum of one item per hour. On Mondays when Tenjin Style is closed, the place becomes Blue Leopard, a *danso* café, from 17:00–22:00). The table charge is 300 yen for ladies, 500 yen for men.

**Hours:** ***15:00–22:00 (Tue–Fri), 12:00–22:00 (weekends and national holidays); closed Mondays*** **Access:** ***2F, 3-8-13 Tenjin, Chuo-ku (seven minutes' walk from Tenjin Station, Kuko subway line)*** **tenjin-style.com**

Tenjin Style is one of the oldest maid cafés in Fukuoka.

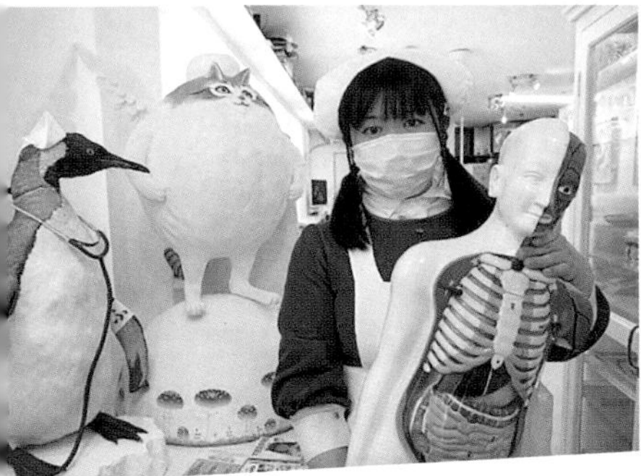

**3 Wonder Museum Sanatorium**
不思議博物館 サナトリウム
Forget all the usual anime bars and maid cafés: this is a truly original place. Made to resemble a germ-free hospital room, this café-cum-gallery is actually the annex of the privately run Wonder Museum (located in Nakagawa-machi), which displays works by artist and sculptor Sumi Takamasa. The all-white interior features all manner of medical apparatus, including a surgical light hanging from the ceiling. The furniture is completed by four anatomical models of the human body and, for some reason, a stuffed penguin wearing a stethoscope. Of course, the staff—or *fushigiko-chan* (Wonder Babes) as they are called here—are dressed like nurses. Even the menu follows a medical theme (e.g., ice cream and jelly served in a metal surgical tray, or a whitish drink that looks like barium). Check out their website for upcoming exhibitions and events.
**Hours:** *12:00–18:30; closed Wednesdays*
**Access:** *3F, 3-3-23 Tenjin, Chuo-ku (five minutes' walk from Tenjin Station, Kuko subway line)*
**bu9t-sm.wixsite.com/html/blank-1**

## Yuriko Tiger: A Unique Idol

The history of Japanese idols is long and fascinating, beginning in 1964 after the French movie *Cherchez l'idole*, starring then-19-year-old *yé-yé* singer Sylvie Vartan, became a hit in Japan and its theme song sold over one million copies. Since then, the term has been applied to cute teenaged girl and boy singers whose popularity is more based on their looks and personality than their singing talent. Girls, in particular, have traditionally conformed to the idealized image of the pure, innocent and chaste woman whose artistic amateurishness, far from being a problem, endears them even more to their fans.

Now more than ever, thousands of girls dream of becoming famous. Among them are an increasing number of foreigners, including Italian-born Yuriko Tiger.

**Where does your name come from?**
Yuriko was inspired by a character in the *Bloody Roar* video game. I've always liked the name Yuriko because it literally means "lily girl." Tiger is a sort of wordplay on Taiga, who is a character in the *Toradora!* light novel/anime/game franchise. It's also a reminder of my rebellious side.

**What took you to Japan?**
I wanted to become a famous pop icon in Japan. I knew that, as a foreigner, achieving my dream was almost impossible, but I wanted to give it a try anyway. I've had this dream since I was introduced to manga and anime at the age of 10. In junior high school I became interested in Japanese music and fashion through YouTube and the Internet. I was fascinated by cosplay, but I thought it was something they did only in Japan. So I was shocked when, at 13, I went to Lucca Comics and came face to face with Italian cosplayers. It was the best thing I had ever seen. For me it was like acting, choosing a character you liked every time. So I began to make my first costumes and took part in national contests.

**When did you come to Japan?**
When I was 19. Just before going to Japan, I attended a once-a-week basic Japanese class for six months. Then I studied in Tokyo for three wonderful months and vowed to return for a longer period as soon as possible. Back in Italy, I was even contacted by a TV program called *Game Time* that offered me a job as an assistant reporter in Tokyo. So I returned to Tokyo for a second six-month stay. The reporting job turned out to be a very small and short-lived experience, but at the same time I got signed by a model agency.

**How did you find that job?**
I had a few good studio photos made, and a Japanese friend helped me write a CV where I listed all my past experience (events, cosplay contests, etc.). Then I had to pass an interview. It's very important to approach your job hunt in a professional way. You

Italian-born Yuriko Tiger's typical working week might involve modeling, acting on television shows, cosplay events, as well as photo or video shoots. She's also working on new music project.

have to show them you are serious and reliable. You can't just send them a selfie, which some people do.

### So Japan really was the wonderland you had always dreamed about.

Yes, at first I was in paradise. But things changed when it was time to sign a contract and I saw a different side of Japanese culture that I knew nothing about. For example, the agency that sponsored my working visa told me I had to leave my Japanese school because now my job came before anything else, including studying. Secondly, I had to move from the shared house where I had lived until then into a condo, which was much more expensive. There were many other things, like having to ask for permission every time I wanted to go out with my friends. Last but not least, I was completely forbidden to have a boyfriend. Eventually I left the agency and began to work with my current manager.

### How and when did your first breakthrough happen?

It was completely by chance. I had been home to Italy for an engagement and on my return to Tokyo I was interviewed at Narita Airport by a popular TV program called *Why Did You Come to Japan?* They ended up devoting the whole 25-minute episode to me, showing my tiny apartment along with my enormous cosplay collection; then we went together to a maid café; and in the end they included a feature about my role as an assistant MC at the World Cosplay Summit in Nagoya. Before this show was filmed I had about 1,000 followers on Twitter, but the night my episode was aired on TV the number of followers suddenly shot up to 10,000 [she has 64,000 followers as of December 2020]. The year after that, 2015, was a banner year for me. So many things happened at once: I debuted on television as a talent, I recorded my first CD single, I did a few idol performances around Japan, and was finally recognized as a professional cosplayer. To be recognized in this way was very important for me, because in Japan foreign cosplayers never get paid jobs.

### Did you find it difficult to obtain a working visa?

Getting a visa as an entertainer wasn't difficult, because it was sponsored by my agency. The problem, though, is that there are quite a lot of restrictions on the kind of jobs you can actually do. That's the reason why most foreigners who work in this field are either married to a Japanese or are biracial *hafu* with Japanese citizenship, so they don't need a visa in order to be able to get work.

### What does a typical working week look like for you?

Recently I've been trying to diversify the things I do and I've been working on developing a more grown-up image. Now I'm more involved in modeling and I've even done a little acting on television. As you can imagine, every day is different, but meetings are a constant. The Japanese seem to really love business meetings, so we have about three or four meetings every week to discuss upcoming engagements. My weekends are usually taken up with photo and video shoots (which can go on for between four and ten hours), cosplay events and so on. On top of all that, I've been going to Sendai in northeastern Japan three to four times a month to work on a new music project with a band called Samurai Apartment, who mix traditional Japanese instruments and pop music.

# EXPLORING KYUSHU

Outside Fukuoka, the cities of Kitakyushu, in the north of Kyushu, and Kumamoto, further south, have worthwhile otaku attractions, including manga museums. Kitakyushu's shopping mall, Aruaru City, in front of JR Kokura Station, houses around 20 otaku attractions including maid and Internet cafés, and a cosplay studio. Unless noted, all shops are open from 11:00 to 20:00.

Maids pose for photographs at Maidreamin maid café.

BELOW Underland is a cosplay studio located on the 4th floor of Aruaru City.

ABOVE Kokura Castle is one of Kitakyushu's famous landmarks.
BELOW Kitakyushu Manga Museum.

## Kitakyushu

**Aruaru City**
**Access:** *Aruaru City, 2-14-5 Asano, Kokura-Kita-ku (five minutes' walk from JR Kokura Station)* **aruarucity.com/floor**

**Maidreamin** (maid café)
**Hours:** *11:30–22:00*
**Media Café Popeye** (manga and Net café) **Hours:** *24/7*
**Jungle** (figures, plamodel)
**Surugaya** (anything otaku)
**Jiku-chushin-ha** 軸中心派 (*moe* and *bishojo* tapestry and illustrations)
**Robot Robot** (figures, character goods)
**Machi Asobi Café** マチ★アソビ (collaboration café)
**G-Stage** (game center)
**Gamers** (anything otaku)
**Gacha Gacha Section** (*gachapon*)
**C-Labo** カードラボ (trading cards)
**Lashinbang** (anything otaku)
**Melonbooks** (anything otaku)
**Animate** (anything otaku)
**Mandarake** (secondhand and collectible items)
**Surugaya #2** (anything otaku)
**Smile Station** (otaku goods)
**UnderLand** (cosplay photo studio)
**Kitakyushu Manga Museum** (see Museums) **Hours:** *11:00–19:00*
**Hologram Theater** (holographic concerts/performances, including idols) **Hours:** *see schedule*
**aruarucity.com/hologramtheater**

# Kitakyushu Museums

### (3•4) Kitakyushu Manga Museum*
北九州市漫画ミュージアム

Though not particularly big, this rather new museum gives you a chance to explore the world of manga from many different angles. There's a corner showcasing the art of honorary director Matsumoto Leiji; an area chronicling the history of postwar manga and another explaining how they are made; a database about Kitakyushu-born comic artists; a Sommelier Corner which introduces recommended works; and, of course, a reading zone with 50,000 books.

**Admission fee:** *400 yen (200 yen for junior and senior high school students, 100 yen for elementary school students)* **Hours:** *11:00–19:00; closed on Tuesdays and at New Year's* **Access:** *5–6F AruAru City, 2-14-5 Asano, Kokurakita-ku, Kitakyushu* **ktqmm.jp**

### (1) Mojiko Watase Seizo Gallery
門司港わたせせいぞうギャラリー

Nothing typifies '80s manga like Watase Seizo's art. The prolific illustrator and comic artist is synonymous with lushly drawn romantic stories set in gorgeous locales. This small gallery gives you a taste of Watase's colorful art.

**Admission fee:** *100 yen (50 yen for elementary and junior high school students)* **Hours:** *9:00–17:00; closed on Tuesdays and New Year's holidays* **Access:** *1F Kyu Osaka Shosen, 7-18 Minato-machi, Moji-ku, Kitakyushu* **mojiko.info/spot/osaka.html**

Kitakyushu Manga Museum explores the world of manga from many different angles.

# Kumamoto Museums

### Koshi Manga Museum
合志マンガミュージアム

Recently opened comic library with a collection of 70,000 volumes, 15,000 of which are displayed on open-stack shelves. They organize manga-related events and workshops, too.

**Admission fee:** *300 yen (100 yen for junior and senior high school students)* **Hours:** *10:00–18:00; closed Mondays, on the last day of the month (unless it's a Saturday, Sunday, or holiday) and at New Year's* **Access:** *1661-271 Miyoshi, Koshi* **city.koshi.lg.jp/life/pub/detail.aspx?c_id=28&id=3024**

### (1) Yunomae Manga Museum
湯前まんが美術館

Comprising three singularly designed buildings that were inspired by a traditional local wooden toy called a *kijima*, this place was originally born as the Nasu Ryosuke Memorial Museum, as it houses a permanent collection of the works of late political cartoonist. Besides the usual well-stocked library, the museum often organizes special exhibitions of Japanese artists.

**Admission fee:** *300 yen (100 yen for junior high and elementary school students)* **Hours:** *9:30–17:00; closed from 12/28 to 1/3* **Access:** *1834-1 Yunomae-machi, Kuma-gun* **yunomae-manga.com**

### Yunomae Manga Festa
ゆのまえ漫画フェスタ

This otaku festival packs a lot of events into just a few hours: stage shows, cosplay, signings, *anison* concerts and talk shows, and the Nasu Ryosuke Manga Award exhibition.

**Admission fee:** *Free* **Dates:** *mid-November* **Hours:** *Saturdays 15:00–17:00; Sundays 9:30–16:00* **Access:** *Near the Yunomae Manga Museum (see above)*

LEFT A taste of the colorful art at Mojiko Watase Seizo Gallery. INSET Poster for the annual Yunomae Manga Festa. RIGHT The Koshi Manga Museum has 15,000 volumes on display.

# TRAVEL TIPS

## When to Go

Nearly every month there are some interesting otaku events and festivals going on in Japan, and the shops in particular are open all year round. Summer, though, can be brutal in most of the country, as the mid-June to mid-July month is the rainy season in most places, and in July and August temperatures often exceed 91°F (33°C) and humidity averages 80 percent, which are not the ideal conditions for walking around with a backpack and bags bursting with manga and toy purchases. Unfortunately, if you are into idols you will have to brave the heatwaves and the biblical crowds and visit in August, because all the main idol festivals take place during that month. Spring is milder (and you may have a chance to see the fabulous cherry blossoms during their brief season between March and April) but the weather can be quite unpredictable. Winter, on the other hand, is cold and often windy but very dry, with mostly blue skies—unless you're traveling to Hokkaido or the west-coast, which get buried under mountains of snow. The first two or three days of the new year are also the one time when almost all shops and museums are going to be closed. Weather-wise, fall is probably the best time to go, as there's a good range of otaku festivals to choose from in that season and the temperatures are pleasant.

## Learn Some Japanese

Finding your way around Japan and communicating effectively can sometimes be a challenge, as most signs are in Japanese and surprisingly few people can speak decent English. While learning the Chinese characters known as kanji can take a lifetime, I recommend you take the time to learn the katakana alphabet, because many shop names and other useful information (things they sell, product names, restaurant menus, etc.) are often written this way. Being able to read this information will make your stay in Japan much easier. For those of you who are interested in studying Japanese, Tuttle Publishing has a wide range of Japanese-language-learning books for students of every level. Check out the website **tuttlepublishing.com**

## Packing

**1.** A backpack is essential for moving around.
**2.** It would be good to bring a spare foldable bag, too. Considering all the things you surely want to buy, it will come handy on your return trip. Just remember not to exceed the maximum total luggage weight or the check-in people at the airport may charge you an extra fee.
**3.** Unless you are planning to go somewhere fancy, casual clothes are generally okay, but try not to look too shabby. In Japan, people are going to judge you by the way you look.
**4.** You are going to walk, walk, walk, so I strongly recommend bringing a change of shoes.
**5.** Don't forget your prescription medication and other necessary medicine you may not find in Japan.

## Jet Lag

When you arrive in Japan you will probably be severely jet-legged, which means by 9:00 pm you won't be able to keep your eyes open, while the day after you will be staring at the ceiling at 3:00 or 4:00 am. So try to stay up as long as you can. The sooner you manage to get back to a normal cycle,

The goods in this shop are organized according to the Japanese hiragana alphabet.

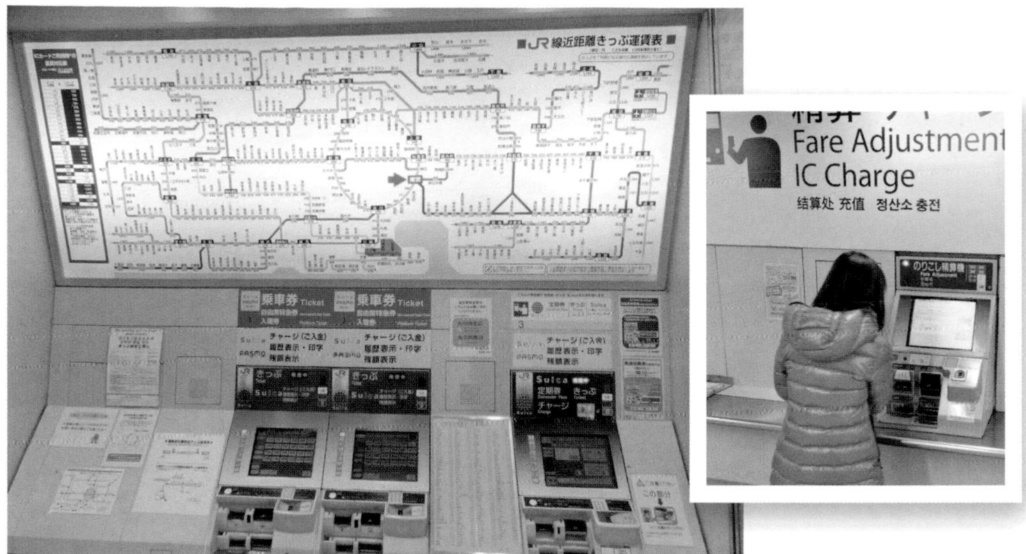


There's no need to calculate your train fare when you purchase a Suica or Pasmo smart card. These smart cards can be charged at fare adjustment machines and ticket vending machines in stations.

the better, because in Japan there's not much you can do early in the morning, and the shops usually open between 10:00 and 11:00.

## Getting Around

Trains are the best way to go anywhere. They are safe, clean, reasonably cheap and show up frequently. During your trip to Japan you'll definitely find yourself using the JR (Japan Railways) system and the local subways, and maybe even some other private train lines. The good news is that you can pay for all your rides with a Suica or Pasmo smart card. These cards can be purchased at any ticket vending machine (just follow the English instructions) and are rechargeable. Even though they are issued by different train companies, they can be used on any train line and also on many buses. Just swipe them on the sensor when entering and exiting. (These cards are really handy—you can even use them to pay for goods at convenience stores and vending machines.) When taking a train, if you are not sure about which track number your train is, you can ask in Japanese: "*Sumimasen*, [place name] *wa nanban desu ka*?" As for train etiquette, talking loudly (especially on your cell phone) and eating on trains is frowned upon. Just don't do it.

If you are on foot and looking for an address, don't hesitate to ask the police. You'll see police boxes on many street corners, and people in Japan use these as information centers.

## Money

While more and more places now accept credit cards, Japan is still very much a cash-only country (this is particularly true of the smaller independent shops). So get some yen before leaving, or exchange some of your currency at the airport when you arrive. Remember to call your credit-card company before leaving and tell them you're going to use it abroad.

You can use your ATM card only at an international ATM. You can find them at Citibank branches and at post offices.

## Shopping

Nonresident foreign customers can take advantage of the duty-free shops. Just remember to take your passport with you. If you buy appliances, be sure to get overseas multilingual models. Many local stores specialize in used games, manga and DVDs, which are an excellent bargain as they are often discounted by around 50 percent. No need to worry, because they only sell these secondhand goods if they are in good condition, and you'll see that many of them could easily pass for brand new items.

If you can't find the price on a particular item, it's usually okay to ask "How much?" in English, but if the clerk doesn't understand you, try the Japanese "*Ikura desu ka*?" and keep paper and pen ready so they can write it down for you.

Prices are pretty much fixed, so don't bother asking for a discount. Haggling is just not part of Japanese culture. However, at shows some sellers are willing to give you a 10 percent (more rarely 20 percent) discount. You may also have an outside chance at a small independent secondhand store, especially if you buy a lot of things.

In restaurants and cafés, you don't have to tip, although in certain places you will be asked to pay a table or seat charge.

## Food and Drink

All the cafés, bars and restaurants included in this guide are otaku-themed eateries, but that doesn't mean you have to eat in such places every day—they are far from cheap. Many of the common restaurants have plastic food displays which make ordering much easier. Eating in Japan is not particularly expensive (as long as you stay away from the high-end fancy restaurants) and, unless you are exceptionally unlucky, on average the food is very good. The ubiquitous convenience stores (*conbini* in Japanese) sell lots of food and drinks too. Most of the food is not particularly healthy, being full of preservatives, but a cheap rice ball or some chocolate can help you fill the hole in your stomach between meals. The added bonus for otaku hunters is that at every conbini there are often anime tie-ins with snack food—a cheap way to expand your collection of toys and character goods. And don't forget all the vending machines selling all kinds of drinks (stay away from English tea and coffee unless you like them extra sweet) and even some snacks.

## Mobile Phones

If you have a mobile phone with 4G technology, you can use it in Japan (ask your telephone carrier how much you will be charged). Otherwise you will need a SIM card that you can get from a vending machine at some airports (e.g. Narita) or Odaiba's Aqua City in Tokyo. It costs about 3,700 yen for one week and around 5,000 for two. They both offer a maximum download speed of 150 megabits per second and 50 MBps as an upload speed. If the data amount exceeds 100 MB a day, the network speed will slow down. You can even buy a smartphone and SIM card together for 13,000 yen. You will need to choose your SIM card size (don't forget to check this information before you travel); pay with your credit card (sorry, no cash); activate your SIM card by scanning your passport at the vending machine, then typing in your email address and contact number in Japan (your hotel phone number will do); go to the "mobile networks" setting and then "access point names." If you have never done this before it might be a little confusing. WARNING: you can't make voice calls with a SIM card purchased this way.

## Toilets

Public toilets are rare (most often found in public parks and gardens); those that you can find are often the old-style squat type, and rather smelly. On the other hand, you can always duck into a department store or convenience store and use the bathroom there. They're generally quite clean, and you don't have to buy anything in order to use them.

## Crime and Safety

Japan is one of the safest places on Earth, even considering how crowded it is. You can go anywhere at all times of day or night without fear of being mugged or attacked by angry hooligans. However, always use your judgment whenever you sense you may find yourself in a bad situation. Most importantly, don't ever get into a fight, especially with a local. The last thing you want to do is to deal with the police. Cops in Japan have a lot of discretionary power and can detain you for up to three days without charging you.

## Hentai (Pornography)

Pornography is part of otaku culture, and Akihabara is Hentai Central. Erotic images are everywhere, with scantily clad teenagers smiling from posters, pillows and mug cups. These things are generally accepted and even actively sought out. This doesn't mean, though, that mainstream shoppers won't be offended by some of the more hardcore stuff. The Japanese moral police have a weird approach to censoring pornography, and even the ubiquitous convenience stores are allowed to sell magazines with stories featuring incest, rape and sex with junior high girls. Just be aware of this and consider yourself warned.

## Taking Photos and Videos

Taking pictures and videos in certain stores—particularly inside game centers and maid cafés—is prohibited (even the Akiba maids who are out in the street advertising their cafés usually don't like to be photographed). In a store, if you want to be on the safe side, ask beforehand (*"shashin totte mo ii desu ka?"*). In a game arcade, be very discreet. The first time you get caught, they'll usually ask you politely to stop. If they catch you again, they will ask you to leave.

## Meeting People

There are several Meetup.com groups devoted to all things otaku. Check to see whether they'll be up to something when you are here.

# OTAKU GLOSSARY

**Akiba-kei** (lit. Akihabara style): Slang term dating back to the early 1980s that is used as a synonym for otaku.

**anikura**: Anime-song club music.

**anison**: Song from an anime show or film.

**bishojo**: Beautiful girl.

**BL/ Boys' Love**: See *yaoi*.

**bromide**: Commercial photographic portrait of a celebrity (singer, actor, etc.).

**burikko**: Woman or girl who acts cute by playing innocent and helpless.

**butler's café**: Cosplay restaurant where well-dressed men cater to a female clientele.

**cameko** (short for camera *kozo*, meaning camera boy): People who like to take cosplay pictures.

**cheki** (lit. small instant camera): A Polaroid picture taken (for a fee) in a maid café.

**chogokin** (lit. "Super Alloy," a fictitious material that appeared in Mazinger Z): A line of Popy/Bandai-made die-cast metal robot and character toys.

**danso**: A girl dressed as a boy.

**dojin**: Independent productions (books, music, films, software) not available through standard commercial outlets.

**dojinshi**: Fanzine.

**fujoshi** (lit. rotten girl): Female fans of manga and novels that feature romantic relationships between men.

**gachagacha**: See *gachapon*.

**gachapon**: Capsule toys dispensed by a vending machine, also called *gachagacha*.

**garage kit**: Model kits, usually cast in polyurethane resin.

**Gunpla**: Gundam plastic models.

**hentai**: Anime and manga pornography.

**itachari**: Bicycle version of an *itasha* (see).

**itasha**: Car decorated with manga, anime or video-game characters (usually cute girls).

**itatansha**: Motorbike version of an *itasha* (see).

**kaiju**: Monster movie.

**layer**: Short for cosplayer.

**light novel**: Short young-adult novel mainly targeting middle and high school girls.

**mecha**: Robots controlled by people (e.g., Mazinger Z, Grandizer, Gundam).

**menko**: Game in which a card is slapped or thrown down to flip over an opponent's card.

**moe** (neologism): Feeling of affection felt for fictional characters from anime, manga and video games; also used to describe a female character who elicits such a feeling.

**niji sosaku**: Fanzine that parodies existing mainstream manga.

**otagei**: See *wotagei*.

**otome** (lit. maiden, young girl): Female otaku

**OVA** (Original Video Animation): An animated film or series made specifically for release in home-video formats without prior showings on television or in theaters.

**plamodel** (also **pla-mo**): Plastic model.

**purikura** (short for "print club"): Stickers made from photo-booth pictures.

**rajikon**: A radio-controlled model.

**shojo manga**: Manga aimed at teenaged female readers.

**shokugan**: Small toy that comes packaged with candy sold at convenience stores and supermarkets.

**shonen manga**: Manga aimed at young male readers.

**situation CD**: A CD featuring an audio drama in which a storyline from an anime, video game, TV series, etc., is continued or expanded.

**sofubi**: Toy figure made from soft vinyl.

**tokusatsu**: Live-action film or TV drama that relies heavily on special effects.

**V-cinema**: Straight-to-video movies.

**visual novel**: Interactive fiction game featuring static, anime-style graphics, multiple storylines and multiple-choice decision points.

**wota**: Fans of idol singers.

**wotagei**: Akiba-style dancing and cheering routines.

**yaoi**: Genre of male-male romance narrative, also called BL or boys' love.

# WORKING IN JAPAN

Today manga and anime are widely available in many languages, thanks to the indefatigable work of many professional and amateur translators. Japanese pop culture is celebrated in countless conventions, while online communities have popped up everywhere. Many countries even have *dojinshi* (fanzine) fairs and cosplay events. In other words, it's become very easy to get your daily fix of your favorite otaku genre.

For some people, the new challenge is to go one step further by moving to Japan to get a job in the Japanese pop-culture industry. The people whose interviews are featured in this book did exactly that. Taken together, their stories clearly show their passion, as well as the challenges one has to meet when living abroad and trying to make sense of a country with very different cultural and social values.

People who aspire to work in anime seem to face the biggest problems. As American-born Henry Thurlow told *BuzzFeed*, a few years ago he managed to get hired by an anime studio only to discover what the term "work hell" really meant: regular six-day work weeks of ten-hour days that turn into six-week nonstop marathons without a single day off when they have to beat a deadline. All this for a salary that—unless you're a top artist—is invariably far below minimum wage. A recent survey by the Japan Animation Creators' Association pegged the average annual income at roughly $10,000, with a few higher-paying studios offering up to $14,000. Eventually Thurlow, in order to keep doing what he loved most without making himself crazy or ill, created his own animation studio, D'Art Shtajio, whose mission is to act as a link between the Japanese animation industry and outside markets, particularly assisting foreigners who want to produce anime-style videos with Japanese studios.

At the other end of the spectrum, independent foreign video-game professionals seem to have prospered in Japan while creating a tightly knit community mainly based in Kyoto (see Expat Game Developers, page 83). They develop their own games and act as localizers and organizers. The key seems to be to avoid working for established publishers, since a lot of mainstream game development seems to be stale and rigid. As veteran game programmer Dale Thomas wrote at *Quora Digest*, "It is really frustrating for foreigners who come in and can easily see how to make things so much better but are not allowed because of the rigidity."

The manga industry seems to be another impregnable bastion, but once in a while a few foreigners do manage to get published. Åsa Ekström moved to Tokyo from Sweden in 2011 and began posting her four-panel comic *Nordic Girl Åsa Discovers the Mysteries of Japan* on her blog while studying graphic design. Eventually her manga was picked up by publishing giant Kadokawa.

Manga artists can't always sustain their initial success. Felipe Smith, an American artist who moved to Tokyo about 10 years ago, created a Japanese-language manga serialized by Japan's largest publisher, Kodansha. Unfortunately, it didn't last, and he moved back to the US a few years later, where he found success working for Nickelodeon and Marvel Comics.

One thing that works in the favor of foreigners is that Japanese publishers and producers, who once focused exclusively on the Japan market, are now more eager to consider overseas tastes. So they have begun welcoming non-Japanese people to help them shape their stories.

Aspiring artists must remember, however, that working in Japan requires a full immersion in Japanese culture. As anime studio Production I.G's PR Francesco Prandoni says, "What most people sending e-mails to our HR department tend to forget is that being proficient in both spoken and written Japanese is not simply a plus, but a sine qua non in order to work in a Japanese company, because that is the only language your coworkers will be using and understand."

Voice acting and singing is another field where a talented foreigner may find lucrative work in Japan. One such example is American-born Diana Garnet, a former exchange student who moved to Japan almost 10 years ago. She got a contract with Sony Music Entertainment after winning an episode of NTV's singing competition *Nodo Jiman the World*. Garnet, who now performs exclusively in Japanese, pointed out in an interview with the *Japan Times* that she had to learn a new style of singing: "J-pop singers project their voice from the front and back of their throat, while English singing comes from down here. I had to build up the right muscle structure so I didn't damage my vocal cords."

So is it easy to have a career in an otaku-related field in Japan? Definitely not. But it's not impossible, either, as long as you have certain qualities and aren't easily discouraged.

# Useful Information

## General Schools

These schools cover the whole spectrum of otaku-related careers, from manga and anime to figure-making, voice acting and singing

Yoyogi Animation Gakuin
**yoani.co.jp/global-en**

Amusement Media Sogo Gakuin
**amgakuin.co.jp**

## Manga

### Manga Schools

**Yokohama Manga Kyoshitsu**
**yokohama-manga.com**

### Manga Competitions

**Japan International Manga Award**
Originally established in order to expand international exchange and global understanding of manga culture, this large-scale international manga competition, run by the Ministry of Foreign Affairs, is the oldest in the business.
**manga-award.mofa.go.jp/index_e.html**

**Morning International Comic Competition**
Run by the publisher Kodansha. This magazine's main audience is adult males, but the competition accepts all genres.
**morningmanga.com/micc**

**Shonen Jump Award**
The best-selling and longest-running (since 1969) weekly manga magazine *Shonen Jump* organizes not one but three different competitions: the Tezuka Award (story manga); the Rookie Award; and the brand new Jump New World Manga Award (with monthly winners). All work must be done in Japanese.
**shonenjump.com/j/mangasho**

**Silent Manga Audition**
Another new international competition. The main rule here is that the artist has to communicate everything via drawings alone.
**manga-audition.com**

**Manga Jiman (UK residents only)**
Organized by the Japanese Embassy in the UK and open to all UK residents aged 14 and over.
**facebook.com/MangaJiman** and **mofa.go.jp/policy/culture/exchange/pop/mangaindex.html**

## Anime

### Animation schools

**Tokyo School of Anime**
**anime.ac.jp/en/school/index.html**

**Tokyo Animation College**
**tokyo-anime.jp/lag/english/index.html**

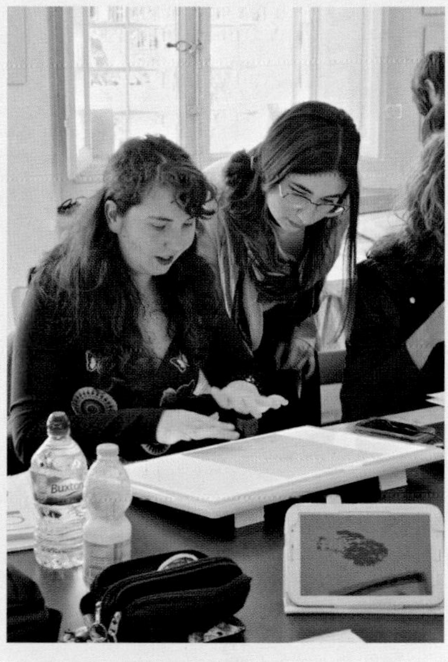

## Voice Acting and Singing

### Talent Agencies

If you are a voice actor, narrator, singer or musician looking for work in Japan, the following agencies are worth a try.

Zenith, Inc. **zenithinc.jp/english.html**
DAG Music **dagmusic.com/en**
Avocado **avocado.co.jp**

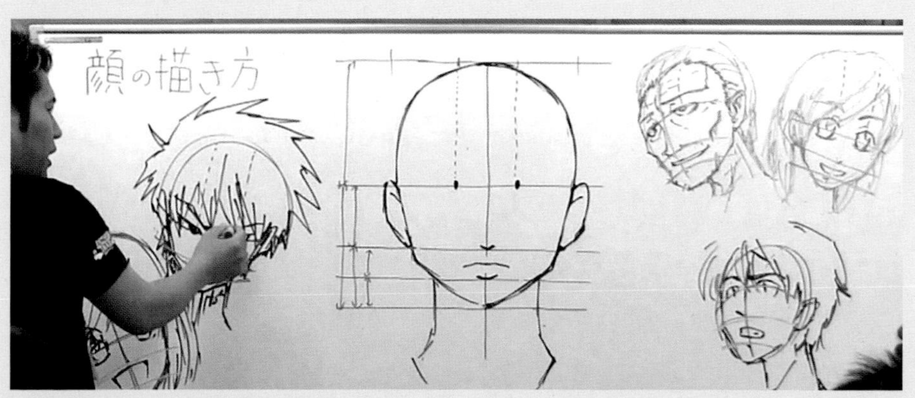

# PHOTO CREDITS

All photos Gianni Simone except: **2 top left** Linriel; **2 bottom right, 18 top right & bottom left, inside back cover left top** Yuichi Kosio; **3 top left, 89 bottom middle & bottom right** John Gillespie; **3 top right** temaki; **3 bottom right, 51 top right, 55 middle right** @Jam Project; **6 bottom left** Taichiro Ueki; **8 top left** Frances Delgado; **8 middle** Nakagawa PROOF; **9 bottom left and right** Meiji University Yonezawa Yoshihiro Memorial Library of Manga and Subcultures; **10 middle** Christian Van Der Henst S.; **10 middle right, 53 middle right & bottom middle** Steve Nagata; **11 top right** Swallowtail; **11 bottom left, 21 bottom, 22 middle** Karl Baron; **11 bottom middle** Ishimoto Ryuta; **14 top** KT/S·N·STP, KT/S·TM; **16-17 bottom** sumiisan; **17 middle right** Yee's photo; **20 bottom right, 31 top middle, 40 top right** Guilhem Vellut; **22 top left** Dick Thomas Johnson; **22 bottom right** Ryo FUKAsawa; **23 middle, 26 middle** kazamatsuri; **26 top right, front cover flap** Shutterstock, beibaoke; **27 top left** Stefan; **27 top middle** Helen Cook; **28 top right** Taco Ekkel; **31 middle right** Big Ben in Japan; **33 middle left, 62 middle right** demiurgo; **33 bottom left** Esa Juntunen; **34 top right** fletcherjcm; **36 middle left** Erik; **36 bottom left** Kim Ahlstrom; **37 top left** Suginami Animation Museum; **37 top middle** Tachikawa Manga Park; **39 bottom middle & bottom right** BL Gakuen; **42 top middle** Stormstill; **42 middle & middle right** Danny Choo; **42-43 top** Hikaru Kazushime; **43 top middle** Kana Natsuno; **52 top left** Kana Natsuno; **43 middle** CrunchyLens; **44 top right** 思弦張; **45 middle left** Super Comic City; **47 bottom right** Matsumoto Katsuji Gallery; **48 top right** Kiichi – Shogakukan; **48 bottom middle** Sora; **49 top right, 79 top right & middle right, inside back cover (Anpanman)** Tomohiro Ohtake; **49 bottom** all Fujiko F Fujio Museum; **52 middle left** Makoto Kojima; **52 bottom right** Japan Amusement Expo; **53 top left, 55 top right** Jump Festa; **54 top middle** Jeremie Eades; **54 middle right** ASL; **54 bottom left** Wonder Festival; **55 top left** World Character Summit in Hanyu; **56 top middle** Walter Lim; **56-57 bottom, 57 top right, 143 Osaka, inside back cover bottom right** Reginald Pentinio; **58 top right** hans-johnson; **58 middle right, inside back cover left center** chopstuey; **58 bottom** Pedro Szekely; **59 top right, 76 bottom left** m-louis; **59 bottom right** Carrie Kellenberger; **61 top** Calvin YC; **61 bottom left** TAKA@P.P.R.S; **61 bottom right** Mike Wyatt; **62 bottom left, 71 middle & middle right** japanexperterna; **62-63 top, 64 bottom left** DocChewbacca; **63 middle** Longneck, Kaitei Majin MOON; **67 bottom right** Zephy Thor; **75 top right** Umeda Arts Theater; **75 bottom right** VR Zone Osaka; **76 top left** John Weiss; **76 middle** Chris Gladis; **80 top middle & bottom left** Olivier Bruchez; **81 top left & bottom right** Danny Foo; **81 top right, middle right & bottom left** Franck Singler; **82 top middle** Nanae Chrono; **82 middle** Yana; **84 top right, 136 bottom left, 143 Kobe** Antonio Tajuelo; **90 bottom right** World Cosplay Summit; **91 bottom left** World Cosplay Summit; **97 top middle** Yasumo; **98 right** public domain, Wikipedia; **100 bottom right** Ishinomori Pro/Toei; **105 top left, middle right & bottom middle** World Cosplay Summit; **105 top right & bottom right** Matias Tukiainen; **106 top right, 107 top right** Adam Pasion; **106 bottom left, 107 top left** Comic Art Tokyo; **110 top right** Rok1966; **118 middle** Kono Fumiyo/Mappa; **120 bottom left** Puffyjet; **130 middle right** ASL; **132 middle right, 133** Yuriko Tiger; **141 top right** Lucca Manga School; **141 bottom** Yoyogi Animation Gakuin; **143** Kyoto, Brian Sterling; Sakaiminato, Mizuki Shigeru; Tokyo, Yoshikazu Takada; **front cover clockwise from top left** ©Klondike, Hagii Kaoru; Shutterstock, Katsumi Yamamoto; dygn; iStock; Adobe Stock #268258420; Shutterstock, Sineenat; Shutterstock, Piyato; Pedro Szekely; Cover Kitchen; Shutterstock, Shuttertong; Cover Kitchen; **back cover bottom left** Cover Kitchen; **inside back cover, right column, center** Brian Sterling.

# ACKNOWLEDGMENTS

Although this book is mainly the result of my personal research, and I am the sole person responsible for any mistakes, I have been lucky enough to be helped, advised and inspired by several amazing people to whom all my gratitude goes.

Working with Cathy Layne is always a pleasure. She has improved my manuscript in so many ways that I should put her name beside mine on the cover. I have worked with many editors, but she is, very simply, the best.

The sidebar on maid cafés is partly based on an essay by pop culture expert and otaku supremo Patrick W. Galbraith: "Maid in Japan: An Ethnographic Account of Alternative Intimacy" (in *Intersections: Gender and Sexuality in Asia and the Pacific*, Issue 25, February 2011).

While I spent my fair share of time and money in countless game centers, Brian Ashcraft's informative and entertaining *Arcade Mania!* gave me a needed historical perspective on the video game industry.

I want to thank all the people who agreed to be interviewed. Special thanks to my man Adam Pasion, and to Rebecca Koga for being an endless source of information on cosplay.

An honorable mention goes to Claude Leblanc, my indefatigable boss at *Zoom Japon* magazine, who keeps having faith in me.

Last but not least, I want to thank my folks for letting me watch the *Grendizer* anime TV series at dinner time one fateful day in April 1978; and my lovely wife Hisako for kicking my butt every time I rest on my laurels.

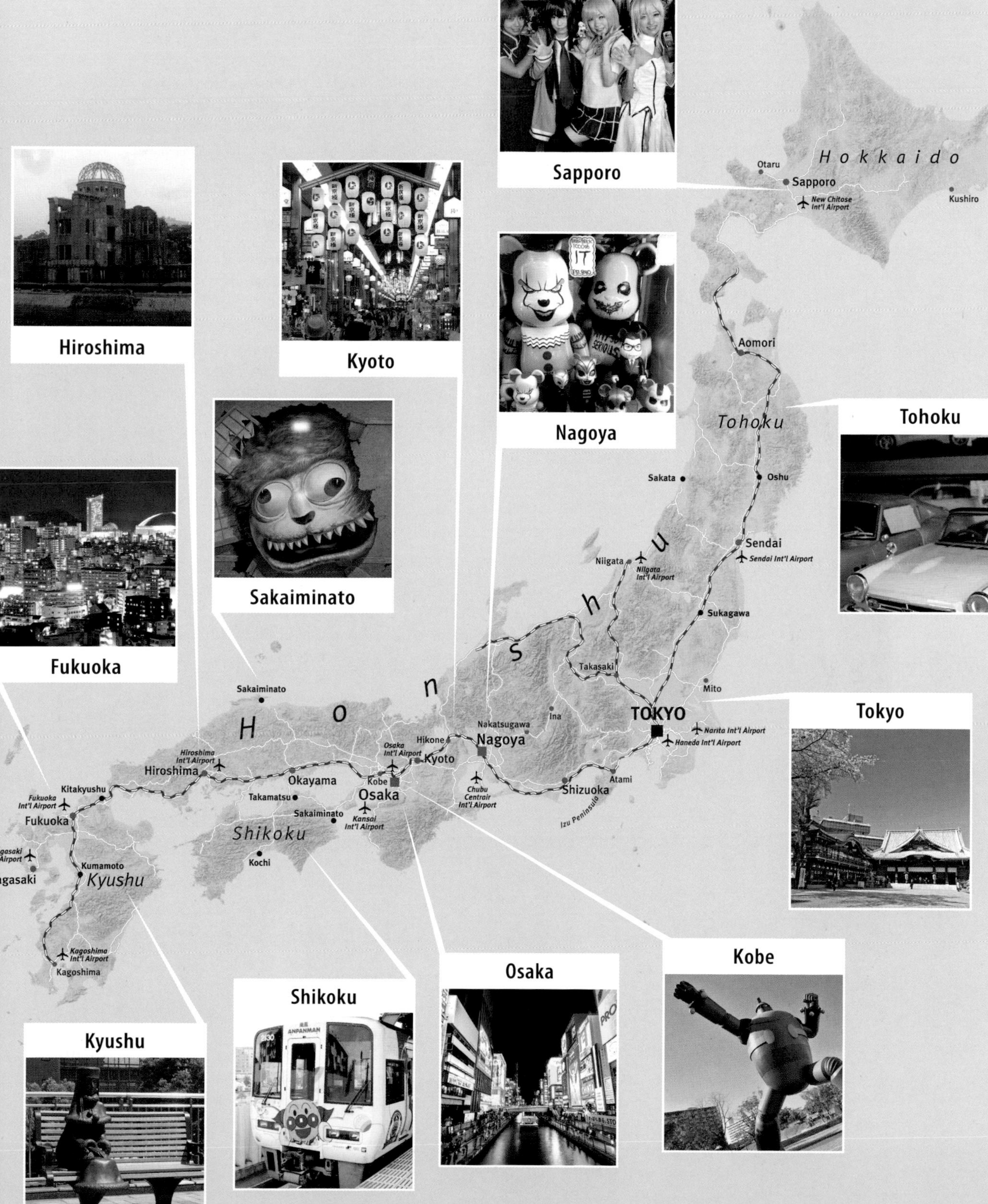

Sapporo
Hiroshima
Kyoto
Nagoya
Sakaiminato
Fukuoka
Tohoku
Tokyo
Kobe
Osaka
Shikoku
Kyushu
Hokkaido
Otaru
Sapporo
New Chitose Int'l Airport
Kushiro
Aomori
Tohoku
Oshu
Sakata
Sendai
Sendai Int'l Airport
Niigata
Niigata Int'l Airport
Sukagawa
Honshu
Takasaki
Mito
TOKYO
Narita Int'l Airport
Haneda Int'l Airport
Ina
Nakatsugawa
Nagoya
Chubu Centrair Int'l Airport
Shizuoka
Atami
Izu Peninsula
Sakaiminato
Hikone
Kyoto
Osaka Int'l Airport
Kobe
Osaka
Kansai Int'l Airport
Sakaiminato
Takamatsu
Okayama
Hiroshima Int'l Airport
Hiroshima
Shikoku
Kochi
Kitakyushu
Fukuoka Int'l Airport
Fukuoka
Nagasaki Int'l Airport
Nagasaki
Kumamoto
Kyushu
Kagoshima Int'l Airport
Kagoshima

Published by Tuttle Publishing, an imprint of Periplus Editions (HK) Ltd

**www.tuttlepublishing.com**



ISBN 978-4-8053-1514-9

Distributed by

**North America, Latin America & Europe**
Tuttle Publishing
364 Innovation Drive, North Clarendon,
VT 05759-9436 U.S.A.
Tel: (802) 773-8930
Fax: (802) 773-6993
info@tuttlepublishing.com
www.tuttlepublishing.com

**Japan**
Tuttle Publishing
Yaekari Building, 3rd Floor,
5-4-12 Osaki, Shinagawa-ku,
Tokyo 141-0032
Tel: (81) 3 5437-0171
Fax: (81) 3 5437-0755
sales@tuttle.co.jp
www.tuttle.co.jp

**Asia Pacific**
Berkeley Books Pte. Ltd.
3 Kallang Sector #04-01
Singapore 349278
Tel: (65) 6741 2178
Fax: (65) 6741 2179
inquiries@periplus.com.sg
www.tuttlepublishing.com

25 24 23 22
10 9 8 7 6 5 4 3 2

Printed in China
2203EP

## "Books to Span the East and West"

**Tuttle Publishing** was founded in 1832 in the small New England town of Rutland, Vermont [USA]. Our core values remain as strong today as they were then—to publish best-in-class books which bring people together one page at a time. In 1948, we established a publishing office in Japan—and Tuttle is now a leader in publishing English-language books about the arts, languages and cultures of Asia. The world has become a much smaller place today and Asia's economic and cultural influence has grown. Yet the need for meaningful dialogue and information about this diverse region has never been greater. Over the past seven decades, Tuttle has published thousands of books on subjects ranging from martial arts and paper crafts to language learning and literature—and our talented authors, illustrators, designers and photographers have won many prestigious awards. We welcome you to explore the wealth of information available on Asia at **www.tuttlepublishing.com**.